Communication in Development

This is a volume in
EUROPEAN MONOGRAPHS IN SOCIAL PSYCHOLOGY

Series Editor: Henri Tajfel

A complete list of titles in this series appears at the end of this volume

EUROPEAN MONOGRAPHS IN SOCIAL PSYCHOLOGY 24
Series Editor: HENRI TAJFEL

Communication in Development

Edited by

W. P. ROBINSON

School of Education, University of Bristol
England

1981

Published in cooperation with
EUROPEAN ASSOCIATION OF EXPERIMENTAL
SOCIAL PSYCHOLOGY
by
ACADEMIC PRESS
A Subsidiary of Harcourt Brace Jovanovich, Publishers
London   New York   Toronto   Sydney   San Francisco

ACADEMIC PRESS INC. (LONDON) LTD.
24/28 Oval Road
London NW1

United States Edition published by
ACADEMIC PRESS INC.
111 Fifth Avenue
New York, New York 10003

British Library Cataloguing in Publication Data
Communication in development. – (European monographs
in social psychology series; no. 24)
1. Child development   2. Children - Language
I. Robinson, W. P.   II. Series
155.4'13   HQ784.C/

ISBN 0-12-590140-2
LCCCN 81-66370

Typeset by Reproduction Drawings Ltd, Sutton, Surrey
Printed in England by Whitstable Litho Ltd., Kent

List of Contributors

CARUGATI, FELICE *Istituto di Psicologia, Facolta di Magistero, Universita di Urbino, Urbino, Italy*

CONDLIFFE, STEPHEN G. *Department of Psychology, University of Bristol, 8–10 Berkeley Square, Bristol BS8 1HH, England*

EMILIANI, FRANCESCA *Istituto di Sociologia, Universita di Bologna, 40126 Bologna, Via Belle Arti 42, Italy*

EMPSON, JANET M. *Department of Social Administration, University of Hull, Cottingham Road, Hull HU6 7RX, England*

FREEMAN, NORMAN H. *Department of Psychology, University of Bristol, 8–10 Berkeley Square, Bristol BS8 1HH, England*

HARTMANN, ELLEN *Institute of Psychology, University of Oslo, Box 1094, Blindern, Oslo 3, Norway*

HAAVIND, HANNE *Institute of Psychology, University of Oslo, Box 1094, Blindern, Oslo 3, Norway*

HEBER, MARGERY *Department of Psychology, University of Southampton, Southampton SO9 5NH, England*

McGLAUGHLIN, ALEX *Department of Social Administration, University of Hull, Cottingham Road, Hull HU6 7RX, England*

MESSER, DAVID J. *Department of Psychology, University of Strathclyde, Turnbull Building, Glasgow, Scotland*

MORRISSEY, MAURA *Department of Social Administration, University of Hull, Cottingham Road, Hull HU6 7RX, England*

PERRET-CLERMONT, ANNE-NELLY *Institute de Psychologie, Université de Neuchâtel, 2000 Neuchâtel, Bassin 7, Switzerland*

ROBINSON, ELIZABETH, J. *Research Unit, School of Education, University of Bristol, 19 Berkeley Square, Bristol BS8 1HF, England*

ROBINSON, W. PETER   *School of Education, University of Bristol, 35 Berkeley Square, Bristol BS8 1JA, England*

SCHUBAUER-LEONI, MARIA-LUISA   *Faculté de Psychologie, Université de Génève, 24 rue Général Dufour, 1211 Geneva 4, Switzerland*

SEVER, JILL   *Department of Social Administration, University of Hull, Cottingham Road, Hull HU6 7RX, England*

SINHA, CHRIS G.   *Department of Psychology, University of Bristol, 8-10 Berkeley Square, Bristol BS8 1HH, England*

SYLVESTER-BRADLEY, BEN   *Faculty of Art and Design, Lanchester Polytechnic, Priory Street, Coventry CV1 5FB, England*

ZANI, BRUNA   *Istituto di Sociologia, Universita di Bologna, 40126 Bologna, Via Belle Arti 42, Italy*

Preface

This book is composed of papers derived from two sources. An International Conference on Social Psychology and Language was held in Bristol in July 1979. Considerations of space rather than merit prevented some of the papers, given in supplementary sessions on language development, from being published in the proceedings – H. Giles, W. P. Robinson and P. M. Smith (eds) (1980). "Language: Social Psychological Perspectives". Pergamon, Oxford. These papers are published in this volume. Also included here are recent and hitherto unpublished papers from European researchers working in the field of language and cognitive development.

I am grateful to Henri Tajfel for so readily agreeing to include this collection in the series *European Monographs in Social Psychology*.

Although this volume is a collection of papers, the whole is more than the sum of its parts. Social psychologists do not work to five- or ten-year plans, but their frames of reference change with time, and this compendium could not have been presented in 1970. Even if it had been, those whose work was then focused on language development would have seen the questions posed and the answers offered as beyond or irrelevant to their concerns. In 1970 'language' was still predominantly presented as an idealised system of syntactic rules located somewhere in Plato's Third World. Human beings were believed to have access to this realm *ab initio*; the Language Acquisition Device of each child was believed to contain the equipment necessary to master the basic rules of syntax, given minimal exposure to primary language data. Such a contention enabled its proponents to dismiss a large number of questions that developmental social psychologists would have posed – or at least to relegate them to the status of matters of performance rather than competence. Then, the proper activity was to chart the progress of syntactic development in young children and to formulate linguistic (psycholinguistic?) rules that would transform base structures into their surface realisation. *Why* the child should change was not asked. *How* it changed was similarly evaded. Thus, with no possible mechanisms of learning within the perspective, and with no principles of learning outside the perspective being seen as having potential application or validity, appeals to the innate characteristics of the child had to become sole and immediate 'explanations'. The perspective of the social psychologist, in contrast, requires him to search the environment more exhaustively before he concedes the impotence of his explanations for development.

Questions about the functions of language were ignored, even to the extent that its nature as a system of communication was forgotten. That investigations of what children used language for might throw light on their mastery of it was neglected. That the use of language began only after the child had already been communicating with others for many months was deemed irrelevant to the problem of how the child combined 'words' to form 'sentences'. 'sentences'.

Language itself at times became synonymous with syntax. Pragmatics, semantics, other components of grammar, and phonology were pared away. That acceptability of syntax is itself a function of individual and social differences at any point in time and that the criteria of acceptability shift through time were forgotten.

The chapters of this volume show that we have escaped from this 'straight-jacket'. The use of this word is not to be construed as uncomplimentary. There have been many general and particular benefits arising during and from the confinement. Able minds were attracted to study children and their development, and significant data were collected and interpreted. Perhaps more importantly, the perspective was defended with both rigour and verve, thereby ensuring that succeeding and competing endeavours be sponsored with corresponding forcefulness; by its very concentration upon particular methods of data collection in the pursuit of particular kinds of answers to a very limited range of questions it spawned the diversity of problems and approaches that we are beginning to tackle and adopt. It opened up the field.

This volume both reflects the emerging diversity and draws attention to some of the general ideas that Chomsky's inspirations neglected. Content ranges from very early non-verbal communication (Sylvester-Bradley; Messer) to the emergence of the child's understanding about referential communication (E. J. Robinson) and to between and within socio-economic status differences in maternal and child behaviour (McGlaughlin; W. P. Robinson). The kinds of verbal and non-verbal experience that promote intellectual development are also considered within the frames of both observed changes within children (Heber; Perret-Clermont and Schubauer-Leoni; E. J. Robinson) and cross-sectional studies of individual differences in mother-child interaction (Hartmann and Haavind). Regrettably under-represented are the relations between what adults actually do with children and the principles they hold that purport to guide their behaviour (Emiliani, Zani and Carugati).

Approaches range from detailed analysis of small numbers, through experiments to surveys, each, however, showing signs of sensitivity to the context or situation in which data are collected.

This concern with the idea that the child's performance is context sensitive is one of the general ideas that is being taken increasingly into account. Two chapters pay close attention to this issue (Freeman, Sinha and Condliffe; Perret-Clermont and Schubauer-Leoni). Neither retreats to an anti-empirical solipsist stance that may become a misguided slogan in the next years; both treat the issue as a challenge to experimental and theoretical ingenuity, recognising that the child is an active participant in situations where he is observed and that the challenge we face is to divine the principles regulating the child's behaviour.

The second common theme emphasises a model of the developing child as a creature coming to make sense of his environment, an environment in which there are people as well as objects (and other forms of life), an environment in which there are events, processes and experiences as well as things. In part the child comes to make sense of this world through the inventions he constructs, the discoveries he makes, and the resolution of incongruities between the inventions and discoveries. He is also aided. Other people create situations for him and serve as models from which he may learn. Other people may tell him what they think the answers are and interact with him in ways that they think will make it easier for him to find out for himself. In late twentieth-century Western societies, the mother remains the primary person enacting this rôle, and it is appropriate that she occupies the rôle of interlocutor in six of the chapters. It is to be regretted that fathers are not represented. But it is also appropriate that teachers, peers and generalised other adults are represented in a lesser measure. Had communication between child and others not been at the heart of every chapter, another title would have been required.

February 1981   W. P. ROBINSON

Contents

1

Negativity in Early Infant-Adult Exchanges and its Developmental Significance

B. Sylvester-Bradley

Adults generally deprecate children's negativities – their rages, their refusals, their rebellions. As Ainsworth, Bell and Stayton (1974) say:

Compliance to commands and prohibitions is generally considered to precede and be at the core of the internalised standards and values that mediate moral behaviour. Until a child – or an adult, for that matter – demonstrates a willingness to comply with the rules, values and proscriptions of his parents – or society in general – he is considered to be asocial and a liability to society, if not indeed antisocial and a menace.

This chapter argues for the opposite point of view – that negativitity plays both a necessary and productive role in development, from the earliest stages of infancy on through adulthood. This argument is based on the fine-grain analysis of infant-adult interactions recorded on video-tape and a theoretical perspective derived from the writings of Baruch Spinoza (Spinoza, 1910 edition; Sylvester-Bradley, 1980).

Initial observations

Although very young infants prefer to look at their mothers more than at strangers (Carpenter, 1974), by about 4 months of age they are found to attend longer to strangers' faces than to the faces of their mothers in a variety of visual preference-tests (Fitzgerald, 1968; Cohen, 1974; LaRoche and Des Biolles, 1976; Bernard and Ramey, 1977). This change is usually explained in terms of the 'discrepancy hypothesis': that perceptual development in infancy consists in the progressive construction of schematic mental representations of the external world (schemata) which become increasingly complex with age. This hypothesis predicts that infants will pay most attention to objects which are moderately dissimilar from the things they already know (i.e. of which they have already formed schemata): stimuli which are very well known or highly discrepant from what they have seen before will receive relatively little attention. Thus Kagan (1970) writes:

As the schema for a human (i.e. the mother's) face becomes well established, between 2 and 4 months of age . . . the strange face becomes optimally discrepant from that schema.

Recent studies of naturalistically recorded infant-adult interactions have suggested that this explanation is incorrect. For example, I (Sylvester-Bradley, 1980) conducted a longitudinal study of five infants between 6 and 26 weeks of age in which I compared attention to mothers, to strangers and to two face-masks – one of which was novel and the other which was seen by the babies at home everyday from four weeks of age. Findings showed a general decline in visual attention to all stimuli after ten weeks of age (Fig. 1a). But while, in accordance with the discrepancy hypothesis, there was a relative increase in attention to the stranger's face over the mother's face, there was also a relatively high level of attention to the face-masks, particularly the familiar face-mask. The discrepancy hypothesis would predict that the trend of attention to the familiar mask should be similar to that for the mother – but that the mask should get less attention overall than the mother's face because it is the less complex stimulus. But, for four of the five babies, more attention was paid to the familiar mask than the mother after 10 weeks of age (Fig. 1b).

This was a surprising finding when the perceivable differences between the masks and people were considered: the mothers' faces were not only larger than the masks, they were more detailed, they moved, they vocalised and they acted contingently upon the babies' actions – all of which have been shown to be attractive stimulus qualities in experimental studies on visual preference (Carpenter, 1974; Haith, 1966; S. J. Hutt, C. Hutt, Lenard, Bernuth and Muntjewerff, 1968; Watson, 1972; H. Papousek and M. Papousek, 1977). Apparently infant attention is not only controlled by cognitive and perceptual parameters but, like adult gaze (Argyle and Cook, 1976), by more complex social factors. In keeping with this suggestion, Trevarthen (1979a) has proposed that the period from 11–20 weeks is a period of 'relative negativity of motivation towards others' which separates an early interest in face-to-face interaction during the second month of life from the development of interpersonal games during the fifth and sixth months such as pat-a-cake, clappa-clappa handies and peek-a-boo (Bruner and Sherwood, 1975; Trevarthen and Hubley,

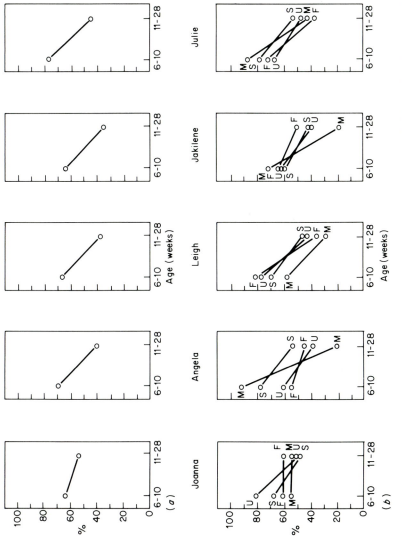

FIG. 1 Proportionate attention to four experimental stimuli by five babies between 6–10 weeks of age and between 11–28 weeks of age. (a) summed for all stimuli, (b) for each different stimulus. M, mother; S, stranger; F, familiar face-mask; U, unfamiliar face-mask. (Mean length of conditions = 251.1 seconds, standard deviation = 81.3 seconds)

1978). Trevarthen's proposal is theoretically important for three reasons. It suggests that infants have functional social sensitivities and motivations from soon after birth. It suggests that infants manifest negativity much earlier than is often supposed. And, more generally, it suggests that, from a very early age, infants have the means to exert active control over their upbringing, provided that this takes place in a 'good enough' (Winnicott, 1960) social environment.

Theoretical views of early negativity

The most influential theories of early negativity are derived from psychoanalysis and stress the importance of conflict. For example, Spitz suggests that infant negativity or 'unpleasure' is the product of frustration caused by a conflict between the infant's wishes and external circumstances. But he goes on to argue that environmental frustration is essential for developmental progress because it leads to improved 'reality–testing':

a precondition for setting up reality-testing is that objects shall have been lost which once brought real satisfaction [Freud, 1925] ... It follows that to deprive the infant of the effect of unpleasure during the first year of life is as harmful as to deprive him of the affect of pleasure ... The importance of frustration for developmental progress cannot be overestimated.   (Spitz and Cobliner, 1965)

A rather different argument is put forward by Melanie Klein (1953a). She suggests that infant negativity is primarily the product of an *internal* conflict – between the self-destructive 'death' instincts and the self-preservative 'life' instincts. Although she stresses that negativity is related by the infant to his or her environment, she sees it as being essentially a defensive projection of innate hate and aggressivity which will occur in the early stages of infancy whatever the infant's circumstances.

Despite their differences, both Spitz and Klein see the transcendence of negativity as playing a necessary part in developmental progress – whether it be achieved by more mature reality-testing or by working through what Klein calls 'the depressive position' [coming to understand that the world cannot justifiably be split into entirely good (loving, supportive) and entirely bad (hateful, persecutory) halves.] This attitude contrasts markedly with the view put forward by some attachment theorists. For example, Ainsworth *et al.* (1974) argue that negative behaviours such as fussiness and disobedience are an avoidable consequence of inappropriate or insensitive mothering techniques. In contradiction of Spitz, they argue that, while negativity is a consequence of frustration by external circumstances, it is developmentally *retrograde*. With a sensitive mother, negativity will not occur, and the infant will naturally grow up into an obedient and easy-going child.

These different theories lead to different predictions about the occurrence of negativity in infancy. Spitz (1975), for example, did not believe that truly purposeful negativity could be observed until 8 or 9 months after birth. This view corresponds to that held by attachment theorists who discuss only the positive aspects of the neonate's behavioural repertoire; those behaviours which permit him or her to *form* a bond with the mother. Behaviours which might disrupt or weaken social realtionships are not discussed as such until babies are more than 6 months old and, even then, the main interest is in negativity towards strangers (e.g. Bowlby, 1969; Ainsworth and Wittig, 1969; Rheingold and Eckerman, 1973; Solomon and Decarie, 1976). Klein (1953b), on the other hand, reports that, in accord with her theory, negativity occurs from birth, and she offers informal evidence that even very young babies will refuse to suck in the feeding situation, struggling and screaming in protest against their mother's attentions.

Empirical reports of negativity

In the light of the theoetical controversy surrounding early negativity one might expect it to have provided the topic for numerous empirical studies. Until recently this was not the case. Nevertheless, the literature contains many incidental reports of early negativity. With respect to the characteristic *forms* of negativity, these reports have a good deal in common. Thus Brazelton, Koslowski and Main (1974) – who report that babies as young as 1 month naturally oscillate between approach and withdrawal during interactions with their mothers – claim that, during the negative part of the cycle, babies use four strategies:

1   Actively withdrawing from their mothers – that is, increasing the physical distance between the stimulus and oneself by changing one's own position, for example, arching, turning, shrinking.
2   Rejecting it (i.e. the stimulus of the mother's face), that is, dealing with it by pushing it away with hands and feet while maintaining one's position.
3   Decreasing its power to disturb by maintaining a presently held position but decreasing sensitively to the stimulus -- looking dull, yawning or withdrawing into a sleep state.

4   Signalling behaviour, for example, fussing or crying, which has the initially unplanned effect of bringing adults or other caregivers to the infant to aid him.

A larger-scale study by Stechler and Carpenter (1967) shows that guided turning-away from the face occurred in all 14 babies they studied between the ages of 2 and 6 weeks, reaching a peak at two or three weeks. They describe these withdrawals of attention as having a 'dramatic and apparently controlled quality'. It took various forms:

lowering of the eye-lids, prolonged closing of the eyes, turning the head toward the periphery of the target, with each of these behaviours interspersed with target orientations whose brevity and precipitous cessation suggest a check in the stimulus field which may then result in further avoidance. The most extreme behaviour is a turning of the whole body so that the head is rotated $80°$ into the side-pillow, often with a rigidly arched back and fussing.

Similar behaviour was reported by Brackbill (1958) in an experiment concerned with the instrumental conditioning of smiling. The subjects (S) were 4-month-olds, and the reinforcement consisted of social and body contact with the experimenter (E). Brackbill's first finding was that, after the cessation of regular reinforcement, the infants' rate of smiling extinguished not to their previous operant rate, but to zero. And

coincident with the beginning of zero response rate was a conspicuous behavioural change: S would no longer fixate the discriminative stimulus (E's face). Instead, S's head turned to one side and remained there – an occurrence that was in distinct contrast to S's persistent fixation during conditioning. When this occurred, immediately preceding the last extinction interval, E propped S's head with rolled blankets or other material, making it impossible for the infant to turn his head to the left or right more than a few degrees. The 'refusal' to fixate persisted even under these conditions; S's eyes then turned toward the ceiling.

In another experiment, Polak, Emde and Spitz (1964) used the smiling response to indicate the onset of depth perception. They discovered that one of the ways infants differentiated between a photograph of a face and a real face was an 'apparently purposeful turning away of the eyes and head'. This

was a common response to the human face in the three to five months age group. Preliminary data on this response suggest a peak of frequency of occurrence of turning away in the third and fourth months.

Their subjects turned away more frequently from the real face than from the photograph.

While varying in detail, these reports suggest that negativity is a distinct type of action occurring from the earliest stages of infancy. But, despite the consensus as to its form, there is some disagreement as to how negativity should be interpreted. For example, Brazelton *et al.* (1974) argue that the behaviours they observed were not so much a product of the quality of stimulation presented by the mother – as originally suggested by Schneirla (1965) – but of a 'basic regulatory mechanism', akin to that which maintains homeostasis in physiological parameters such as body temperature, allowing infants to maintain some control over visual stimulation. Stern (1971, 1977) and Stechler and Carpenter take a similar view, suggesting that gaze aversion and all its accompaniments are methods of limiting visual stimulation to manageable proportions:

it appears that the very young baby has to regulate intake or confrontation in relation to his developing schemas. The frequent almost surreptitious glancing back at the target while holding the head averted [cf. 'fractional glances', p.11 below], would support the idea that in some way he knows that the stimulus is there, that he is drawn to it, but can handle it only in small doses.   (Stechler and Carpenter, 1967)

The use of physiological concepts, such as homeostasis and arousal, and statements that negative behaviours are affected by the quantity but not the quality of the visual stimulation to which infants are exposed, suggests that early negativity is an automatic process which does not involve the infant's purposes. This view has been seriously challenged by a series of studies which show that infant negativity can be experimentally controlled (e.g. Tatam, 1974; Brazelton *et al.*, 1975; Tronick, Als and Adamson, 1979; Murray, 1980).

For example, Murray (1980) has found that, by asking mothers to go blank-faced during mother-infant interactions, 2-month-olds are made to stop smiling, avert gaze from the mother's face, show facial expressions of distress, peculiar grimaces of the mouth, increased handling of the clothes, touching the face, sucking the thumb or fingers and crying. Murray has also shown that differences emerge from comparisons between infants' behaviours when interacting with their mothers in 'live' closed-circuit television and the behaviours of the same infants when watching a replay of their mothers' behaviour. In the second condition, when – while being visually identical – the mothers' behaviours are not coordinated with the behaviours of their babies, the babies will more often turn away from the TV-image 'looking puzzled and frowning, making more prolonged grimacing movements, touching their clothes and face and yawning more often'.

These results show that negativity *is* related to the quality of stimulation to which infants are exposed and is not an automatic response to perceptual overload. But why do babies find their mothers aversive when the normal structure of mother-infant inter-action is changed? The simplest proposal is that infants have an expectation that people will interact with them when in a position to do so and that, when this expectation is violated, negativity will occur. However, some workers claim, on the basis of earlier experimental work with non-social stimuli (e.g. Papousek, 1969; Watson, 1972), that these results provide further evidence for the existence of 'a funda-mental cognitive response system' which underlies all infant behaviour, having as its aim the comprehension and control of all environmental stimulation (Papousek, 1975; Watson, 1977). In terms of this hypo-thesis, pleasure or happiness results from increased control or compre-hension and unpleasure or negativity results from reduced control or incomprehension of the environment. Thus, because the experimental perturbations of mother-infant interactions have effects which are incomprehensible to the baby and therefore reduce the social efficacy of their behaviours, negativity results. On the other hand, normal mother-infant interaction gives infants pleasure simply because it enables them to learn about and thus gain control over a fertile source of environmental stimulation.

Murray argues against the view put forward by Papousek and Watson on the basis that, if one takes the *form* of infants' expressions into account, their negative reactions appear to be 'protests or solicit-ations for responsiveness'. She also reports that there is a marked difference between infants' reactions when their mothers go blank-faced and when interaction with their mothers is *naturally* inter-rupted by the entrance of a second adult who engages the mother in conversation – distress being much less apparent in the latter condition.

Murray's view is not incompatible with Papousek and Watson's provided one accepts that:

1   babies have a natural understanding of or sensitivity to per-sonal interaction – or, as Trevarthen (1979b) puts it 'an innate faculty for intersubjectivity', and

2   that it is *babies*, not impersonal 'cognitive response systems', who have a natural tendency to increase their understanding of and control over the environment – expressing pleasure when they are successful and distress when they are not.

Thus the 'blank-faced' behaviour of mothers is more distressing to infants than natural interruptions because blank-facedness is more incomprehensible to infants than is interruption.

Recast in personal terms, what Papousek and Watson refer to as a 'fundamental cognitive response system'should be seen as a formulation of what is seen in philosophical circles as *will*. Spinoza saw 'will' as the essential attribute of the psyche in that the essence of every living thing is 'the endeavour wherewith it endeavours to persist in its own being' (1910, Part 3, prop. VII); 'will' being the mental attribute of this endeavour. Thus the conclusion to be drawn from 'unnatural' experimental perturbations of infant-adult exchanges is that *early negativity results from the frustration of infants' wills*.

While all the empirical evidence reviewed in this section – with the possible exception of Brazelton *et al*'s (1974) – is compatible with the conclusion, it has important limitations. In the first place, it is based entirely on *experimental* evidence. This means that we still do not know what role negativity plays in normal development. We know that, experimentally, young infants can *be made* to express negativity. But do they express negativity under normal circumstances? And, if so, is it of the same sort as that produced in experimental circumstances? Secondly, this conclusion offers no clear explanation of the observations reported in section one of this chapter: as they stand these observations can throw no light on Trevarthen's suggestion that there is an increase in infant negativity between 2 and 6 months of age because they are of insufficient empirical detail.

With these questions in mind, I present sixteen detailed examples of naturally-occurring negativity as recorded on video-tape in the course of the study already mentioned (Sylvester-Bradley, 1980).

Naturally-occurring negativity

In my study, interactions potentially including negativity by babies were initially identified by analysis of mothers' babytalk. While the examples located were 'unnatural' in the sense that they took place in front of video-cameras, the interactions gave rise to them spontaneously, without any intervention by the experimenter. The interactions took place in a brightly furnished room at the Department of Psychology, Edinburgh University. On arrival, the babies were secured in a specially-designed baby-chair by a broad elastic waistband which allowed them maximum freedom of limb-movement. The mothers were then asked simply to chat with their babies while recording took place. A great variety of behaviours ensued, the different tones of the interactions being well reflected in the structure and content of the mothers' babytalk (Sylvester-Bradley and Trevarthen, 1978). (Mean interaction length = 280.7 secs; s.d. = 67.3).

If one listens to maternal babytalk, one soon becomes aware that mothers do not perceive their infants' actions as wholly positive. Thus one quite frequently hears comments such as: 'You're fed up with me', 'Aren't you talking to Mummy?', 'Come on, look at me!' 'Are you fed up with this game?' and 'You'll probably be happier on your own'. Between eight and twenty percent of maternal utterances were of this type in the study of five mother-infant pairs between 6 and 28 weeks of age (Sylvester-Bradley, 1980). By following up the most explicit maternal attributions, sixteen interactions potentially including negativity were located and analysed in detail. In the course of these analyses, nine different patterns of movements were identified as expressions of negativity.

(i) *Gaze aversion*: when the baby spent a disproportionately short time during the interaction looking at her mother. Gaze aversion could be of two types – *passive* and *active*.

Passive gaze aversion was recorded when a baby spent a disproportionately long time staring at nothing in particular – a simple object or an area of the floor. For example, Angela (aged 23 weeks) spent only 6% of a 288 second interaction looking at her mother. For 94% of the time she adopted a fixed hunched-up posture, looking at her feet or the floor directly below them (Plate 1). When she did look at her mother, her looks were shot up from under her eyebrows and were very brief (mean length $(\overline{X})$ = 0.9 seconds, standard deviation (s.d.) = 0.5 seconds, N = 9).

In contrast to passive gaze aversion, active gaze aversion was when a baby showed a disproportionately *high* visual interest in her surroundings, looking at everything but the mother. Thus Leigh (aged 20 weeks) spent only 8.1% of the first 100 seconds of an interaction looking at her mother while the mother spent 90.1 seconds looking at her. But Leigh spent only 20.3 percent of this time in a hunched posture (e.g. looking at her hand, Plate 2); the rest of the time she was very active visually, making 86 fixations of stimuli other than her mother (i.e 51.6 per minute, *forty times* more than Angela – 1.3 times per minute). All but one of Leigh's seven looks at her mother were under 1 second long ($\overline{X}$ = 0.7 seconds), whereas Leigh's other looks were, on average, longer than 1 second ($\overline{X}$ = 1.1 seconds).

(ii) *A hunched posture*: this was often associated with passive gaze aversion, where the baby would look at the floor, her own feet, her clothes or hands for long periods of time ('self-regard') – looking at her mother only briefly from under her eyebrows.

(*iii*) *Active resistance to adult's coercion*: this was often associated with (*ii*): when an adult attempted to coerce the child to make eye-contact, there would be a very visible attempt on the part of the child to resist. (Hutt and Ounsted, 1970, report similar behaviour in autistic children).

For example, during Angela's interaction with her mother, the mother made three attempts to force Angela's head back so that they were face-to-face. Only once, the first time, was this coercion at all 'successful' – in the sense that Angela did briefly look at her mother – although she almost immediately looked away (after 1.1 seconds), arching her back as she did so (Plate 3). The second struggle lasted 5.5 seconds, and even though the mother did manage to get Angela's head into an upright position, Angela hooded her eyes so that no eye-contact was made (Plate 4: Babytalk: 'Angela. Mummy's goin' – Hello, darling. There. Now you sit up properly. Be a good girl. What is the matter?' etc.). Interestingly, Angela did look at her mother during this struggle, but only while her mother was looking away (duration = 0.3 seconds). The mother's third attempt at coercion was equally unsuccessful in that Angela immediately re-adopted her hunched position after her mother's attentions.

(*iv*) *Fractional glances*: these are also described by Hutt and Ounsted in autistic children, whom they found to collect visual information by means of peripheral vision, but also by 'paranoid, darting looks': glances which usually last a fraction of a second only, which begin a fraction of a second after the co-interactant has looked away from the baby and end a fraction of a second after the other has begun to look back at her.

Both Leigh and Angela made fractional glances. For example, towards the end of the 100 seconds under discussion, Leigh began to arch her back and vocalise negatively with an 'angry' cry-face (Plate 5; Ekman and Friesen, 1978). But, after 94 seconds, she simultaneously looked away from her mother at the right-hand wall and stopped crying. The mother, who had been admonishing her ('Eh-eh! Eh-eh! Eh!'), turned to follow Leigh's gaze, saying 'What's that?' Almost immediately, Leigh turned back from the wall to look at her mother (Plate 8). But, as soon as her mother began to look back at Leigh, Leigh turned away to the wall again (Plates 7–9 and Plates 10–12).

(*v*) *Protesting vocalisation*: usually of relatively low intensity (i.e. not continuous and not loud) and suggesting frustration in that a simple change of stimulus makes them cease. These appear homologous with the vocalisations in ten-month-olds described by Zelazo, Kagan and Hartmann (1975) which they found to be a product of boredom as opposed to excitement.

(*vi*) *Facial expressions*: typically babies would adopt a fixed, 'blank', non-smiling expression if not crying. When crying they would not infrequently protrude their lower lip in an expression commonly described as a 'pout' or 'pet lip' by Edinburgh mothers and used by them as an indication of 'temper' as opposed to a genuine grievance (Plate 6). Occasionally this 'pet lip' expression would occur without crying – associated with an angry or otherwise 'blank' face (cf. Ekman and Friesen, 1978; Eibl-Eibesfeldt, 1975).

(*vii*) *Trunk movements*: including threshing and struggling movements and back-arching, as reported by Schaffer and Emerson (1964), Thoman (1975) and Brazelton *et al.* (1974) (see Plate 5).

(*viii*)*Biting*: one instance of apparently intentional biting was recorded, when Angela moved her mouth towards the mother's thumb, the mother let her take it in and the baby bit it. Melanie Klein would probably view this as a symbolic attack on the bad breast (oral aggression); but, however one views it, it certainly proved painful for the mother: 'There we are. Are you having a look around? Ouch!! [self-conscious laugh] You nearly bit my finger!'

(*ix*) *Comparisons*: whether or not an action was an instance of negativity could often be determined by comparing it with the infant's behaviour in the conditions recorded immediately before and after the interaction in question. For example, it can be shown that Angela's lack of interest in her mother was not simply a product of boredom with the experimental situation as a whole because the second greatest amount of attention to an experimental stimulus was given in the condition immediately following the mother-condition – with the familiar face-mask (i.e. 6% *vs* 28%). Indeed, as soon as the experimenter entered the recording-studio at the end of the interaction with the mother, Angela ceased hunching, sat up and looked at him and, subsequently, at the familiar face-mask which replaced her mother (Plates 13–15). She also ceased the frequent 'frustrated' vocalisations she had been making throughout the interaction with her mother as soon as her mother left the room: having vocalised so often that there were no more than 15 seconds of continuous silence from her when with her mother, Angela only vocalised twice in the first 208 seconds with the familiar mask.

As well as describing a range of negative behaviours occurring spontaneously in the first six months of life, I also reported a number of more general findings (Sylvester-Bradley, 1980).

1   *First, it would be mistaken to suggest that negativity is only found in interactions between babies and their mothers – it is also to be observed in interactions between babies and other adults.* For example, a 16-week-old baby, Joanna, spent only 17.8% of a 334 second interaction looking at a stranger, having spent 69.2% of the previous interaction looking at her mother (duration = 327 seconds). She had spent more than 60 seconds smiling at her mother, whereas, with the stranger, she did not smile at all, adopting for the most part a sulky, impassive facial expression, with a slight pout, down-turned lip corners and looking somewhat below the stranger's face (Plate 16). In subsequent conditions, with the face-masks, she looked considerably more than with the stranger (unfamiliar mask = 47.3%; familiar mask = 39.5%). She also smiled at both the face masks (for 2.6 and 1.1 seconds respectively). Joanna's attention appeared to be attracted away from the stranger's face by the pattern on her dress. But as soon as the stranger transferred *her* attention to the dress, Joanna made a fractional glance (Plates 16–18).

2   *Often it appeared that negativity was a result of frustration with purely conversational face-to-face interaction.* Babies would often act negatively if adults only chatted with them, but as soon as the adult started to do something other than chat, the baby would perk up and take an interest. Thus Joanna (aged 26 weeks) spent only 15.6% of a 373 second interaction looking at her mother. And, while she did not cry, she made frequent protesting vocalisations (i.e. vocalisations in conjunction with elements of an 'angry' cry-face; Plate 19). Her behaviour was not wholly negative however. She smiled at least once a minute throughout the interaction (for a total of 20.5 seconds) and the mother soon found that she could capture Joanna's attention by holding up her hand in Joanna's line of vision and waving her fingers. Joanna would be fascinated by this, looking at the fingers continuously and ceasing all vocal protests (Plates 19–21). Her interest was also awakened by less conscious efforts to entertain her. For example, after a period of 17 seconds during which Joanna had not looked or smiled at her mother at all, had avoided an attempt by her mother to achieve eye-contact by stooping to look into Joanna's face (Plates 22–24) and had made five protesting vocalisations, her interest suddenly rekindled on seeing her mother start to scratch the side of her (the mother's) nose (Plates 25–27). Nevertheless, as soon as these various finger-displays ceased and normal babytalk resumed, Joanna, with hardly another look or smile at her

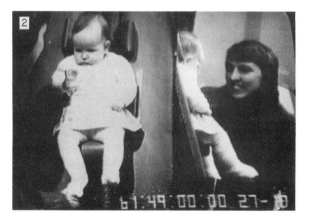

PLATE 1 Hunched posture (Angela, aged 23 weeks). PLATE 2 Hunched posture with hand regard (Leigh, aged 20 weeks). PLATE 3 Resistance to mother's attempt to coerce face-to-face interaction (Angela aged 23 weeks).

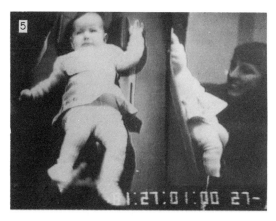

PLATE 4 Resistance to mother's attempt to coerce face-to-face interaction (Angela aged 23 weeks). PLATE 5 'Angry' cry-face with back-arching (Leigh, aged 20 weeks). PLATE 6 Cry-face with 'pout' (Sarah aged 13 weeks).

16

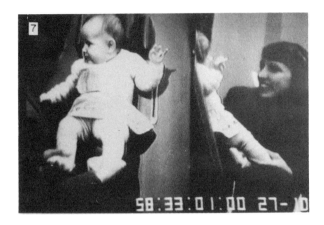

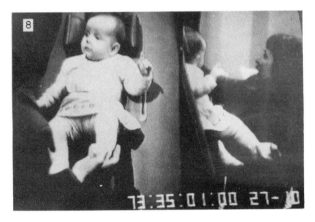

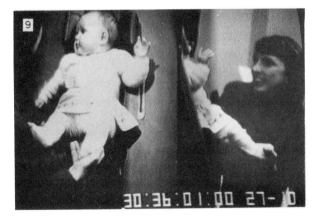

PLATES 7–9 A 'fractional glance' by Leigh (aged 20 weeks)

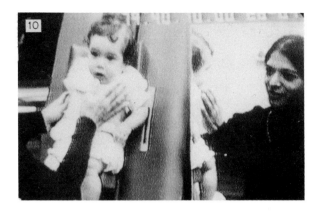

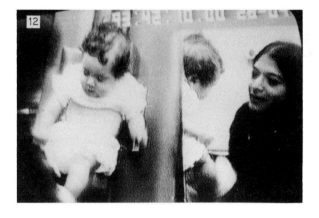

PLATES 10-12   A 'fractional glance' by Angela (aged 23 weeks)

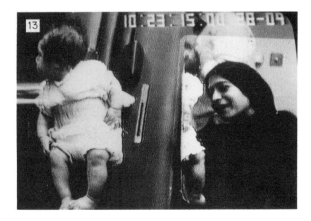

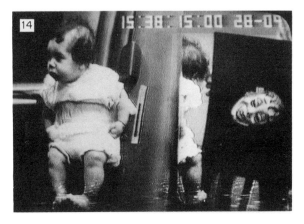

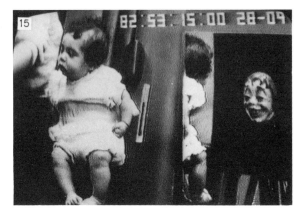

PLATES 13-15 Transformation in Angela's posture and attention on the experimenter's entrance to the recording-studio (13) and the substitution of the mother by a familiar face-mask (aged 23 weeks)

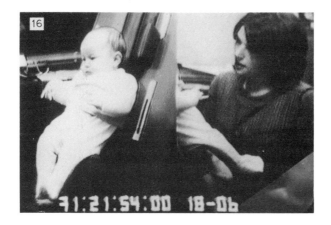

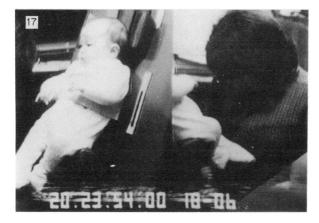

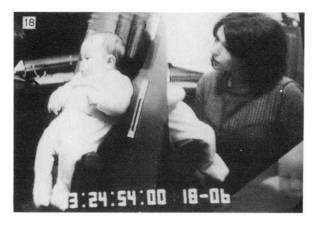

PLATES 16-18   A 'fractional glance' by Joanna (aged 16 weeks)

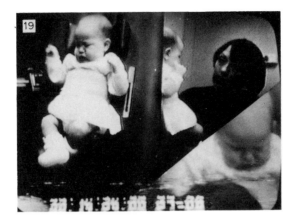

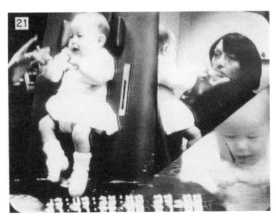

PLATES 19–21 Joanna's expressions of negativity contrasted with her interest in her mother's fingers (aged 26 weeks)

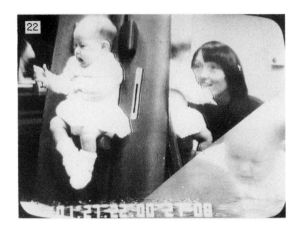

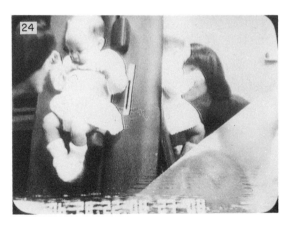

PLATES 22–24   Joanna's response to her mother's attempt to make eye-contact (aged 26 weeks)

22

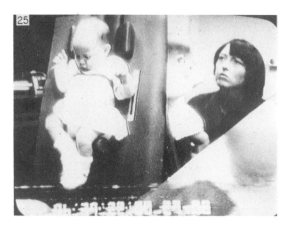

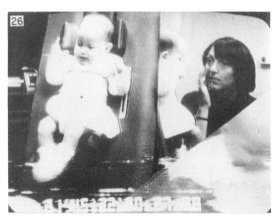

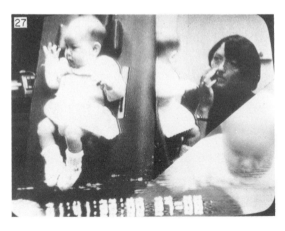

PLATES 25-27   Joanna's response to her mother scratching the side of her (the mother's) nose (aged 26 weeks)

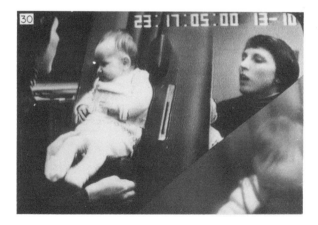

PLATES 28–30 A 'fractional glance' by Leigh (aged 18 weeks)

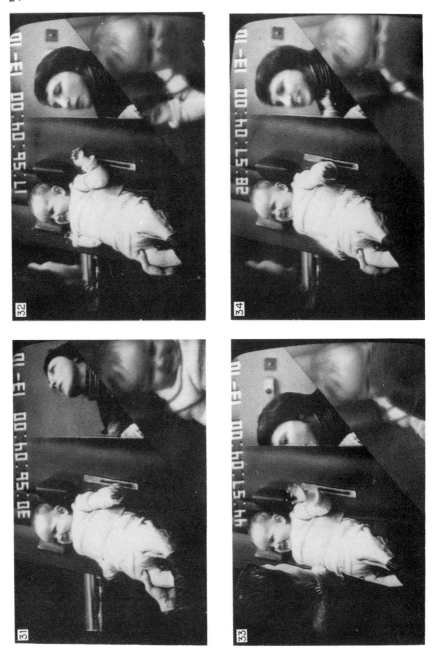

PLATES 31–34 One bout of a person-person game played by Leigh (aged 18 weeks) and her mother

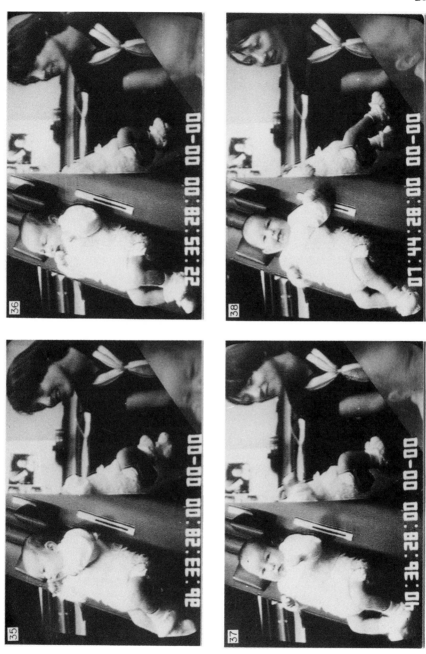

PLATES 35-38 Transformation in Joanna's expressions, whilst interacting with her mother, on seeing a stranger standing by the door of the recording-studio (aged 15 weeks)

26

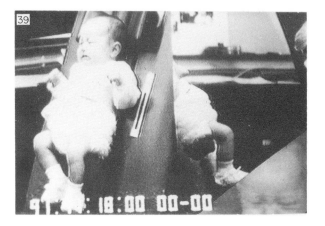

PLATES 39–41 Transformation in Joanna's expression, whilst in the presence of an unfamiliar face-mask, on seeing her mother standing by the door of the recording-studio (aged 15 weeks)

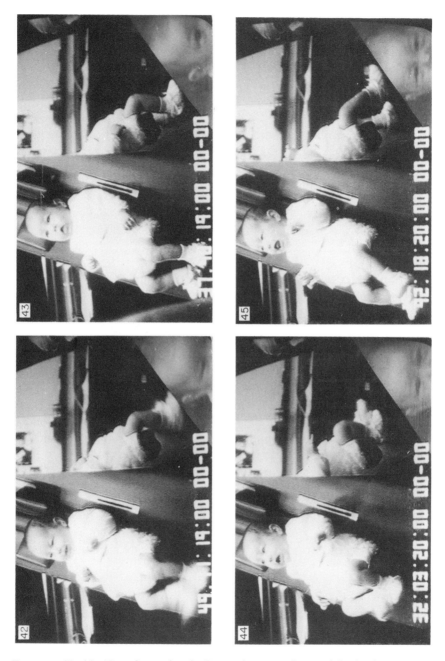

PLATES 42–45 Transformation in Joanna's expressions, whilst in the presence of an unfamiliar face-mask, on seeing her mother disappear from the door of the recording-studio (aged 15 weeks)

mother, would re-adopt a hunched, uninterested posture and start
to protest. She finally found satisfaction by turning away from her
mother and sucking her thumb.

3   *The most consistently successful means of interesting a baby
during an otherwise negative interaction was the playing of interpersonal games.* An example is an interaction between Leigh and
her mother at 18 weeks. This interaction included the greatest
proportion of smiling recorded in any single condition throughout
the case-study (27.9%). But this was associated with three fractional
glances, with concealed 'under the eyebrows' looks, with back-
arching, with resistance of an attempt by the mother to force Leigh
into a position in which Leigh would look at her face and with protesting 'frustrated' vocalisations.

These two sets of behaviours were clearly segregated. Their segre-
gation is well reflected in the different lengths of Leigh's looks at her
mother. She looked at her mother 22 times: 13 of these looks were
less than 1 second long, six were between 1 and 5 seconds long and
three were over 13 seconds long. The four longest looks (i.e. 4.6,
13.9, 14.7, 17.3 seconds) were all associated with the playing of
games. They all began within 2 seconds of the mother starting a game,
and they all finished only after the mother had finished playing the
game and resumed normal conversation. In each case, their onset was
followed by smiling within between 1 and 6 seconds, whereas only
one of the shorter looks was associated with smiling (this was a
fractional glance, 0.4 seconds long, made 3 seconds after the mother
had interrupted a game to clean up Leigh's mouth. The smile ended
0.1 seconds after the beginning of the look; (Plates 28–30). In fact,
there were only four instances of smiling – coinciding with the four
longest looks.

The mother only initiated a game on four separate occasions during
this interaction – and each of these coincided with a long look and
smile from Leigh. In each case the game consisted of a repeated
sequence of actions and nonsensical noises, beginning with the mother
making a gargling noise, with five or six narrowly separated stresses.
Having made this noise one or two times, she would repeat it with
more dramatic gestures – shaking her head from side-to-side and
bringing her face close up to Leigh's. Finally she began to sway
right away from Leigh at the start of each bout, throwing her head
back to look up at the ceiling and breaking eye-contact. At the end
of each bout, marked by one noise-action cycle, she would pause in
a normal conversational position and smile at Leigh (Plates 31–34).
There were many examples like this.

4 *Negativity could not be described as a purely social phenom-enon – with only social causes.* It was sometimes caused simply by the baby's frustration with the conditions in which she was having to sit, not by frustration with people. Indirectly, because people can understand babies and because people usually have control over babies' environments, negativity will *constitute* a social phenomenon. But one can observe occasions when, for example, a baby who has been protesting because the sun is in her eyes, is relieved just as effectively by non-social means (a cloud obscures the sun) as by social means (her father moves the pram). This sort of example shows that negativity is, essentially, a protest 'against the current state of the universe', not, as it often appears to be, a 'complaint to mother' or 'to father'.

The best illustration of this point is to be found in an interaction between Joanna and her mother at 15 weeks. Joanna cried consider-ably less during this interaction than she had in the previous two conditions, and smiled more. However, she spent less than 13% of the interaction looking at her mother. The mother made two com-ments attributing rejection to Joanna. They came after Joanna had turned away from her, beginning to cry, but then focused on an unfamiliar adult standing by the door of the recording-studio, and immediately stopped crying (Plates 35–38).

Are you going to talk to me? Are you? Are you going to talk to me? (Joanna begins to turn away) You're going to start crying again aren't you. [Joanna begins to cry] Yes. Yes. [Joanna sees the stranger and stops crying] See – there's someone to look at! Hello. [Joanna smiles at the stranger] *Oh, you're fed up with your Mummy aren't you! You're just fed up with your Mummy now aren't you!*

During this interaction Joanna spent more than twice as much time looking at the stranger as at her mother (32.7% *vs* 12.7%), her looks at the stranger were, on average, considerably longer than those at the mother ($\bar{X}$(M) = 2.0 seconds, s.d. = 1.4 seconds, N = 18; $\bar{X}$(S) = 10.0 seconds, s.d. = 13.7 seconds, N = 9), and she smiled for a higher proportion of the time she was looking at the stranger (3% (M) *vs* 8% (S)). She cried, proportionately, twice as much at her mother as at the stranger (22% (M) *vs* 11% (S)).

From both the mother's babytalk and empirical measures, it se ned that Joanna's negativity during this interaction was the p.oduct of a relative preference for interaction with the stranger over her mother. Subsequent analysis showed that this was not the case however.

Joanna cried a lot during this visit to the laboratory. But her mother and the experimenter agreed that her crying was not due to any physical suffering. This impression was reinforced by Joanna's behaviour with the unfamiliar face-mask. At two points, this condition was broken by the mother going into the recording studio to dis- cover why Joanna was distressed (for 62 and 25 seconds respectively). On both occasions, Joanna stopped crying as soon as she saw her mother and, within 3 seconds, smiled at her (e.g. Plates 39–41). In the 30 seconds before the first break, Joanna cried for 94% of the time. In the first 30 seconds of the break she did not cry at all and smiled for 9 seconds, having not smiled at all with the face-mask. Indeed, she only cried once during this break (1.1%) – despite spending 6.8 seconds looking at the face-mask. This showed that the face-mask only elicited crying under certain circumstances.

Joanna spent 73.4% of this break looking at her mother. As soon as she saw that her mother had left the room she started crying again. She cried for 87% of the next 23 seconds – looking at the mask for 56.6% of the time. Then her mother returned – whereupon her behaviour was again transformed (32% smiling, 73% looking at mother, 0% crying). Her mother's second exit was followed by renewed crying (Plates 42–45).

The next condition, with the familiar face-mask, contained almost continuous crying and was interrupted after 69 seconds by the mother's attempt to comfort Joanna. It was this attempt which led to the mother-infant interaction described above.

Taken in conjunction with her behaviour with the unfamiliar face-mask, Joanna's behaviour in the interaction with her mother suggested that she was not protesting because she was 'fed up' with her mother – as the mother thought – but because she wished to be taken out of the baby-chair. In both these conditions, her positive behaviour was directed at someone standing by the door and, usually, people didn't appear at the door unless they were going to attend to her needs. Thus, on both occasions, it appeared that she stopped crying and started smiling in anticipation of being picked up. This impression was supported by the frustrated sound of her cries – the fact that they were generally of low intensity and discontinuous. It was also supported by the observation that, on the two occasions when preparations were made to take her out of the chair during the final interaction (i.e. when the waist-band was undone) she stopped crying – only to restart when it was refastened. As the mother's babytalk shows, by the end of this mother-infant interaction Joanna was looking from face to face, crying at stranger, mother and experimenter alike – as if she had 'given up hope' of any person liberating her:

(as Joanna cried at the experimenter) No, he's not going to help you. (as Joanna cried at the stranger) No, nobody's going to help you.

Discussion

While my analyses are far from exhaustive, they do enable us to address a number of points that emerge from the literature concerning early negativity.

In the first place, we can reject Spitz's explicit assumption that negativity does not occur in the first 6 months of life under normal circumstances. We can also reject Spitz's equation of negativity with a simple behavioural pattern akin to rooting (i.e. lateral gaze-aversion). Early negativity has a variety of different behavioural characteristics which can be combined in a variety of different ways. Although these do often include low levels of eye-contact, 'gaze-aversion' is far from being a stereotyped action-pattern: low eye-contact may be the result of active scanning of the environment as well as passive 'staring at nothing'. In this and in a number of other respects the behaviour patterns characterising early negativity resemble those characterising childhood autism as described by Hutt and Ounsted (1970).

Secondly, in all the examples reviewed here, negativity appeared to be specific to particular circumstances – the infant was fed up with interacting with her mother but was happy to talk to a stranger or vice versa, the infant disliked being in the baby-chair but cheered up as soon as she thought she was being taken out, the infant was fed up with talking to people but was quite happy to look at masks, the infant disliked conversational interaction but was easily amused by the playing of games, etc. In other words, early negativity appears to be related to the quality of stimulation to which infants are exposed. This finding runs counter to statements made by Klein, Brazelton *et al.*, Stechler and Carpenter, and Stern. On the other hand, the lability of infants' reactions to very similar circumstances – sometimes accepting games and sometimes rejecting them, being interested in finger-movement but not tongue-clicking or vice versa – suggests that negativity has a significant 'internal component'. However, in the light of this lability it seems that the internal component of negativity should not be conceived in terms of stable physiological processes such as 'instincts' (Freud, Spitz, Klein) or 'basic regulatory mechanisms' (Brazelton *et al.*, Stechler and Carpenter and Stern). It would be better to conclude – in *psychological* terms – that infants have varying interests or moods.

This conclusion shows up an important weakness in current formu-

lations of attachment theory as an explanation of early social development (e.g Bowlby, 1969; Ainsworth *et al.*, 1974). Generally speaking,
attachment theorists focus only on the positive aspects of the young
infant's repertoire of social behaviours (smiling, clinging, following,
looking, crying-for-contact, etc.). The work reported in this chapter
shows that young infants also manifest a wide range of contact-
denying behaviours. Attachment theorists usually view these behaviours as the product of unsatisfactory mothering techniques
(insensitivity, inappropriateness of response, unavailability for
interaction) and thus offer no account for the importance of infants'
'moods' or changing interests in determining the occurrence of early
negativity.

It would seem that all the results reported in this chapter are compatible with the conclusion that early negativity results from the
frustration of infants' wills or interests by external circumstances,
providing one acknowledges that infants' interests are labile. This
conclusion suggests an explanation for the observations reported
in the first section of this chapter – that there was a general decline
in infant attention to a range of experimental stimuli in the 10–28
week period, a decline which was particularly marked in attention to
the mother's face (contrary to predictions derived from the discrepancy hypothesis: Kagan, 1970).

In the first place, it is well known that, between 3 and 5 months
of age, the infant's visual capacity reaches adult levels of competence
(e.g. Haith, 1977) and that their ability to grasp and control reachable
objects also becomes functional during this period (White, Castle and
Held, 1964; van Hofsten, 1979). These developments would naturally
increase the infant's interest in exploring their surroundings. Thus,
if we accept, as argued, that infants derive pleasure from increasing
their knowledge about and active control over the environment, one
would expect a general decline in attention to the experimental
stimuli as reported in section one. And, in so far as a reduction of
control over the environment leads to displeasure, the relatively low
proportion of attention paid to mothers would reflect a conflict of
interests: the mother, having been instructed to chat with her daughter,
would see the baby's increasingly active investigations of the surroundings as counter-productive and attempt to frustrate them. The
baby, thus frustrated, would, through innate obstinacy of purpose
('negativity'), make more persistent attempts to evade her mother's
attentions. Strangers would generally fare better than the mothers
because, in the first place, they would have 'novelty value' and,
secondly, because they would be less sure of themselves with the

babies, less assertive and, therefore, less frustrating than the mothers. The masks would fare better simply because they 'allowed' the babies to investigate what they wanted.

The proposition that infants derive pleasure from increasing their control over the understanding of the environment would also explain their increasing preference for games over normal 'conversational' interactions – because, in games, adults make their actions more obviously predictable to and controllable by the infant with whom the game is being played. Thus, in playing games, infants can adopt a more active – and therefore enjoyable – rôle than is possible in adult-like interactions.

Conclusion: asocial and social negativity

At first sight, it might be thought that negativity was essentially counter-productive so far as social development is concerned, tending to reduce inter-personal exchange, to lead to separateness and to cause sadness, guilt and depression in others. In the light of the argument presented in this chapter however – where development is seen in Spinozan terms, as the fulfilment of invididuals' natural tendency to increase their powers of self-determination – it seems that negativity need not be unproductive so far as either infants or their caretakers are concerned. Early negativity appears to be a product of infants' inabilities to act in the way they want or 'to maintain their will' in the face of frustrating external circumstances. Understood as such, it should not provoke distress in others but rather it should provoke active attempts to discover and facilitate the fulfilment of the infant's purposes (whenever these are compatible with the care-taker's own purposes). In this event, negativity will have productive consequences for both infant and caretaker. It is only when caretakers misunderstand the nature of negativity – taking it to be a 'personal comment' for example (see e.g. the comments of Joanna's mother, p.29) – that it is distressing for them and developmentally unproductive for their charge.

The argument that negativity is essentially an asocial phenomenon has its limitations however. In the first place, its existence is combined with an acute social sensitivity in young infants (see the empirical reports reviewed earlier and Trevarthen, 1979b). And, secondly, as infants grow older, one begins to observe a type of negativity which does appear to be essentially social. The best-known early examples are of the toddler's obstinate opposition to all adult suggestions (Spitz, 1957). For example:

Do you want to go out or do you want to stay indoors?
No.

Later comes the so-called 'adolescent rebellion' where, once again, parents' wishes and those of other authority-figures are systematically rejected by the child.

In the light of our argument, these social negativities must reflect the child's growing awareness that, amongst the major sources of frustration to his or her powers of self-determination are social expectations and rôle-requirements. It is for this reason that one finds social negativity to be more frequently observed where either parental expectations (Zinner and Shapiro, 1972) or broader, economically-determined social conditions and politically-determined forms of social control (Hall and Jefferson, 1975) are particularly debilitating to the individual. Perhaps we should conclude, therefore, that the asocial negativities of young infants in interaction with their mothers represent the first precursors of political awareness in adulthood.

Acknowledgements

The research by Sylvester-Bradley (1980) reported in this chapter was supported by an M.R.C. Studentship and supervised by Dr C. B. Trevarthen and Dr M. Manning.

References

Ainsworth, M. D. S., Bell, S. M. and Stayton, D. J. (1974). Infant-mother attachment and social development: 'socialization' as a product of reciprocal responsiveness to signals. In "The Integration of a Child into a Social World" (M. P. M. Richards', Ed.). Cambridge University Press, Cambridge
Ainsworth, M. D. S. and Wittig, B. A. (1969). Attachment and exploratory behaviour of one-year-olds in a strange situation. In "Determinants of Infant Behaviour" (B. M. Foss, Ed.) Vol. 4. Methuen, London
Argyle, M. and Cook, M. (1976). "Gaze and Mutual Gaze". Cambridge University Press, Cambridge
Bernard, J. A. and Ramey, C. T. (1977). Visual regard of familiar and unfamiliar persons in the first six months of infancy. Merrill-Palmer Quarterly 23, 121–127
Bowlby, J. (1969). "Attachment and Loss", Vol. 1, "Attachment". Hogarth, London

Brackbill, Y. (1958). Extinction of the smiling response in infants as a function of reinforcement schedule. *Child Development* 29, 115-124

Brazelton, T. B., Koslowski, B. and Main, M. (1974). The origins of reciprocity: the early mother-infant interaction. *In* "The Effect of the Infant on Its Caregiver" (M. Lewis and L. A. Rosenblum, Eds). Wiley, New York

Brazelton, T. B., Tronick, E., Adamson, L., Als, H. and Wise, S. (1975). Early mother-infant reciprocity. *In* "Parent-Infant Interaction" (R. Porter and M. O'Connor, Ed.) Ciba Foundation Symposia 33 (new series). Elsevier (ASP), Amsterdam

Bruner, J. S. and Sherwood, V. (1975). Peekaboo and the learning of rule-structures. *In* "Play - Its Role in Development and Evolution" (J. S. Bruner, A. Jolly and K. Sylva, Eds). Penguin, Harmondsworth

Carpenter, G. C. (1974). Visual regard to moving and stationary faces in early infancy. *Merrill-Palmer Quarterly* 20, 181-194

Cohen, S. W. (1974). Developmental differences in infants' attentional responses to face-voice incongruity of mother and stranger. *Child Development* 45, 1155-1158

Eibl-Eibesfeldt, I. (1975). "Ethology: The Biology of Behaviour", 2nd edn. Holt, Rinehart and Winston, New York

Ekman, P. and Friesen, W. V. (1978). "Manual for the Facial Action Coding System". Consulting Psychologists Press, Palo Alto, California

Fitzgerald, H. E. (1968). Autonomic pupillary reflex activity during early infancy and its relation to social and non-social visual stimuli. *Journal of Experimental Child Psychology* 6, 470-482

Freud, S. (1925). Negation. *In* "The Standard Edition of the Complete Psychological Works of Sigmund Freud" (J. Strachey and A. Freud, Eds) Vol. 19. Hogarth, London

Haith, M. H. (1966). The response of the human newborn to visual movement. *Journal of Experimental Child Psychology* 3, 235-243

Haith, M. H. (1977). Visual competence in early infancy. *In* "Handbook of Sensory Physiology" (R. Held, H. Leibowitz and H. L. Teuber, Eds) Vol. 8. Springer-Verlag, Berlin

Hall, S. and Jefferson, T. (Eds) (1975). "Resistance Through Rituals: Youth Subcultures in Post-War Britain". Hutchinson, London

Hutt, C. and Ounsted, C. (1970). Gaze aversion and its significance in childhood autism. *In* "Behaviour Studies in Psychiatry" (S.J. Hutt and C. Hutt, Eds). Pergamon, Oxford

Hutt, S. J., Hutt, C., Lenard, H. G., Bernuth, H. von and Muntjewerff, W. J. (1968). Auditory responsivity in the human neonate. *Nature* 218, 888-890

Kagan, J. (1970). Attention and psychological change in the young child. *Science* 70, 826-832

Klein, M. (1953a). Some theoretical conclusions regarding the emotional life of the infant. *In* "Envy and Gratitude and Other Works, 1946-1963". Hogarth, London

Klein, M. (1953b). On observing the behaviour of young infants. *In* "Envy and Gratitude and Other Works, 1946-1963". Hogarth, London

LaRoche, J. L. and Des Biolles, Q. Z. (1976). Stability of the differentiation between mother and stranger in the young child. *Enfance* 1-2, 63-75

Murray, L. (1980). The Sensitivities and Expressive Capacities of Young Infants in Communication with their Mothers. Ph.D. Thesis, University of Edinburgh

Papousek, H. (1969). Individual variability in learned responses in human infants. *In* "Brain and Early Behaviour: Development in the Fetus and Infant" (R. J. Robinson, Ed.). Academic Press, New York

Papousek, H. (1975). Cognitive aspects of preverbal and social interaction between human infants and adults. *In* "Parent-Infant Interaction" (R. Porter and M. O'Connor, Eds). Ciba Foundation Symposia 33 (new series). Elsevier (ASP), Amsterdam

Papousek, H. and Papousek, M. (1977). Mothering and the cognitive head-start: Psychobiological considerations. *In* "Studies in Mother-Infant Interaction" (H. R. Schaffer, Ed.). Academic Press, New York.

Polak, P. R., Emde, R. N. and Spitz, R. A. (1964). The smiling response II: visual discrimination and the onset of depth perception. *Journal of Nervous and Mental Diseases* 139, 407–415

Rheingold, H. L. and Eckerman, C. O. (1973). Fear of strangers: a critical examination. *In* "Advances in Child Development and Behaviour" (H. W. Reese, Ed.) Vol. 8. Academic Press, New York

Schaffer, H. R. and Emerson, P. E. (1964). Patterns of response to physical contact in early human development. *Journal of Child Psychology and Psychiatry* 5, 1–13

Schneirla, T. C. (1965). Aspects of stimulation and organization in approach/ withdrawal processes underlying vertebrate behavioural development. *In* "Advances in the Study of Behaviour" (D. Lehrman, R. A. Hinde and E. Shaw, Eds). Vol. 1.Academic Press, New York

Solomon, R. and Decarie, T. G. (1976). Fear of strangers: a developmental milestone or an overstudied phenomenon? *Canadian Journal of Behavioural Science* 8, 351–363

Spinoza, B. (1910). "Ethics". Everyman, New York

Spitz, R. A. (1957). "No and Yes: on the Genesis of Human Communication". International Universities Press, New York

Spitz, R. A. and Cobliner, W. G. (1965). "The First Year of Life: a Psychoanalytic Study of Normal and Deviant Development of Object Relations". International Universities Press, New York

Stechler, G. and Carpenter, G. (1967). A viewpoint on early affective development. *In* "The Exceptional Infant" (J. Hellmuth, Ed.). Vol. 1. Special Child, Seattle

Stern, D. N. (1971). A micro-analysis of mother-infant interaction: behaviour regulating social contact between a mother and her $3\frac{1}{2}$-month-old twins. *Journal of the American Academy of Child Psychiatry* 13, 402–421

Stern, D. N. (1977). "The First Relationship: Infant and Mother". Fontana/ Open Books, Glasgow

Sylvester-Bradley, B. (1980). A Study of Young Infants as Social Beings. Ph.D. Thesis, University of Edinburgh

Sylvester-Bradley, B. and Trevarthen, C. B. (1978). Babytalk as an adaptation to the infant's communication. *In* "The Development of Communication" (N. Waterson and C. Snow, Eds). Wiley, London

Tatam, J. (1974). The Effects of Inappropriate Partner on Infant Sociability. M.A. Dissertation, University of Edinburgh

Thoman, E. B. (1975). How a rejecting baby affects mother-infant synchrony. *In* "Parent-Infant Interactions" (R. Porter and M. O'Connor, Eds). Ciba Foundation Symposia 33 (new series). Elsevier (ASP), Amsterdam

Trevarthen, C. B. (1979a). The primary motives for cooperative understanding. Address to B. P. S. Developmental Psychology Section Conference, 16th September, 1979, Southampton

Trevarthen, C. B. (1979b). Communication and cooperation in early infancy: a description of primary intersubjectivity. *In* "Before Speech: the Beginning of Interpersonal Communication" (M. Bullowa, Ed.). Cambridge University Press, Cambridge

Trevarthen, C. B. and Hubley, P. A. (1978). Secondary intersubjectivity: confidence, confiding and acts of meaning in the first year. *In* "Action, Gesture and Symbol: The Emergence of Language" (A. Lock, Ed.). Academic Press, New York

Tronick, E., Als, H. and Adamson, L. (1979). Structure of early face-to-face communicative interactions. *In* "Before Speech: the Beginning of Interpersonal Communication" (M. Bullowa, ed.) Cambridge University Press, Cambridge

von Hofsten, C. (1979). Development of visually directed reaching: the approach phase. *Journal of Human Movement Studies* 5, 160–178

Watson, J. S. (1972). Smiling, cooing and "the game". *Merrill-Palmer Quarterly* 18, 323–339

Watson, J. S. (1977). Perception of contingency as a determinant of social responsiveness. *In* "Origins of the Infant's Social Responsiveness" (E. B. Thoman, Ed.). Wiley, New Jersey

White, B. L., Castle, P. and Held, R. (1964). Observations on the development of visually directed reaching. *Child Development* 35, 349–364

Winnicott, D. W. (1960). Ego distortion in terms of true and false self. *In* "The Maturational Processes and the Facilitating Environment: Studies in the Theory of Emotional Development". Hogarth, London

Zelazo, P. R., Kagan, J. and Hartmann, R. (1975). Excitement and boredom as determinants of vocalisation in infants. *Journal of Genetic Psychology* 126, 107–117

Zinner, J. and Shapiro, R. (1972). Projective identification as a mode of perception and behaviour in families of adolescents. *International Journal of Psychoanalysis* 53, 523–530

2

Non-Linguistic Information which could assist the Young Child's Interpretation of Adults' Speech

D. J. Messer

Introduction

Much of recent research with young children has attempted to identify features of the child's environment which could assist the process of language acquisition. Attention has been concentrated largely either on the modification of adults' speech to children (see Landes, 1975; Snow, 1977) or on pre-verbal patterns of adult-child interaction which may be relevant to the development of speech (see Schaffer, 1977a; Lock, 1978). In contrast to the considerable advances in these two areas our knowledge of the interface between them, that is the integration of linguistic with non-linguistic behaviour, is limited. Yet it is precisely this relationship which may enable infants to crack the linguistic code, for a simplified linguistic input and an existing knowledge of non-linguistic communication, by themselves, cannot provide the necessary information.

The integration of speech with other social behaviour can be examined from a variety of perspectives, but perhaps one of the most interesting questions to ask concerns the way non-linguistic events can help the comprehension of speech about objects. This is not only because of the highly referential nature of adults' speech to children but also because the child's vocabulary contains a high proportion of nouns (Nelson, 1973; Phillips, 1973). The comprehension of referential speech presents the listener with a number of difficulties (Ogden and Richards, 1923; Bruner, 1975a). These include the problem of identifying the referential word in the speaker's utterance and of locating the physical referent in the environment. This study examines the way that non-linguistic behaviour could help the child overcome such problems.

What forms of non-linguistic behaviour would ensure that children are in a position to relate adults' speech to objects in the immediate environment? Manipulation of objects is a good candidate because it often coordinates the interest of adults and children. For example, monitoring a child's manipulation of objects can provide information which will allow an adult to integrate speech with the child's activity; alternatively adult manipulation of an object can be used to direct the child's interest to objects that the adult wishes to talk about. During adult-child play manipulation is a particularly suitable behaviour to coordinate interest, because it has the advantage of clearly indicating the object an individual is interested in and of providing an almost constant stream of relevant information. Already there is evidence which suggests that adult speech may be closely integrated with the manipulation objects. Howe (1975) found that on half the occasions when mothers named a toy the child was touching the appropriate object within two and a half seconds of the start of the utterance. Similarly, in this investigation an examination is made of whether the fine timing of the adults' utterances ensures that speech coincides with the manipulation of the appropriate object.

The cues provided by simultaneous behaviour may not be the only ones that can assist the identification of the referent. Studies of early social interaction suggest that the redundancy present in the sequential organisation of behaviour puts infants in a better position to predict which behaviour will occur next (Fogel, 1977; Kaye, 1977; Stern, Beebe, Jaffe and Bennett, 1977). Typically maternal behaviour is highly repetitive, and these repetitions are grouped together into distinct episodes.

A similar organisation may be present in object related speech to children. Repeated reference to the same object in successive adult utterances would increase its redundancy and thereby make prediction of the next referent less difficult. The following example illustrates this; the utterances are organised into what will be termed *verbal episodes* – that is a string of successive utterances which all refer to the same object irrespective of the form of reference used. In the example, Utterance 1 and 2 together would constitute one verbal episode, and Utterances 3 to 5 another one; in Utterances 1 and 2 there is repeated reference to the same object, and in Utterances 3 to 5 to a different one.

1   that's horsey
2   clip clop, he's coming to see you Andrew
3   there's a nice dolly
4   I don't think she can stand though
5   she's got lovely hair, hasn't she?

Awareness of this organization would make it easier for children to predict the referent of the next utterance in the verbal episode. Accordingly, the second issue addressed in this investigation concerns the importance of verbal episodes in adult's speech to children. However, this behaviour would be of limited utility unless young children were also given non-linguistic markers to help them recognise the beginning of verbal episodes. Without the change in verbal episodes being clearly indicated a young child could continue to believe erroneously that an object previously spoken about was still the current referent. Therefore, it was necessary to examine whether non-linguistic events highlight the start of verbal episodes in adults' speech to children.

If children are to acquire referential words they also need to be able to pick out the name of the object from the stream of adult vocalisations. One solution which would make the problem less difficult would be for names to occur in one word utterances. However, as this appears to occur infrequently (Broen, 1972) some other cues must be available to assist children in identifying these words.

Acoustic amplitude is often used by adults to emphasise important words. In addition, young children are also likely to find words of a higher acoustic amplitude to be more attention worthy; not only do mothers tend to use loudness to mark important events (Kaye, 1977), but many species orientate to loud sounds, and communication systems tend to treat signals of low amplitude as background noise. Thus, part of the following study was devoted to examining whether auditory amplitude was used to emphasise the names of objects in maternal speech to young children.

To summarise, the research presented here is concerned with investigating various ways in which non-linguistic information can assist the comprehension of referential speech. Three topics are considered. First, an examination is made of the relationship between reference and the simultaneous manipulation of objects. Second, the sequential organisation of social interaction is studied to discover whether non-verbal events mark out those utterances which refer to the same object. Lastly, an investigation is made into the mother's use of emphasis to see if this could assist the identification of referential words.

Observations were obtained from two separate studies. The data from Study 1 was analysed in relation to the first two topics. The data from the second study was collected to answer the question posed by the third topic.

Study 1: Contiguity of reference and manipulation

METHOD

Subjects

There were three age groups, 11 months, 14 months and 24 months (+/− 10 days) with 14 mother-child pairs in each group (seven male and seven female). Thus there was a group of pre-verbal children, a group just beginning to use words, and a group of more sophisticated verbal ability (a classification based on the usual verbal abilities of children at these ages which was confirmed by maternal reports). The sample was recruited from predominantly middle-class/upper-working-class areas.

Procedure

Subjects were recruited by telephone. The purpose of the study was given as an interest in the way mothers and children of different ages play with toys. The nature of the task was explained, and it was stressed that the interest was in recording behaviour similar to that which might occur at home.

Prior to the observations an attempt was made to eliminate any anxieties the mothers may have had about the situation. The nature of the observations was outlined again. The mother was asked to play with her child just as she wished. The first play session of 5 minutes with four building blocks allowed the pair to become accustomed to the surroundings. There followed another 5 minute session which consisted of play with seven toys. Data were obtained only from the second session.

Apparatus

The toys consisted of a red 'Matchbox' bus, a red plastic car, a 'bendy' dog (Pluto), a small doll, a green plastic fish, a small plastic horse, and a yellow teddy bear. Play took place on a table which had a tray with raised edges clamped to it. The child was seated on the mother's lap. The sessions were recorded on video-tape at a child welfare clinic. The camera was placed on a tripod two to three metres from the mother and child. All other equipment was hidden behind a screen.

Data extraction

The video-tapes were first analysed to provide a record of the sequence in which the toys were manipulated; a note was also made of whether the mother, the child, or both held the object. Secondly, the mother's verbal utterances were transcribed onto the data sheets in a way that preserved the temporal relationship between speech and manipulative behaviour. Subsequently, the transcriptions were categorised. Utterances which referred to a toy were categorised as containing a 'name', 'pronoun' or 'indirect reference', and utterances not referring to a toy were placed in a separate category. Naming occurred when a common, proper or baby language noun was employed to refer to a toy. A pronoun was defined as a word for which the name of a specific toy could be substituted (e.g. this, he, her, it). A reference to a toy which did not involve a name or a pronoun was termed an indirect reference. In such cases the semantic content of the utterance had to involve a specific toy: this could include a behaviour performed on a toy (e.g. 'Look'), or a reference to an aspect of the toy (e.g. 'See the wheels'). The referent of an utterance was determined from the semantic content of speech; if there was doubt about the toy's identity, then eye gaze was used as an additional cue.

Only the most specific reference to a toy was coded, and on those occasions when three or more toys were referred to (e.g. 'Look at them') the utterance was treated as if it did not contain a reference. Consequently, for each utterance the data sheets contained a record of the most specific form of reference that was used about a particular toy, the identity of that toy, and information about who was manipulating which toy at the time.

When the coding was finished the tapes were re-analysed to ensure that the categories had been used consistently. One month later a reliability study was conducted by the author on one subject randomly chosen from each age group. If after coding an item as categorised differently from the original transcript, or if an item was out of place, this was regarded as an error. The percentage agreement between the two transcripts for 11 months was 79.9%, for 14 months 79.4% and for 24 months 89.9% (percentage agreement = 100 − total errors × 100/ total number of observations).

RESULTS

Maternal speech

The corpus of maternal speech consisted of 1074, 1095 and 1253 utterances in the 11 month, 14 month and 24 month age groups. The mothers' mean length of utterance in each age group was 3.3, 3.0 and 3.2 words respectively. No significant differences between age groups were found in the mean length of utterances (one way analysis of variance, $F = 1.71$, d.f. $= 2,39$).

The relationship between reference and manipulation

Could information from the manipulation of toys assist the identification of the referent in maternal speech? The data necessary to answer this question were obtained by constructing seven by seven contingency tables. These were prepared by cross-classifying utterances according to the identity of which of the seven toys was referred to and according to which of the seven toys was being simultaneously manipulated. Thus the entries in the cells of one of the diagonals of these tables represent the number of occasions when a reference was made to a toy that was being held at the time. Contingency tables were constructed for each age group, each reference type, and identity of individual (mother or child) manipulating the toy (a total of 18 tables).

A high proportion of references was to toys that were being simultaneously manipulated (between 73% and 96% depending on reference types, age group and who held the toy). Does this indicate that verbal reference was synchronised with the manipulation of the appropriate toy more often than expected by chance? Because these co-occurrences comprise the entries in the cells on one of the diagonals of the contingency tables, this relationship can be examined by calculating a *kappa* coefficient (Fleiss, 1973), which takes into account chance agreement between the identity of the toy referred to and the identity of the toy being manipulated. In each of the eighteen tables the size of the *kappa* coefficients revealed that mothers referred to the toy being manipulated at the same time more often than would be expected by chance. Furthermore, in each case the *z* score shows that the probability of this occurring by chance was less than 0.0001.

The possible importance of manipulation as a clue about the identity of the referent was highlighted when information theory (Attneave, 1959) was applied to the data. Uncertainty about events is greatest when only the number of possibilities are known; there were seven toys so the maximum uncertainty about which toy would be referred to was $\log_2 7 = 2.81$ bits. If each of the possibilities were not equally likely then knowledge of their probabilities would reduce uncertainty, i.e. if references were made only to one of the seven toys then an observer would be reasonably certain about the referent of any utterance. Knowledge about the probability of each toy being referred to only decreased the maximum uncertainty by between 1% and 4%, which indicates that there was no toy to which reference was especially likely to be made (the 'rawbias' method was employed to obtain unbiased estimates of uncertainty). Further reductions in uncertainty are possible if concurrent (or previous) events are associated with particular outcomes. When the identity of the toy being played with is known, uncertainty about which toy was being referred to was reduced by between 57% and 89% (depending on age, reference type, and who held the toy).

These analyses have drawn attention to the degree of redundancy between speech and manipulation during play. It was found that knowledge about the identity of the toy being manipulated appreciably reduced the uncertainty about the toy to which a reference was made. Consequently, ongoing activities could have made an important contribution to the comprehension of maternal speech.

The timing of speech and manipulation   Did a temporal relationship exist between speech and manipulation? To investigate this question the sequence in which toys were manipulated was established, then the timing of utterances was examined in relation to the sequence. It was predicted that most references would be to toys manipulated at the same time, that there would be fewer references to toys held during preceding or subsequent manipulations of the appropriate toy, and the least number of references would be to toys held at other times. Using Page's L-test (Bradley, 1968) these predictions were found to be true in each age group and for each form of reference ($p < 0.001$ in every one of the nine comparisons). Consequently, as time for contact with the toy increases, so the probability it would be referred to decreased.

The use of double references   If mothers were to refer to several objects in one utterance then this might be expected to make referential speech more difficult for children to comprehend because the children would have problems in combining information from different sources (Sugerman, 1973). Consequently, it is also of interest to examine the mothers' use of double references (the reference to two different toys in the same utterance, e.g. 'Put the doll on the car' or 'Put it on the car'). Perhaps the two most important aspects of the employment of double references to note are that they were used infrequently and that their use increased in frequency with the age of the child (see Table 1). This suggests that the mothers had an awareness of the cognitive and linguistic capabilities of their children.

It is perhaps of greater interest that the use of double references appeared to be influenced by contextual factors. For example, the frequency of double references was related to who held the toys, there being more double references when the child held one or both of the relevant toys (see Table 1).

TABLE 1

The use of maternal double references as a function of
position of toys

Position of toys	Age of child (months)		
	11	14	24
Both held by infant	2	3	21
Both held by mother	4	2	2
One on table, one held by infant	0	7	27
One on table, one held by mother	3	0	21
One held by infant, one held by mother	0	1	14
Both on table	0	0	2
Total	9	13	90[a]

[a]Includes 3 instances when one of the toys was held by both

Furthermore, when one toy was on the table and the other was being manipulated by the mother or the child, then the toy on the table (which would be more difficult to identify) was named more often: the toy on the table was named 3, 7, 29 times and the toy being manipulated was named 0, 0, 6 times, at 11, 14 and 24 months respectively. Thus mothers appeared to organise their speech so that they took account of the possible difficulty of interpreting double references.

Summary   The first analysis of the data from Study 1 has revealed that the manipulation of objects could provide a useful clue about the toy to which verbal reference was being made. In most cases the relevant object was being manipulated at the same time, and even in those instances when this did not occur, references tended to occur either shortly before or after the object was handled. This relationship was maintained in all three age groups, for all three types of reference, and for whether the mother or child was manipulating the toy. A similar sensitivity was shown in the mother's use of double references; these tended to be integrated with play in a way that would maximise the child's chances of understanding this more complex form of speech.

The sequential organisation of behaviour

The data obtained from the investigation described in the previous section were subjected to a second analysis to determine whether sequential as well as simultaneous events could assist the interpretation of speech. Here it was of interest to determine whether speech was organised so that utterances which referred to the same object tended to occur together and to establish whether non-verbal behaviour marked out this structure.

For the purpose of this analysis when a double reference occurred only one of the references was analysed. The reference category which was examined was the one that concerned a toy which had already been referred to in the previous utterance, or if there was no continuity between utterances it was the most specific reference in the utterance.

Verbal episodes   Was maternal speech organised into verbal episodes? To put it another way was there a tendency for successive maternal utterances to refer to the same object? To examine this possibility transition tables were constructed by cross-classifying pairs of successive maternal utterances according to the identity of the toy referred to in the first utterance, and the identity of the toy referred to in the next utterance. A 7×7 table of transition frequencies was produced for each age group. In transitions between successive utterances over half of them contained a reference to the same toy as the previous utterance (between 59% and 64%, depending on age group). Moreover, such a result was unlikely to occur by chance. A *kappa* coefficient (Fleiss, 1973) was calculated from the transition table of each mother-child pair; these *kappa* scores indicated that in each case the observed frequency of utterance transitions was greater than the expected one, and in every case the z score indicated a level of significance of 0.001%.

The reduction of uncertainty about the identity of the referent was calculated by the use of information theory (Attneave, 1959). As before the maximum uncertainty about which toy would be referred to was $\log_2 7 = 2.381$ bits, and this was reduced by between 1% and 4% when the frequency of references to the different toys was known; in contrast, knowledge of the identity of the toy referred to in the previous utterance reduced the maximum uncertainty about which toy was being referred to by between 43% and 48% (depending on the age group).

Thus speech was organised into *verbal episodes*, that is sequences of successive utterances which all referred to the same object. Knowledge about this arrangement could be used to assist the identification of the object which would be referred to next. Was non-verbal information available to help linguistically unsophisticated children identify the introduction of a new referent into a sequence of utterances?

Toy manipulation and the beginning of verbal episodes   The beginning of a new verbal episode would be less difficult to identify if it followed the manipulation of a new toy. A high proportion of verbal episodes began after there had been a change in the identity of the toy being manipulated (70% at 11 months, 71.1% at 14 months and 45.9% at 24 months). Was a toy change more likely to occur before the start of verbal episodes than at other times? A comparison was made of the observed and expected frequency of toy changes before the start of verbal episodes. This entailed constructing 2 × 2 contingency tables by cross-classifying utterances according to whether they were at the beginning of a verbal episode and whether the toy being held was the same as the toy held when the previous utterance occurred. The expected frequency of toy changes could then be calculated from the marginal totals of the contingency tables in the normal manner. The observed and expected frequencies were calculated for each mother. In every age group there was a significant number of mother-infant pairs for whom the observed frequency exceeded that expected by chance. The mean frequency of toy changes that preceded the start of verbal episodes were: 11 months; observed 9.6, expected 4.5, $p < 0.002$; 14 months; observed 9.6, expected 4.3, $p < 0.002$; 24 months; observed 7.2, expected 4.8, $p < 0.058$ (two-tailed *Sign Test*). Thus, the start of verbal episodes was marked out by the manipulation of new objects.

The inter-utterance interval between episodes   If a long pause preceded the start of verbal episodes, this would also give a clue as to when the change in referent was made. To investigate this possibility six mother-child pairs were randomly chosen from each age group. The length of the inter-utterance intervals was timed separately for those pairs of utterance which referred to the same toy and those that referred to different toys.

Reliable measure of inter-utterance intervals to the nearest second can be obtained by the use of a stop watch (Schaffer, Collis and Parsons, 1977). Use of a Lexicon Varispeech cassette recorder permitted the recordings to be replayed at half the normal speed with corrections being made to the pitch which ensured that the slower speech was intelligible. This increased the accuracy of the method so that it was possible to time utterances to the nearest tenth of a second. The interval between utterances which referred to different toys was on average twice as long as the interval between utterances which referred to the same toy (mean interval in seconds between utterances: 11 months; same toys 3.3, different toys 7.2; 14 months; same toys 3.1, different toys 9.4; 24 months; same toys

2.0, different toys 5.4). Furthermore, the mean interval between utterances which referred to different toys was for every subject the longer one (for each age group $p < 0.032$; two tailed *Sign Test*). Thus the time between utterances could also be used to help identify when a new verbal episode began.

Summary   The second set of analyses of the data from Study 1 revealed that non-verbal behaviour marked out those sequences of utterances which referred to the same object. Verbal episodes tended to occur after a change in the identity of the toy being manipulated and after a longer than usual inter-utterance interval. As a result non-linguistic behaviour made it easier to detect the sequential organisation present in maternal speech about objects. This could reduce the difficulty the child would have in understanding referential speech. There was an indication that at 24 months the children received less assistance in this task; manipulation no longer gave such a clear indication about the start of verbal episodes. Apart from this, similar behaviour was observed in all three age groups.

Study 2: The emphasis of names of objects

The two previous sets of analyses indicated that non-linguistic behaviour could be used to assist the identification of the physical referent of maternal speech. An additional study was conducted to determine whether non-linguistic behaviour such as acoustic amplitude is used by adults in a way that could assist the identification of the verbal referent by children.

METHOD

Subjects

Fifteen mother-infant pairs were observed; eight children were female and seven were male. The sample was drawn from a predominantly middle-class area. The age at which children are starting to produce words would seem to be the one at which adults are most likely to emphasise the names of objects. Consequently, 14-month-old children were observed (+/– 12 days).

Procedure

The procedure was similar to that of the previous study. The only difference being that a longer session of eight minutes was recorded for analysis, and that all the video equipment was placed behind a one-way mirror.

Apparatus

The study was conducted in a mobile laboratory which was sited at a child welfare clinic. To reduce the possibility of noise the play sessions took place on a padded table top and soft toys were provided: a teddy, a car, a duck and a ladybird. The pair were seated around the table. A microphone placed near to the pair supplied an audio signal which was converted by an electronic device into a visual display, this was mixed onto the video recording. The amplitude of the auditory signal correlated with the number of lights that were illuminated. The system gave a flat response to signals of a constant voltage over a frequency range of between 1.0 and 5.0 kHz, and the use of light emitting diodes in the visual display minimised the response latency of the equipment.

Data analysis

The sample used for analysis consisted of all maternal utterances which contained the name of a toy. These uttereances were transcribed along with any non-linguistic vocalisations, such as 'Oh', 'Ooo', or 'Mhh'; such expressions were treated as 'words'. The words were classified either as *names* of toys or as *non-names*. For each utterance the *loudest* word was also located, this was accomplished by manually turning the video reels so that the maximum sound level of each word could be identified from the visual display of light emitting diodes.

RESULTS

The corpus of speech was made up of 739 utterances. It was necessary to discard 14% of the sample because extraneous noise prevented the loudest word from being identified. In 20% of the utterances the loudest word could not be identified because the speech was either so loud that the maximum response was obtained from the light emitting diodes, or so soft that no response was produced. Thus the analysis is based on a sample of 487 utterances which contained a total of 1850 words.

Were names marked out as being the loudest word in an utterance? Words were classified into the categories given in Table 2. For each category a calculation was made of the probability that it would be the loudest word in an utterance (probability = number of occurrences of the word as a loudest word/total number of times the category was used). Names were most frequently the loudest word in an utterance and had the highest probability of being the loudest word in an utterance.

TABLE 2

The probability that a word would be the loudest in an utterance

	Total no. of vocalisations	Total no. of loudest vocalisations	Mean probability[a]
Names of toys	511	250	0.47
Qualifiers	106	39	0.40
Non-verbal expressions	51	24	0.36
Interrogatives	96	37	0.34
Other nouns	87	33	0.23
Verbs	364	67	0.16
All other words	65	11	0.14
Locatives	163	15	0.10
Pronouns	126	8	0.08
Articles	281	3	0.03
Total	1850	487	

[a]Calculated from the individual probabilities of each mother

In this corpus of speech 28% of all words were names, yet nearly 50% of these names were the loudest word of an utterance, suggesting that this behaviour occurred more frequently than would be expected from a random association of naming and loudness. A more formal test of this possibility was made by cross-classifying utterances according to the position of the loudest word in the utterance and the position of the name, so that the cells on the diagonal of these tables contained the number of occasions when names were the loudest word in the utterance. Separate tables were constructed for each utterance length and for each mother. The expected frequencies were calculated from the marginal totals in the normal way. The observed frequency of utterances where the loudest word was a name consistently exceeded that expected by chance (mean frequencies: observed 15.9, expected 13.0; $p < 0.002$ (two-tailed *Sign Test*)).

Were there circumstances in which names were especially likely to be the loudest word in an utterance? The sequential analysis of speech has indicated that non-verbal behaviour marked out verbal episodes. Consequently, this is likely to be a time when young children are attending to the referent; moreover, previous experience of non-verbal interaction may have taught them that the establishment of a topic usually precedes comment about it. Therefore, the emphasis of names at the beginning of verbal episodes might be particularly effective in drawing the child's attention to these words.

To examine this possibility, 2 × 2 tables were constructed for each mother by cross-classifying utterances according to whether they contained a loudest name, and whether they were the first utterance after a change of topic. Analysis revealed that utterances immediately following a change in referent were more likely than other utterances to contain loudest names. The Mantel-Haenzel procedure (Fleiss, 1973) was used to combine the evidence from the sample of subjects; the *Chi-square* of association from this analysis was 10.89 and the summary odds ratio was 1.91. The homogeneity term is also significant, indicating that individual differences existed; however, inspection of the data showed that the summary odds ratio and its associated *Chi-square* adequately represented the group average.

Summary   The observation of maternal speech in the second study indicated that referential names had a high probability of being the loudest word in an utterance and that the emphasis of names was especially likely to occur at the beginning of verbal episodes. This relationship between words and acoustic amplitude should help the child to relate the name of a toy to the object on which his or her attention is focused.

DISCUSSION

The present findings suggest that non-linguistic behaviour could have an important role to play in assisting the child's comprehension of speech. Both preceding and simultaneous events gave an indication of which object was being talked about, and the use of emphasis gave an indication of which word referred to the object. Thus, not only are children presented with speech in a simplified form (Landes, 1975; Snow, 1977), but non-linguistic information appears to be available to assist the comprehension of this simplified speech.

In this discussion attention will be paid to three topics. First, an examination is made of whether children are likely to make use of non-linguistic behaviour such as that described here to help them interpret speech. Second, theories of language acquisition are examined to discover whether this behaviour would be predicted to assist children during the initial stages of acquisition. Third, a consideration is made of whether the behaviour could continue to contribute to the development of older children's speech.

The relevance of non-linguistic behaviour to children

Were children likely to utilise information provided by these different forms of non-linguistic behaviour? Various studies have indicated that by the end of their first year children are able to use and respond to verbal and non-verbal behaviour in a relatively sophisticated manner (Bruner, 1975b, 1977; Clark, 1977; Macnamara, 1977). In particular, children of this age can follow forms of indication such as eye gaze and pointing (Scaife and Bruner, 1975; Lempers, E. R. Flavell and J. H. Flavell, 1977; Murphy and Messer, 1977). If children can respond to these relatively complex forms of indication, it would seem likely that they will also have some understanding of the importance of manipulative events. Children may also be able to utilise the redundancy provided by the organisation of speech into verbal episodes. They are exposed to repetitive behaviour from the first months of life (Kaye, 1977; Stern, Beebe, Jaffe and Bennett, 1977) and this experience may cue them to other forms of redundancy which are present in social interaction at a later age. As regards acoustic amplitude, mothers often use this form of emphasis to high-light important events (Bruner, 1975a; Kaye, 1977) so children could come to attach particular significance to words that are stressed.

In addition, the nature of the relationship between speech and non-linguistic behaviour was likely to ensure that infants paid attention to information from both sources. The link between speech and non-linguistic behaviour did not simply occur as discrete events which would aid the interpretation of particular utterances. Instead, speech was integrated with non-verbal processes which were basic to social interaction and information concerning speech was continuously available from the very organisation of social interaction. In the case of speech and manipulation an important relationship existed between verbal reference and the object being held at the time. This fundamental relationship appeared to occur throughout the observation sessions and was not simply related to the activities of one member of the dyad or tied to specific behaviours. The structure of speech was made easier to detect by the redundancy provided by verbal episodes and by the use of non-verbal behaviour to mark out this structure. However, no one event made this sequential organisation easier to detect but the very organisation of interaction could have played a rôle in this process. Emphasis did tend simply to indicate the identity of the referential word. Even so, loudest names were not equally likely to occur in any utterance, they were especially likely to be positioned at the beginning of verbal episodes. Consequently, although emphasis may not have provided a continuous stream of information about the identity of the referential word, neither was it the case that the use of emphasis was separate from other aspects of social interaction.

Thus, linguistic and non-linguistic actions appear to have been united in a common organisation rather than one form of behaviour being structured around the other. An important point is that the infants were part of this organisation: they were not likely to have been passive observers left to deduce the meaning of speech from non-linguistic events (see Bruner, 1975b). Therefore it can also be argued that children would attend to and try to make sense of non-linguistic behaviour because these events were part of the communication system in which the children were involved. This is not to deny that certain behaviours may have had more relevance than others, but to point out that the development of language could depend on a whole range of non-verbal as well as verbal behaviours.

Other more specific findings indicate that information from manipulative acts may be used by older children to assist the comprehension of speech. Children of 3–4 years have been reported to have difficulty in following instructions when the subject of a sentence is a toy other than the one being held (Bem, 1970). After training, the children made few mistakes so it would seem likely that the confusion was not due to cognitive limitations, but may have been due to the children simply assuming that the object they held was usually the subject of a sentence. What is surprising is that discrepancies between speech and its non-verbal context even affect older children. Huttenlocher, Eisenberg and Strauss (1968) found that children of the 4th grade were slowest when following instructions in which the grammatical subject and the perceived subject did not coincide, and quickest when the two did coincide. The implication of this is that children in the second year of life who possess fewer verbal skills are likely to be even more dependent on contextual information when interpreting speech. It might even be speculated that this early dependency on non-linguistic information results in the development of comprehension strategies which are seen in older children. More mature children also appear to respond to words of a higher acoustic amplitude. The use of this device makes it more likely that words will be recalled (Frith, 1969; Hermelin and O'Conner, 1970; Weener, 1971; Shepard and Asher, 1973). The implication is that acoustic amplitude would have a similar impact on young children.

Thus, three lines of argument point to young children being able to utilise the information from the non-linguistic behaviour described here. First, children by the second year of life respond to other relatively complex forms of non-linguistic communication. Second, the children did not appear to have to work out the significance of behaviours that would occur like 'bolts out of the blue'. Instead their involvement in social interaction may have given them a participant's perspective of the way non-linguistic behaviour fitted together with speech. Third, research with older children suggests that even they may rely on non-linguistic information when processing speech.

The initial acquisition of words

What role might non-linguistic behaviour play in the initial acquisition of words? As the relationship between words and objects varies from culture to culture *a priori* reasoning can show that word acquisition, that is the process whereby children come to produce the appropriate label in relation to certain objects or events, will occur through children using information in their environment to identify referential words and their physical referents. Therefore, some form of non-linguistic behaviour, perhaps similar to that observed here, must be available to help the child with these tasks. However, though the importance of the environmental input is self evident, only limited attention has been paid to specifying the parameters which would enable the acquisition of words to take place. In particular, it is not clear what forms of behaviour are necessary for the acquisition of words, how frequently they would need to be repeated, and whether this would need to occur over a certain age range.

If acquisition occurred by infants learning to associate a word with features which are common to a group of objects, then the contingencies described in this study would be suitable to play a part in this process. However, the child is not just learning the relationship between a word and an object, but also coming to understand that a word is a sign referring to a class of objects, and that a word can be used to obtain certain ends. Thus acquiring names will not involve a simple mechanical stamping in of associations between words and objects, with the child being a passive recipient of this process. Rather the learning of this relationship only becomes important when it can be integrated, by a process of active hypothesis testing, with existing knowledge – such as appropriate concepts and appropriate communicative abilities. Piaget's writings have often emphasised such a process, he has written that 'the organising activity of the subject must be considered just as important as the connections inherent in the external stimuli, for the subject becomes aware of these connections only to the degree that he can assimilate them by means of his existing structures' (Piaget and Inhelder, 1969, p. 5).

One possibility is that acquisition is only limited by the development of cognitive and communicative abilities. In such a case children might only need a brief exposure to the relationship between words and referents, consequently, the non-linguistic behaviour seen here would only have a limited importance for the acquistion process. Support for such a view comes from the fact that prior to the use of words children clearly have some of the capacities necessary for this task. Schaffer (1977b) has pointed out that one can identify the following forms of continuity between pre-verbal and verbal communication: those of constituent skills (intentionality, role alternation), those of function (the wish to obtain certain goals), and situational similarities (the development of communication skills in certain contexts). If we assume, for the moment, that these abilities are a limiting factor for word acquisition then one might expect there would be a rapid change in behaviour when the child first realises the relevance of the relationship between names and objects. However, the observations of children at the time of word acquisition do not report any sudden differences in behaviour at the onset of word use (Bloom, 1971, 1973; Bates, Camaioni and Volterra, 1973; Sugerman, 1973; Dore, 1974, 1975; Lock, 1975). Indeed, Bates et al. (1973, p. 220) have written that 'we found a gradual passage from vocalisation, to vocalisation as signal, to word as signal, to word as a proposition with a referential value'.

Thus, although important cognitive and communicative developments have to take place before word acquisition can occur, observations suggest that at first the child's cognitive developments are not sufficient to enable him or her to fully understand the communicative significance of words. Because of this children are likely to require repeated exposure to the appropriate relationships between names and objects over a relatively long period of time, before they will be able to use words effectively for some communicative purpose. This form of behaviour was observed here.

A similar perspective also emerges from a number of theories that provide accounts of the role of the environment in the development of language. These theories emphasise the complex nature of the acquisition task. Clark (1975, p. 77) has suggested that the problem for the child is to 'segment sound sequences . . . and then work out how they are related to the situation around him'. It is assumed that this will be possible because adults talk about the 'here and now' and because children have the appropriate conceptual structures to decode this speech. Nelson (1974) has also discussed the relevance of the environmental input. She has postulated that for acquisition to take place the child must notice that a word is used consistently with an object for which he or she has already formed a concept. Bruner (1975a, b, 1977) has emphasised that the problem of reference is to develop procedures to construct and use a limited taxonomy. More-over, he points out that the ability to use reference 'is dependent not only on mastering a relationship between a sign and a significate, but upon an understanding of social rules for achieving dialogue in which that relationship can be realised' (Ninio and Bruner, 1978, p. 15).

These accounts make it clear that the child should repeatedly be able to pick out the appropriate relationship between words and their physical referents, for if too many incorrect identifications or discrepancies occurred then the child's initial use of words would bear little or no relation to that of adults. Furthermore, the impli-cation from these writings is that the acquisition process is a gradual one, the child 'works out' (Clark, 1975) or 'notices' (Nelson, 1974) consistencies between words and objects, and has also to place this relationship within gradually emerging cognitive and communications systems (Nelson, 1974; Bruner, 1977).

To summarise: the early stages of language development might be assisted by behaviour similar to that observed here. To acquire words, children initially have to be able to relate words to the appropriate non-linguistic events. Analysis revealed that information from man-ipulation and the sequential organisation of interaction was able to assist the identification of the physical referent in the environment, and information from the use of acoustic amplitude could have assisted the identification of the referential words in maternal speech. Consequently, non-linguistic events could have drawn the child's attention to the relevant parameters.

Theories and observations of speech development suggest that word acquisition does not occur rapidly, the child slowly assimilates the relationships between words and referents to existing cognitive and communicative functions. The behaviour observed here is suit-able for a process of this nature. Behaviour which would assist the identification of the referent was observed over a broad age range. Examination of the use of emphasis was only made with a group of 14-month-olds, but there is no reason to believe that the behaviour only occurs with children of this age. These behaviours also occurred repeatedly during the sessions which suggested that children were given many opportunities to recognise the appropriate connections.

The role of non-linguistic behaviour in later language acquisition

The possible relevance, to children, of the behaviour observed here is not confined to the initial acquisition of words. The basic relation-ship between speech and non-lingusitic behaviour was also present in the 24-month-old group. Initially one might not expect interaction to continue to be organised so that information was available to assist the identification of the referent. However, a more careful consideration of this problem suggests that there are a number of reasons for, and benefits from, interaction continuing to be organised in this way.

It is possible that even at the end of the second year the existence of a relationship between verbal and non-verbal events is necessary for language development. This is because the expansion of the child's vocabulary would still require appropriate relationships to exist between words and objects. Moreover, the relationship between speech and non-linguistic behaviour may not only help older children to acquire new names but may also help the acquisition of other words. In this respect it is interesting that mothers in the oldest age group appeared to refer to aspects or parts of toys more often than mothers of younger children; similar results have also been reported by Murphy (1978). Therefore, the identification of the object being talked about in relation to all *three* forms of reference may have become more relevant to language acquisition as the child's own linguistic knowledge increased.

There is another way that the relationship between speech and non-linguistic behaviour may be important for the child's linguistic development. It is generally accepted that when children first use a word in connection with a group of objects, the word is applied in an over-restricted or over-extended manner and the supposition is often made that continuing exposure to the word, in the presence of the appropriate class of objects, results in the child coming to use the word in a more conventional manner. There is still a debate about the mechanism and status of these developments (Barrett, 1978; Clark, 1973, 1975; Nelson, 1974), but the significant point is that repeated exposure to appropriate relationship between words and objects might be necessary for the child's use of words to become more similiar to that of the adult. Admittedly in this study it was not possible to observe whether mothers organised speech so that a word usually accompanied the manipulation of different members of the same class; however, the implication from the findings is that this would occur. Thus the presence of appropriate relationship between speech and non-linguistic behaviour may play a fundamental role in assisting the internal development of the child's vocabulary.

The identification of the relationship between utterances also is likely to make the acquisition of language less difficult. For example, detection of this relationship would make anaphoric utterances, elliptical utterances, pronouns and the use of indirect references easier for children to understand. Consequently, the organisation of maternal speech into verbal episodes might assist the acquisition of those linguistic expressions that require the listener to be able to relate the present utterance to past or future ones.

It is also worth considering the relevances that these findings have to the acquisition of syntax. Psychologists tend to stress developmental continuities in language acquisition and argue that pre-lingusitic processes are of relevance to this process (Sinclair, 1969; Bruner, 1975a, 1977). They emphasise that the acquisition of syntax must be seen in relation to the development of other abilities; of these, the relevance of semantic understanding has often been stressed (Macnamara, 1972; Ervin-Tripp, 1973; Bloom, 1973; Bruner, 1975a, b). For example, Macnamara (1972, p. 7) has written that 'prior knowledge of vocabulary items and their referents is basic to the learning of syntax' and Ervin-Tripp (1973, p. 261) that 'the learner must know the referent for learning of language to occur' (italics omitted). Thus the development of referential proficiency is often seen as providing one of the foundations for the later development of syntax, and so it is possible to see a tenuous connection between the behaviour observed here and the later use of syntax.

Information from ongoing behaviour may also have a more direct relevance. Slobin (1973, p. 186) has argued that:

In order to acquire language, the child must attend to speech and the contexts in which speech occurs – that is, he must be trying to understand what he hears, and be trying to express the intentions of which he is capable. This means that he must have both cognitive and linguistic discovery procedures available – in order to formulate internal structures which are capable of assimilating and relating both linguistic and non-linguistic data.

Macnamara (1972) has put the point more forcibly. He reasons that because the same syntactic device can have several different semantic structures, and vice versa, a recourse to contextual information is essential if children are to establish the status of syntactic variations. He also says that 'the thrust to learn syntax comes mainly from meaning' and stresses that the understanding of a speech act requires information about the context in which speech occurs. Thus the continuing integration of speech and non-linguistic behaviour may not just be relevant to the identification of the referent but may also be necessary for the child to understand the communicative intentions present in speech, and for him to relate syntactic structures to these communicative intentions.

Acknowledgements

This research was supported by a grant from the Social Science Research Council to Professor H. R. Schaffer. The author would like to acknowledge the help, advice, and encouragement of Glyn Collis and Professor Schaffer which made completion of this paper possible; and to Martha Zaslow for her thoughtful comments on this paper.

References

Attneave, F. (1959). "Applications of Information Theory to Psychology". Holt, New York

Barrett, M. D. (1978). Lexical development and overextension in child language. *Journal of Child Language* 5, 205–219

Bates, E., Camaioni, L., and Volterra, V. (1973). The acquisition of performatives prior to speech. *Merrill-Palmer Quarterly* 21, 205–226

Bem, S. L. (1970). The role of comprehension in children's problem solving. *Developmental Psychology* 2, 351–358

Bloom, L. (1971). Why not pivot grammar? *Journal of Speech and Hearing Disorders* 36, 40–50

Bloom, L. (1973). "One Word at a Time". Mouton, The Hague

Bradley, J. V. (1968). "Distribution-free Statistical Tests". Prentice-Hall, New Jersey

Broen, P. A. (1972). The verbal environment of the language learning child. *Monograph of the American Speech and Hearing Association*, No. 17

Brown, R. and Bellugi, U. (1964). Three processes in child's acquisition of syntax. *In* "New Directions in the Study of Language" (E. H. Lenneberg, Ed.). M.I.T. Press, Massachusetts

Bruner, J. S. (1975a). The ontogenesis of speech acts. *Journal of Child Language* 2, 1–19

Bruner, J. S. (1975b). From communication to language – a psychological perspective. *Cognition* 3, 255–287

Bruner, J. S. (1977). Early social interaction and language acquisition. *In* "Studies in Mother-Infant Interaction" (H. R. Schaffer, Ed.). Academic Press, London

Clark, E. V. (1973). What's in a word? On the child's acquisition of semantics in his first language. *In* "Cognitive Development and the Acquisition of Language" (T. E. Moore, Ed.). Academic Press, London

Clark, E. V. (1975). Knowledge, context, and strategy in the acquisition of meaning. *In* "Georgetown University Round Table on Language and Linguistics" (D. P. Dato, Ed.) Georgetown University Press, Washington, D.C.

Clark, E. V. (1977). Strategies and the mapping problem in first language acquisition. *In* "Language Learning and Thought" (J. Macnamara, Ed.). Academic Press, New York

Dore, J. (1973). "The Development of Speech Acts". Unpublished doctoral dissertation. City University of New York, New York

Dore, J. (1974). A pragmatic description of early language development. *Journal of Psycholinguistic Research* 4, 343–350

Dore, J. (1975). Holophrases, speech acts and language universals. *Journal of Child Language* 2, 21–40

Ervin-Tripp, S. M. (1973). Some strategies for the first two years. *In* "Cognitive Development and the Acquisition of Language" (T. E. Moore, Ed.). Academic Press, New York

Fleiss, J. L. (1973). "Statistical Methods for Rates and Proportions". Wiley, New York

Fogel, A. (1977). Temporal organization in mother-father face-to-face interaction. *In* "Studies in Mother-Infant Interaction" (H. R. Schaffer, Ed.) Academic Press, London

Frith, U. (1969). Emphasis and meaning in normal and autistic children. *Language and Speech* 12, 29–38

Hermelin, B. and O'Connor, N. (1970). "Psychological Experiments with Autistic Children". Pergamon Press, Oxford

Howe, C. J. (1975). "The Nature and Origins of Social Class Differences in the Prepositions Expressed by Young Children". Unpublished doctoral dissertation, University of Cambridge, Cambridge

Huttenlocher, J., Eisenberg, S. and Strauss, S. (1968). Comprehension: Relation between perceived actor and logical subject. *Journal of Verbal Learning and Verbal Behaviour* 7, 527–530

Kaye, K. (1977). Toward the origin of dialogue. *In* "Studies in Mother-Infant Interaction" (H. R. Schaffer, Ed.). Academic Press, London

Landes, J. (1975). Speech addressed to children. *Language Learning* 25, 355–379

Lempers, J. D., Flavell, E. R. and Flavell, J. H. (1977). The development in very young children of tacit knowledge concerning visual perception. *Genetic Psychology Monographs* 95, 3–53

Lock, A. (Ed.) (1978). "Action, Gesture and Symbol". Academic Press, London

Lock, A. (1975). "On being picked up". Paper presented at A.S.A.B. symposium Mother-Child interaction in man and the higher mammals, London

Macnamara, J. (1972). Cognitive basis of language learning in infants. *Psychological Review* 79, 1–11

Macnamara, J. (Ed.) (1977). "Language Learning and Thought." Academic Press, New York

Murphy, C. M. (1978). Pointing in the context of a shared activity. *Child Development* 49, 371–380

Murphy, C. M. and Messer, D. J. (1977). Mothers, infants, and pointing: A study of a gesture. *In* "Studies in Mother-Infant Interaction" (H. R. Schaffer, Ed.). Academic Press, London

Nelson, K. (1973). Structure and strategy in learning to talk. *Monographs of the Society for Research in Child Development* 38, Nos. 1–2, Serial No. 149

Nelson, K. (1974). Concept, word, and sentence: Interrelations in acquisition and development. *Psychological Review* 81, 267–285

Ninio, A. and Bruner, J. (1978). The achievement and antecedents of labelling. *Journal of Child Language* 5, 1–15

Ogden, C. K. and Richards, I. A. (1923). "The Meaning of Meaning". Routhedge and Kegan Paul, London

Piaget, J. and Inhelder, B. (1969). "The Psychology of the Child". Routledge and Kegan Paul, London (originally published in 1966)

Phillips, J. R. (1973). Syntax and vocabulary of mothers' speech to young children: Age and sex comparisons. *Child Development* 44, 182–185

Scaife, M. and Bruner, J. S. (1975). The capacity for joint visual attention in the infant. *Nature* 253, 265–266

Schaffer, H. R. (Ed.) (1977a). "Studies in Mother-Infant Interaction". Academic Press, London

Schaffer, H. R. (1977b). Early interactive development. *In* "Studies in Mother-Infant Interaction" (H. R. Schaffer, Ed.). Academic Press, London

Schaffer, H. R., Collis, G. M. and Parsons, G. (1977). Vocal interchange and visual regard in verbal and pre-verbal children. *In* "Studies in Mother-Infant Interaction" (H. R. Schaffer, Ed.). Academic Press, London

Shepard, W. and Ascher, L. M. (1973). Effects of linguistic rule conformity on free recall in children and adults. *Developmental Psychology* 8, 139

Sinclair, H. (1969). Developmental psycholinguistics. *In* "Studies on Cognitive Development" (D. Elkind and J. Flavell, Eds). Oxford University Press, New York

Slobin, D. I. (1973). Cognitive prerequisities for the development of grammar. *In* "Studies of Child Language Development" (C. A. Ferguson and D. I. Slobin, Eds). Holt, Rinehart and Winston, New York

Snow, C. E. (1977). Mothers' speech research: From input to interaction. *In* "Talking to Children" (C. E. Snow and C. A. Ferguson, Eds). Cambridge University Press, Cambridge

Stern, D. N., Beebe, B., Jaffe, J. and Bennett, S. L. (1977). The infant's stimulus world during social interaction: A study of caregiver behaviours with particular reference to repetition and timing. *In* "Studies in Mother-Infant Interaction" (H. R. Schaffer, Ed.). Academic Press, London

Sugerman, S. (1973). A description of communicative development in the prelanguage child. Unpublished honors thesis. Hampshire College. *Cited* in Bates, E., Camaioni, L. and Volterra, V. The acquisition of performatives prior to speech. *Merrill-Palmer Quarterly* 21, 205–226

Weener, P. (1971). Language structure and the free recall of verbal messages by children. *Developmental Pscyhology* 5, 237–243

3

Collaboration and Confrontation with Young Children in Language Comprehension Testing

N. H. Freeman, C. G. Sinha and S. G. Condliffe

Introduction

Whenever one tests children who are not fully socialised into adult discourse rules, there is a real problem to cope with. Let us put it formally: given that the adult and child enter into a social relationship involving compliance by the children with adult directives, under what conditions can one diagnose with confidence the children's level of linguistic competence independently of the social relations into which they enter? The adult trades a great deal on the cooperative goodwill of the child, yet one simply does not know how to formalise this at present. What presuppositions do the children typically bring to the experimental episode? Often it is of little use to have an intelligent conversation with them afterwards: they do not know how to formulate presuppositions any more than we do.

The experimenter knows more than the children: and if knowledge is power, then there is a most unequal power relationship. The experimenter has set up a situation, and the children's job is to investigate it to find out roughly what is expected of them. So they have to find out to a certain extent what is in the experimenter's mind, so as to distinguish between what will be accepted as cooperation and what will be construed as evasion or 'playing about'. Many experiments must feel like 'playing about', especially if the experimenter has kindly provided toys. How do children find out what is really to be done? How do they diagnose the task and find out whether the diagnosis accords reasonably with the adult's intentions?

PROBLEMS OF THE PILOT PHASE

The following examples from our work are only slightly edited. If we come out of it badly, we trust that the data reported later will restore our credit.

First example   The experimenter puts down a hollow cube on its side and asks a 2-year-old to put a brick on top of the cube. The child retreats. The cycle is gone through again and the same thing happens, twice. The adults briefly confer. The experimenter thinks that the child might not understand the referential meaning of the word 'on'. The mother thinks that her child had got the impression that she was going to be allowed to play with bricks and was not ready to negotiate a change in joint enterprise. The observer thinks that the child was not going to let anyone tell her what to do. After sorting out these problems, the researchers wonder how they are going to classify the behaviour of a whole sample of children.

Second example   Another 2-year-old is perfectly willing and able to obey 'in' and 'on' requests at the cube. He is then asked to put a small brick on top of an inverted cup. He goes to the trouble of turning the cup upright, putting the brick inside it. This happens twice more. The experimenter thinks that the child's grasp of 'on' is rather unstable and can easily be thrown off by a conflicting cue (the canonical orientation of the cup: which way up it 'ought to be'). The mother thinks that the child was not properly listening, since he knew what cups are for, not registering that the experimenter really meant the cup to be kept inverted. The observer thinks that since this was the first time that the experimenter had asked for an object to be manifestly misused, the child was either showing that he trusted the experimenter enough not to believe that violation of normal rules were being asked for, or that he did not trust the experimenter enough to engage in a joint enterprise of normal-rule violation. They all wonder if these are not really the same explanation in different guises. The researchers drive off arguing about theory.

Third example   The same child is tested three months later. All goes well, and the child manages to put a brick on the inverted cup, and in the upright cup; but when asked to put the brick *in* the inverted cup, reaches out and puts it on. This happens again. The experimenter thinks that this is an index of developmental advance: the tyranny of canonical orientation has given way to an ability to search for abstract features, such as a 'flat surface' or 'cavity' regardless of the symbolic nature of the target, inducing a new kind of processing problem. The mother thinks that the child is trying to comply so much that he takes it for granted that the request can be fulfilled without interfering with the experimenter's arrangement of the target. The observer thinks that the child was merely doing the simplest action necessary to show willing. A few probes eliminate this last possibility, but the others remain.

Fourth example   A 3-year-old passes all tests of 'in' and 'on' with bricks, cubes, cups etc., and laughs as he realises that he has to invert a cup to comply with the request to put a brick under it. The researchers are pleased that 3-year-olds are easy to work with.

Fifth example   The experimenter and observer are with a $4\frac{1}{2}$-year-old in a nursery school. They play imitation games, getting the child to put a brick in and on a cup, when upright as well as inverted, as quickly as he can. The child enjoys the game. Then they give verbal requests and the child correctly puts a brick in the upright cup and on the inverted cup. The experimenter then inverts the cup and asks the child to put the brick in it. The child burst into tears. The adults are galvanised into consolatory activity. They ask the child if he wants to go back to the classroom and he says no. So they again play imitation games showing that all the things that can be done with a cup and a brick are really permissable. Again 'language comprehension' conditions are introduced and again the child performs well until asked to put the brick in the inverted cup, when his lip trembles. He is swiftly consoled and rewarded. Later, the teacher expresses surprise that the child should get upset at all, and consoles the researchers who had been getting on so well for so many sessions at the school. All agree that 4-year-olds are much more subtle than 3-year-olds and could be expected occasionally to experience as conflict what the 3-year-olds see merely as a delightful puzzle.

Sixth example   The observer is holding his daughter, aged 2 years 3 months. He gives her a cup of milk at her request and says, as usual, 'tell me when you have had enough'. For the first time Anna simply says 'No'. The observer looks surprised, fortunately, for it galvanises the child to explain 'Cos I'm going to drink it all up'. This makes it clear that the 'No' meant that the presuppositions of the request did not apply to the current situation, rather than an acceptance of the presupposition and denial of the social conventions governing its consequence.

This last example brings out the dilemma in accounting for the previous examples. To what extent should one analyse young children's behaviour in terms of the presuppositions they bring to the situation, to what extent in terms of acquired suppositions about their current social relationship with the adult, and to what extent in terms of their efficiency at decoding the referential content of the utterances? Whenever a child shows success, failure or odd responses in putting behaviour under the linguistic control of an adult, this always happens against a rich backcloth of socially established conventions. Why is it difficult to get some children to apply their knowledge of language to over-ride their knowledge of what objects are *typically* for and how people *typically* interact over objects? It is obviously no good always asking for typical behaviour (e.g. putting a brick in an upright cup) because that might be what the child would do in the absence of linguistic comprehension.

THERE IS NO SUCH THING AS A 'PURE REFERENTIAL-LANGUAGE COMPREHENSION TEST'

Now we may focus on previous research into 'purely referential comprehension'. The first question is what presuppositions children might have and how they may go about checking whether these remain appropriate to the situation at hand. One speaks of 'establishing rapport with children', a sort of 'getting on the same wavelength'. The experimenter trades on the set of general-purpose coping strategies that the children have built up through extensive previous experience with unequal power relations. It is easy to guess what one strategy might be. The child might put its trust in the adult not to demand something out of the child's sphere of competence, and to go ahead assuming that the materials are to be used according to normal rules of usage. This makes intuitive sense in many situations. When Wilcox and Palermo (1974) provided a toy table and teapot, these are conventionally 'congruent' for a relationship of support, and indeed the children were readier to put the teapot on the table than under it, on request.

Another obvious coping strategy is 'lying low', doing the minimum, leaving it to the experimenter to do the work of making clearer just what he wants. Again, Wilcox and Palermo identify a bias something like this.

Finally, another strategy would be one of 'jumping the gun', avoiding taking in too much information until the experimenter makes it clear that he has provided an important utterance, then to make some literal-minded action trusting that the experimenter can hardly disapprove. When Grieve, Hoogenraad and Murray (1977) conspicuously called the same cube either 'bath' or 'table', the child might well assume that here was the cue for inference about the spatial relations that the cube was meant to enter into, sanctioned by the authority of the adult. They would thus tend to put something *in* the bath even when the experimenter said *on*. Grieve *et al.* say that such an incorrect response may not result from lexical incomprehension, but stem from 'a conflict between the child's understanding of the preposition and what he believes to be an appropriate response in that situation' (p. 237). We shall later show a weakness in their design and improve on it.

Experimenters may well interpret data in accordance with salient theoretical categories without capturing the essence of the evidence. They may legislate that the data are primarily indices of 'language comprehension' plus 'noise' but may actually have been recording the outcomes of a mixed set of coping strategies with subtle cues acting to shift their balance. Certainly it would be a fair inference that the children possessed virtually perfect language comprehension if they made no errors in misusing materials. But errors are the raw materials of analysis for a developmental account, and one must generally distinguish coping strategies which mask comprehension from these which index faulty lexical comprehension.

In the course of diagnosing a situation, the child will almost inevitably receive conflicting cues about what to do. An experimenter putting a large cup and a small brick on the table, saying that he wants the brick to *go on* the cup (that he thinks the brick ought to go on the cup) is certainly providing conflicting cues. The adult presupposition is that the referential content of the words 'mean what they sound like meaning', *on* means 'contact and support but not *in*' and *cup* means 'this object which we both recognise is indeed one of those things you have often seen used for keeping something safely *in*'. The conflict remains even if the experimenter does not name the object, for that merely shifts the modality of the conflict. *All* 'referential comprehension tests' involve cue-competition for control over behaviour, and 'good comprehension' involves receptive-language-driven control over competing cues. Errors may have different *levels* of origin as competing cues are processed. Even when children are conscious of a conflict (e.g. between 'bath' and 'on') they may lack the discourse skills to explain their problems.

Finally there is the vexed question of the mode of administration of a task. This can vary from confrontation to collaboration. Whenever power and knowledge are unequally apportioned it becomes a prime task to find out how different practices of task presentation during the task affect results. This is axiomatic for social psychology. Accordingly, we shall present the results of giving a 'standard language comprehension test' in different ways, and make an evaluation according to levels of error and types of error. Two findings will receive particular attention: active involvement of the child in collaborative activity may not alter the error level for the better but it reliably alters the distribution of error types. Secondly. there is an association of error level and error type which enables one to identify a bias associated with good performance. We can then ask what the adaptive significance of the bias might be for language acquisition. We shall focus on the issue of contextual sensitivity.

SOME STRENGTHS AND WEAKNESSES OF PREVIOUS WORK

Clear scoring of errors is one thing, their interpretation is an altogether different enterprise, as we have seen. With the advantage of hindsight we can scrutinise some of the assumptions in earlier research so as to reject the weaknesses but also see what is worth preserving: after all, we don't want to throw out the baby with the bathwater.

At the start of the 'semantics revolution', the issue of 'reference' was seen as an asocial one, as though there were direct correspondence between distinctions of meaning within the linguistic system and the elementary perceptual distinctions that the human being is predisposed to make (e.g. size and shape). Developments were to make this view untenable. The work of Bruner (1975), Halliday (1975) and others has demonstrated that reference needs to be analysed according to the transactions between the individual and both the physical and interpersonal context. Nonetheless, the earlier view did present a refreshingly simple model of language acquisition. The child's task was seen to be to strive *directly* towards mastery of the meaning system by the continual checking of hypotheses about the distinctions relevant to word meaning against adult consensus. It is not surprising therefore that errors were taken to be evidence of pitfalls on the way to semantic competence: pitfalls which could temporarily arrest the headlong rush to linguistic mastery. Errors were therefore treated as *primitive* and unsophisticated, evidencing a lack of semantic knowledge or that unfortunate tendency in children to fall prey to competing nonlinguistic biases.

The work of Brown (1973) well illustrates this:

We found an initial tendency in the children to persist in using an object according to its customary use, and so put things *in* cups, ashtrays, boxes and the like even when the experimenter said *on*. However, this was a very transient rigidity, and after a few trials the children all responded appropriately to the contrast between *in* and *on*. Therefore I conclude that they understood the semantic distinctions but were briefly thrown off by the request to use an object of fixed function in an unaccustomed way (p. 378).

This 'transient rigidity', which seems to be the product of an elementary coping strategy, is thus set down as 'noise' in the data, of little theoretical relevance. But what may be 'transient' in one age-group may well be a relic of a dominant process in a younger group.

Eve Clark (1973) followed a similar line, although she was less inclined than Brown to attribute lexical knowledge to children. A correct response might be the outcome of a correct linguistic hypothesis or of a non-linguistic 'rule' which fortuitously happens to give a response identical to a lexically-driven one. Errors were taken as evidencing non-linguistic rules in operation: these Clark assumed to be primitive, elementary biases operating independently of language. To demonstrate them, Clark asked young children to put a toy animal *in*, *on* or *under* other objects such as bridges and boxes. The data indicated that the particular rules in operation were a tendency to respond (*a*) to cavities and (*b*) to flat surfaces, ordered so that the second is only used if there is no cavity available for the operation of the first rule. Clark went further, proposing a developmental hypothesis: 'The children can best be viewed as progressing through three stages: A stage where they rely on non-linguistic strategies plus partial semantic knowledge of the words; a transition stage; and a stage where they rely on full semantic knowledge of the words' (p. 177).

There are a number of weaknesses in the work. Clark offers no independent evidence for deciding whether non-linguistic strategies operate as coping strategies when lexical knowledge is poor, or whether they can mask a high level of comprehension (cf. Brown). Without such evidence the developmental statements cannot be strictly grounded in the data base.

Certainly very young children have little lexical knowledge, hence must rely on non-linguistic response mechanisms. It is equally evident that they eventually act in a linguistically-driven manner. It follows that the acquisition of these terms must occur between these extremes: but it gets one no further just to call it a 'transition stage', and no evidence is offered on this. Do children alternate rapidly between non-linguistic and linguistic strategy? Do they apply linguistic strategies with some materials but not others? Do they operate non-linguistic strategies only when tired or bored or what? The real issue of language acquisition is left in the air. Unfortunately Clark presents her data in a form which is the least helpful for answering these questions, as pooled data for age-groups. We can surely expect individual variation in both age of acquisition of the terms and in the fine-grain of strategies. Of particular interest would be data on any other differences to be found between children who made very few errors and those who made many. Individual data would also allow a test of the rule-ordering hypothesis; are *all* children subject to a cavity-bias, with no minority obverse bias? In the next section we shall present evidence on these points.

The study of Wilcox and Palermo (1974) was intended to clear up some of the outstanding problems. They pointed out that the *motor* difficulty of a particular response may well affect performance, they used a thematically 'neutral' object to try and unconfound simple rule-ordering from a tendency to place objects in customary relationships, and they analysed some of the data at the level of individual response consistency. Unfortunately this work too has its methodological faults, some of which are referred to later (for detailed account and critique, see Hoogenraad, Grieve, Baldwin and Campbell, 1976).

The other pioneering study is by Grieve *et al.* referred to in the previous section. They used a 'neutral' target, called by a name which implied a socially-acceptable function for it; and found that the performance was influenced by prior naming. Their theoretical statements reflect pragmatics theory and the 'sophisticated child' approach:

... the young child of 1½ or 2 years, say, has reason to be generally less confident of his understanding of language than he is of his apperception and construal of the extralinguistic world. This may lead him to neglect his understanding of the utterance (to the extent that he does understand it of course) when it seems to him to conflict with what he believes, on the basis of his construal of the context, to be the appropriate interpretation of what is required ... an incorrect response cannot be taken as proof of lack of understanding, since it may result from a conflict between the child's understanding of the preposition and what he believes to be an appropriate response in that situation. This conflict he resolves by ignoring the preposition's meaning in favour of his understanding of the context, of which he has reason to be more confident. (p. 237).

Although theoretically advanced, this study too has weaknesses. The procedure for producing conflict was to provide two potentially competing utterances: prior naming and the placement instruction. This is incredibly difficult to theorise for subjects who are acquiring language, for it elides the distinction between language acquisition and language processing. Certainly Grieve *et al.* took pains to ensure that the children had indeed processed the first utterance, by requiring them to speak the name of the object, but this procedure had a negative effect: there were only seven two-years-old to start with, and only *one* of these passed the screening test for inclusion in the naming conditions. Thus the data come from children over 3 years old, who must be well on the road to mastery of these terms (Brown, 1973; Clark, 1973). It seems that the study may well have produced a sufficiently complex procedure to confuse older children at the expense of having little to say about *early* acquisition. Finally, the conclusions of Grieve *et al.* are excessively pessimistic *vis-à-vis* the possibility of ever constructing a truly developmental story: if we can *never* decide on the extent to which lexical knowledge enters into correct responses and into errors, we cannot by definition investigate the acquisition of lexical knowledge.

Finally, one weakness of all the previous studies is the cavalier attitude taken to the physical scaling of the stimuli. Since relationships like containment and support occur within spatial constraints, these must be controlled by rigorous measurement. It would be ludicrous as a test of the contrastive status of *in* and *on* to use unscaled targets where the cavity was far greater in area than the support surface. In the Clark and Wilcox-Palermo studies, physical characteristics were not made orthogonal to the symbolic content of the targets. True, Grieve *et al.* held the physical characteristics of their cubes constant whilst signalling different symbolic functions, but they made things worse by 'scattering the objects on the table' so that the orientation of the objects and complexity of motor responses necessary to fulfil an end-state representation remained completely uncontrolled.

Now to suggest the way forward. Clark's account is *developmental* but hopelessly *asocial*, Grieve *et al.*'s approach is *social* but offers little to a story of *development*. There must be a way to amalgamate the two.

On development

Children do not acquire knowledge of locative prepositions overnight: there must be some transition between a pre-linguistic level of response and the lexically driven mode. The above studies have not got to the heart of the developmental process, nor can we hope to do more than scratch the surface. However, we shall focus on the most elusive problem of all: can we hope to catch children who have *nearly* acquired the trick of allowing themselves to be referentially language driven, and if so, do they show a typical type of lapse which distinguishes them from other children? Only then can a developmental account be launched, one which will focus eventually on the relationship between 'expressive' and 'referential' functions of language (Nelson, 1973).

On social and situational variables

How do we go about studying an ingenious being who is taking in a wide range of information (previous experience, the physical factors of the situation, the social relationships obtaining in the situation) and then making a personal interpretation of the demand characteristics? How can we as researchers gain privileged access to the child's mind to determine the fine-grain mechanisms of this construal? After pointing to the riddle, Grieve *et al.* left it for others to solve. Other workers have adopted a purely observational approach. Goodwin (1980, p. 209) says that 'Good experiments have certainly been done but, at every stage, the main thrust has come from the nursery rather than the laboratory'. Perhaps, yet strictly controlled experiment is still the best way to obtain precise information on the mechanisms of cognition, as long as it is designed to simplify the input to the child, not further complicate it. We must devise techniques to convey simple, specifiable information to the child and not simply load in complex, competing information as Grieve *et al.* did. One experiment will not suffice: instead we need to devise a matrix of experiments, each differing slightly and systematically from the others.

On the social front, we must also vary the method of task administration. This step was not taken in previous research, yet it is vital to have the information to answer questions such as 'Under what (social) conditions is situational, contextual information salient to the child?'.

On the standardisation of the target

We must ensure that the physical properties of the stimuli used are controlled for, so as to unconfound the symbolic character of the target from its physical characteristics.

On the adaptive significance of strategies

There must be some strategies which interfere with performance and some which aid it. It should be possible to find a condition in which the more able children will make one particular type of error which is contextually-primed. Utterances which refer to physical contexts might cue the child into looking for the contextual support of the adult utterances. This would be a strategy of adaptive value, for mastery over discourse involves sensitivity to the relations between utterances and context.

The experiments described below capitalise on the points raised. They are not definitive: at least we hope not, for we have done many more studies which await writing-up. But they do address the problems and give rise to two very sensitive findings.

Pilot studies

CONTEXTUAL SENSITIVITY, JOINT ACTIVITY AND
COMPREHENSION

We are going to try to negotiate with young children over the context for in- and on- placements. We shall play simple games just prior to a *standardised* test for comprehension. The games are designed to bring to the notice of the child *one* of the to-be-tested relationships in such a way that the child is free to ignore this information but equally, might feel socially obliged to take it into account in formulating a response to the locative instruction. Thus we can determine the physical and social situations under which a child might make a contextually-primed error. We might expect a game to influence the children in so far as it may provide cues to enable the children to construe what the experimenter seems 'really to be getting at'.

In all the experiments, comprehension tests were carried out with two hollow cubes: a large one (7.5 cm) as target, and a small one (3.5 cm). The placement instruction was always 'Put your block in (on) this one' (pointing to the target). The target was *always on its side with the cavity facing towards the child*. Thus the cavity and flat surface were equally visible, providing precisely equal area at which to aim. The in- and on- placements at such a target are motorically very similar. Furthermore, no strong relation of congruency holds between two cubes (unlike, say, a table and teapot). A pilot study by Bob Carabine did show a slight tendency for children to prefer to construct *in* relationships between cubes but, as we shall demonstrate, such a bias cannot by itself account for the data.

Two pilot experiments represent extreme conditions, useful for bracketing the main experiments which follow. The first is a *reductio ad absurdum* of the Grieve *et al.* study: flooding children with contextual information around an invariant target. Prior to the comprehension test a game was played with two large cylindrical waste paper bins (radius 25 cm). This inelegant apparatus is ideal for conveying contrasting ideas of containment and support. When upright, they present truly massive cavities which are just asking to have something thrown in them (the experimenter's response sheet was frequently thrown in by the children). When inverted, they present respectable flat surfaces which can be thumped or used as a table. The subjects were 24 children aged from 1;11 to 3;0 years. The experimenter introduced the bins either both upright or both inverted and asked the child 'Show me what you can do with these'. No strict protocol was followed, the experimenter was usually kept busy just maintaining the bins' orientation. When the child had explored containment or support, the target was inserted between the bins, the small cube put in the child's hand, and both an in- and on- placement asked for. Then the second game began, this time with the bins in the orientation not yet experienced, followed by another test of the two locatives. Finally, the bins were removed and after a short distracting break, a 'neutral' post-test was run: a simple in/on test to the target on its own. Naturally, the order of presentation of upright and inverted bins and *in* and *on* instructions was counterbalanced.

There were only 5 children who avoided error altogether. The important question is whether the type of game affected individual error in the rest of the children. Consider first the error pattern after games, as shown in Table 1 (the totals column).

There is a lawful pattern here. Of the 9 children who made *two errors* out of the 4 context-embedded trials, only one gave an error pattern that showed any influence of the game (that is, an error to *in*, with a flat surface present and to *on* with a cavity present). Of the remaining two-error children, 6 always put the cube in (an in-bias) and 2 always on (on-bias). In perfect contrast, of the 8 children who made a *single error* in the 4 trials, 6 of them occurred when the game was not congruent with the request and only 2 when congruent (the 8-1/2-6 contrast between one-and two- error children is reliable at $p < 0.025$, *Fisher Exact Probability Test*). The suggestion is that being influenced by the context goes along with relatively *good* performance (in the sense of making only one error, not two, over the four trials). We have an independent check of this. The post-test gave a rough measure of an individual's competence with the target cube on its own. The trend is towards 'innishness', but more important is the link between post-test performance and performance immediately following the games (Table 1). Of the children who were *errorless* on the post-test, 6 were 'context-sensitive' and 2 were not: whereas of the children who made a post-test error, only 1 was context-sensitive, 8 were in- or on-biased and 2 were errorless. Thus two lines of evidence converge: context-sensitivity is associated with children who are really quite good at acting in accord with the locative instruction. Splitting the sample into age-groups around the median gave no trace of an age-related effect in the data: division by error-level seems more sensitive than by chronological age. Children who are close to being lexically driven may be contextually sensitive.

We now pass on to another *reductio ad absurdum*. This is to mimic the Wilcox-Palermo approach whereby the potential symbolic significance of the target is altered at the test without a priming-up

TABLE 1
Individuals showing particular response patterns in the first
pilot experiment

Task errors	Pre-test performance		Totals
	Errorless ($N = 8$)	Error ($N = 11$)	
None	0	2	2
IN-bias	0	6	6
ON-bias	0	2	2
2 C.S.	1	0	1
1 C.S.	5	1	6
1 N.S.	2	0	2
3 errors	0	0	0
4 errors	0	0	0

In-bias: two errors, both with ON request
On-bias: two errors, both with IN request
C.S.: contextual sensitivity, error only when game mismatches test request
N.S.: not context sensitive, the error occurs with a game-test match

contrasting message being given to a child. The simplest method that we and Bob Carabine could think of was to give the standard cubes-in- and on- test, only having the target flanked by two toy tables or by two cups. Would the children scan the array and show any tendency to classify the cube as a support when it was flanked by tables and a container when it was flanked by cups?

There were 35 children, 19 at 2;6 and 16 at 3;0. They were tested with the cube on its own, then after a break, with the cube flanked by cups (tables), then after another break with it flanked by tables (cups). Twenty-five children sailed through all the tests. Ten fell down on the pre-test, always with the *on* request, and nine of these made errors on the main test, with four making one error, four making two (and one making three). It is not very satisfactory to have two groups of but four a piece to compare, yet the tiny data were encouraging. The two-error group were totally 'innish' regardless of the context, the one-error group were contextually primed. This took the form of only managing to get *on* right within the table context. So rather like the previous study there is an association between in-bias for the two-error group and its inhibition by context-sensitivity for the one-error group, and in fact the 4-0/0-4 contrast happens to be reliable (p 0.025, *Fisher Test*), though it is so tiny that no-one could feel at all happy. All the same, there must surely be some symbolically-primed effect on placement to be found if even such a pared-down design can give a glimmer of the same effect as in the first experiment.

The problems with the above pilot studies are that the first is rather too messy with too much unspecifiable information being thrown at the child and the second, though tidier, gave extremely weak effects. The experiments do, however, justify our adoption of a working hypothesis for the main experiment: an association between error-level and error-type.

Main experiments

Bob Carabine had the feeling that the children found it easy to ignore the cups/tables context because the 'conceptual distance' between cubes and cups/tables is too great. The obvious next step was to design an experiment where we might expect the children to see some resemblance between context and target. The best of resemblances is, of course, a cube to a cube: and with an all-cube design we also have a technique for ordering the information available to the child (cubes can be stacked, nested, scattered around cavity-up or down and so on). Furthermore, we can start to home in on the social variables of the task, for cube arrays can be built in a number of different ways, with the child's active cooperation or without it. The main experiment manipulated a number of these variables within a matrix of 6 conditions. We shall give the results of the two conditions which are relevant here.

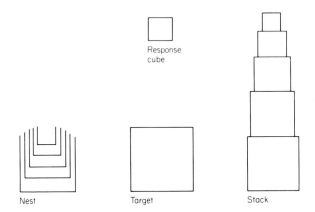

FIG. 1   Target cube, response cube and the flanks (relative sizes)

Active condition   The children were encouraged cooperatively to build two *stacks* or two *nests*, the details of which can be seen in Fig. 1. Then the target cube was inserted in the gap between the two stacks (nests), on its side as usual, and in- or on- placement requested. After a response, the array was completely dismantled and the next one built. Thus there were four trials, *in* or *on* asked for after stacking or nesting games. This condition was designed to present information about possible cube relationships in the context of active cooperation.

Passive condition   The experimenter placed two prepared stacks or nests on the ground, inserted the target between them, and then asked for a placement at the target. The nests had been constructed so that each nested cube protruded slightly over the lip of the cube containing it so as to make the cubes-within-cubes property of this array evident. Again there were four trials; *in* and *on* asked for with stacks and nests present, this time without cooperative activity. The experimenter confronted the child with information.

In sum, the end-state arrays at the time of the comprehension tests were *identical* for both active and passive conditions: a target cube on its side flanked by two stacks or two nests. All that differed was the method of arrival at the end-state: either through cooperative building or by the imposition of the array with absolutely no child involvement.

The order of presentation of the stacks (nests) and of the *in/on* instruction was counterbalanced within each condition over all the children. 48 children took part, aged between 1;11 and 3;1.

TABLE 2

Individual error patterns with passive/active
stack (nest) conditions of the first main
experiment ($N = 48$)

| Error level | Experimental condition | | | |
| | Passive | | Active | |
	C.S.	N.S.	C.S.	N.S.
One error	13	1	6	4
Two errors	1	15	0	20
Errorless	17		17	
Three errors	1		1	
Four errors	0		0	

C.S.: context sensitive; N.S.: not sensitive

First, we shall consider the results from the *passive* condition, shown in Table 2.

The *one-error* children overwhelmingly made their error when the contextual array which had been placed flanking the target was *incongruent* with the request: 13/14 of them (reliable at $p < 0.001$, *Binomial Test*, one-tailed). These *one error* children were certainly sensitive to the context of the placement instruction. In contrast, *two-error* children made errors which were not consistently related to the type of flanking array: 11 in-bias, 2 on-bias, 2 where both errors completely contradicted the flank and *only one* fully commensurate with the flank type. The 13-1/1-15 contrast between the one-error group as context-sensitive and the two error group as not, was reliable below the 1% level (*Fisher Test*). But for the *active* condition, whereas the two-error group gave the same picture of bias (17/20 children in-biased and 3 on-biased), the one-error group gave a different pattern: a 6–4 split between context-sensitive and non-sensitive: not a reliable group contrast.

The conclusion is that if one is searching for an association between error-level and error-type, look first to the *passive* conditions. Active, cooperative stack (nest) building seems greatly to weaken any tendency for the children to take account of the context in formulating a response to the locative instruction. This result is also very useful for another purpose: it is entirely the converse of that predicted by any motor-transfer account of 'context-sensitivity'. If the effect of prior games is simply to set up a low-level motor-plan to put *on* after stacking and *in* after nesting, we should expect no 'context-sensitivity' if the child were not involved in constructive activity and plenty if the child had actually built the stacks (nests). That we found the opposite demonstrates that 'context-sensitivity' must be mediated at a higher level.

This experiment has confirmed the association of error-level and error-type. The sample splits into three roughly equal groups: 17/48 errorless on the passive task, 14/48 making one error (predominantly context-sensitive) and 16/48 making two errors (predominantly to a particular instruction and not the context). This pattern cuts across chronological age, and seems to reflect a developmental trend from 'primitive' bias, through context sensitivity, to a very good grasp of the meaning of the locatives. Can it be that children who are inclined to take account of the context, as in the passive condition, are those on the verge of full lexical mastery? To prove this it would have to be the case that these context-sensitive children are *consistently good* at such tasks and the biased children *consistently poor*:

we might, after all, be dealing with a flash-in-the-pan. Remember that the passive condition was part of a matrix of others which have not been cited. In all, each child experienced 12 trials with *in* and 12 with *on*. Figure 2 shows that the context-sensitive children averaged

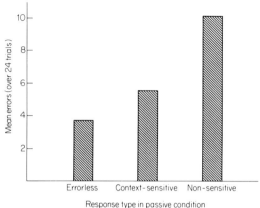

FIG. 2   Errors over 6 conditions by children giving three patterns of performance in the passive stacks (nests) condition

only half the errors of the non-sensitive children (who reliably maintained their bias over most of the other conditions). The children who were *errorless* in the passive condition, and who we might presume to be the closest of all to full lexical mastery, only lapsed occasionally in the other conditions. Intriguingly, the children who were context-sensitive in the passive condition were far closer in mean error level to these children than to the non-sensitive children. Surely this demonstrates the association of context-sensitivity with very good lexical grasp.

The next step must be to enquire more closely into the active/passive distinction. In the conditions just reviewed, this distinction was confounded. Not only did the level of experimenter-child cooperation differ, but also the overall level of child motor activity, the amount of time spent setting up the context, and also the type of information available to the child (in the passive condition this was purely *visual*, in the active condition there was a component of constructing cube relationships). An experiment is needed which unconfounds these variables a little. This is easy to devise.

The subjects were 12 children age 2;3 ± 1 month and 12 children age 2;9 ± 1 month. In the *active seriation* condition, the children were required to build two horizontal lines of cubes laid out in order

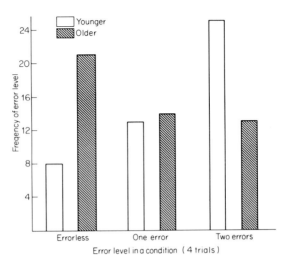

FIG. 3   The frequency of three error levels over the four conditions of the second main experiment

TABLE 3

Error level and error type in the stacks (nest) and horizontal seriation conditions of the second main experiment ($N = 24$)

Experimental condition	Arrangement of materials					
	Errorless	1-error		2-error		3 or more errors
		C.S.	N.S.	C.S.	N.S.	
		(a) Stack (nest)				
Passive	6	7	1	2	8	0
Active	7	2	4	1	9	1
		(b) Horizontal seriation				
Passive	8	7	1	0	8	0
Active	8	4	1	0	10	1

C.S.: context sensitive; N.S.: not sensitive

of size, all with either cavities or flat surfaces upwards. The target was placed between the lines for the comprehension test. In the *passive seriation* condition, the children sat and watched the experimenter build the lines. Each of these conditions had four trials: *in* or *on* asked with cavities up or down. Now both the active and passive conditions are strung out over time, and in neither case are the functions of cubes as support or container being directly demonstrated, nor are the motor patterns for these functions being practised. The other two conditions of this experiment were a replication of *active stacking (nesting)* and *passive stacking (nesting)*.

For the first time there were definite age-related differences as shown in Fig. 3. In all conditions, there were *fewer* errorless younger children and *more* younger children showing a consistent in- or on-bias. Note, however, that there was little difference between the two groups in the number of children who gave only one error in a condition. This is a very encouraging pattern. Earlier we advanced the hypothesis that children pass through three stages: a stage where they have little ability to avoid strong biases of the Clarkian type: a stage where they are on the verge of becoming fully lexically driven but are prone to some context-sensitivity: and a stage where they are fully able to act in accord with the locative. The age-related difference here shown precisely fits this hypothesis. The younger sample gave errors which were predominantly either biased or, as we shall see, context-sensitive. The older sample were, in the main, errorless or context-sensitive: there were very few examples of consistent bias from these children. We do not know why we hit upon a chronological age difference in this experiment but not the others, since in all cases the samples were selected at random from a pool acquired by widely distributed subject appeals. Our hypothesis, which was previously founded on an appeal to error levels as reflecting development, now finds some confirmation in the form of an age-related trend.

Having pointed out the differences, we may now amalgamate the two groups for the usual consideration of error-level and error-type. Table 3 shows the data.

Taking the replication passive stacks (nests) condition first, we see the usual pattern: an association of context-sensitivity with the one-error group but not the two-error group. The split of 7 sensitive to 1 not sensitive in the one-error group is reliable at p 0.035 (*Binomial Test*) and the opposing splits of 7-1/2-8 between one-and-two error groups is reliable (p 0.025, *Fisher Test*). Yet again, reliable context-sensitivity is associated with children who are better at the task. In the *active stacks (nests)* condition we expected from previous data a weakening of context-sensitivity: there was, in fact, a reversal of error-type in the one-error group such that only 2/6 gave a context-sensitive error and 4/6 gave an error when the context and instruction were congruent. The number of one-error children was small; but nonetheless, this result suggests that context-sensitivity is considerably weakened by active stacking (nesting). All in all, these two conditions replicate the findings of the main experiment in almost all respects.

Now to the new horizontal seriation conditions. Here we see a reliable level of context-sensitivity for the one-error group after *passive* seriation: a 7-1 split (p 0.035, *Binomial Test*). As we expect by now, this reliably contrasts with non-sensitive bias in the two-error group (7-1/0-8 split, p 0.005, *Fisher Test*). This condition shows that the children do not have to see the relationships demonstrated in the form of cubes in and on other cubes before they show context-sensitivity: children can take their cues from cubes in a line, cavity up or down. As usual, it is better children who seem more inclined to utilise contextual information. The *active seriation*, however, gave results that are rather more ambiguous. Only a few of the children gave one error: five in all. Of these, four were context-sensitive but one was not, an unreliable result. Thus although the trend is in the direction of context-sensitivity, we can say little without more data.

The final experiment was somewhat different from those above. This time the target was varied as well as the context. The children *actively* built a stack (nest) and then a large and small cube were extracted from the finished construction. The large cube was used as a target and placed either cavity up or cavity down. The small cube was placed in the child's hand and the placement request made. Clearly, in some trials the target was in an orientation suited to the lexical item in the instruction: in these direct-placement trials the children would just have to reach out and place their cube to be correct. In other trials, they would have to turn over the target if they were to act in accord with the instruction: these have been labelled +T trials (plus transformation). There were 39 children aged between 1;4 and 2;2 ($\bar{X}$ = 1;9) and 56 children between 2;4 and 3;8 ($\bar{X}$ = 3;0).

Table 4 shows that children of all ages found direct-placement easier than transformation trials, as one would expect. Interestingly, when adjusted for sample size, the overall error level found in the previous experiments with the cube-on-its-side target fell precisely midway between the error levels of the direct-placement and +T trials of this experiment. This certainly shows that scaling of target difficulty is a practical possibility, but, more important, it strongly re-emphasises the criticism of previous work that the effects found may well have been partially an artefact of the lack of control over target physical properties and/or orientation. In addition, context-sensitivity was in evidence. This is most easily seen with the amalgamated data. For both groups there were more errors to the *on*-request following nesting than stacking and more errors to the *in*-request following stacking than nesting. For the older group there was indeed a full cross-over effect. Limitation of space precludes analysis of the detail of differences between this experiment and the others. All we wish to demonstrate is that, under some circumstances, context-sensitivity *can* occur following joint cooperative stacking (nesting) games. This shows that it cannot be activity or cooperation *per se* which acts so as to destroy context-sensitivity in some of the above experiments, nor can this be a function of the children having to construct cube relationships in the active stacking (nesting). A wider explanation will be pursued in the next section.

TABLE 4
Errors following stacking and nesting in the transformation experiment

Response pattern	Age group						
	Younger (N = 39)				Older (N = 56)		
	Stack		Nest		Stack		Nest	
	$\overline{T}$	+T	$\overline{T}$	+T	$\overline{T}$	+T	$\overline{T}$	+T
In✓On✗	4	9	5	12	1	8	3	10
In✗On✓	3	7	0	3	6	10	0	7
With $\overline{T}$ and + T pooled							
	Stack		Nest		Stack		Nest	
In✓On✗	13		17		9		13	
In✗On✓	10		3		16		7	

✓, correct; ✗, wrong; $\overline{T}$, no transformation; + T, plus transformation

Conclusions and wider issues

The most important point is the developmental story which casts light on the transition to lexical mastery. This does not involve non-linguistic biases simply dying away to a vestigial 'transient rigidity'. Rather, they give way to contextually-primed bias before full mastery. To put it formally, a precursor of full semantic specification for relational terms is responsiveness to their episodic context of application. The analysis of error-level and error-type is a prime tool for such research.

The second issue is that of the conditions under which such a tendency will be manifest: the issue of collaboration and confrontation. To recapitulate, it seems as if context-sensitivity is found in the confrontation ('passive') conditions. After the experimenter had imposed the array on the children, about a third of them were prone to give context-congruent error patterns with both stacks (nests) and horizontal seriation. Collaboration exerts a more complex effect. If two stacks (nests) were built before a response was required to an independent target, then context-sensitivity was destroyed: but if the target had been extracted from a child-constructed stack or nest, then context-sensitivity was present. Following active horizontal seriation there were traces of context-sensitivity: it was not completely destroyed.

The process of confronting children with extraneous information seems invariably to lead to a proportion of them feeling obliged to take this information into account in formulating a response. McGarrigle and Donaldson (1974) have shown how Piagetian conservation tests tend to confront the children with an adult-imposed manipulation of materials and can lead them to answer a somewhat different question to the one the adult had intended, whereas the more collaborative procedure of 'checking-up' after a toy teddy bear has destroyed the rows of counters leads to better conservation of number. This single study is by no means definitive, but it points in the same direction as our own. To our explanation of context-sensitivity we can now add a social determinant: any tendency for presuppositions regarding the overall topic of discourse to override referential knowledge of the words used is strengthened when the interactive pattern between the adult and child is one of confrontation. One need not look far to see why this is so. Remember that the child is in a very disadvantaged position relative to the experimenter: the power relationship is a one-sided affair. Remember also that when an adult and child interact there is often an ulterior motive, in the sense that adults will try to teach, cajole, show the child new ways for dealing with problems and so on. Further, social psychology has shown that we as adults have a presupposition that others will act in a purposive and rational manner unless we have evidence to the contrary. Assuming that young children are sensitive to these factors, then contextually-primed responses can be seen as a natural outcome of the child's awareness of the possible intentions of the adult. If a child sees an adult going to all the trouble of putting out a stack of cubes, or laying out a line of them all in the same orientation then it is perfectly reasonable for the child to assume that this information will be relevant to the task in which she will shortly be asked to participate. Thus in situations of confrontation, where the child is not able to attempt to negotiate the information, its relevance to the task must seem very strong indeed: here is a quota of information that the child must take as given.

Collaboration is altogether more complex than confrontation. An act of collaboration might be aimed at negotiating and making clear some aspect of shared knowledge or it might simply be an interaction for interaction's sake, a true game. Hence the child's task is more difficult from the outset: to decide when an adult means a game as *really* a game, and when it is to be taken as a lesson with something to be learned. Adults have a propensity for turning the most innocuous little games into 'learning experiences'. Given that the power relationship in the situation is one-sided, it is reasonable to suppose that the child will be on the look-out for the intentions of the adult even in a collaborative situation. We suggest that the child can only be really confident that a game was really intended as such when the adult will allow the child to finish it without intervening (i.e. without confronting the child with a supposed lesson or moral of the game). Thus in the active stacks (nests) condition, the child built one stack (nest) and then another. The adult went on to ask the child to do something else without explicitly drawing attention to the completed game. Here the child was allowed to complete the game without confrontation and then went on to something different. But in the final stack (nest) experiment where the cubes were extracted from the completed construction, there was an element of confrontation. The construction had been completed to be sure, but the adult then insisted on pulling it apart. In a sense the adult confronted the child with materials which may have seemed intended to draw the child's attention back to the game. In the active horizontal seriation task, where the trend was in the direction of context-sensitivity, the child was not allowed to take the game to its conclusion. All the cubes had been placed in a neat line in the same orientation, just right to go on to stacking or nesting. At that point, the experimenter intervened, thus confronting the child with an unfinished situation which was crying out to have something further done. In the bins pilot experiment the child's exploration of the materials was interrupted by the adult for a formal test.

If this tentative account be reasonable, context-sensitivity has its origins in confrontation. Collaboration is a complex process which may or may not contain the seeds of confrontation: the child's task is to determine when the social interaction seems to lead to a lesson about the materials used and when it seems to be aimless. One cue which can influence this decision is whether or not the adult allows the game to be finished: if it is finished it may be considered as over and done with, but if the adult intervenes as if to stress particular aspects of the game then it may be taken as a cue that this information is salient to the next step of the proceedings.

Finally, it is important to deal with the wider issue of whether there will ever be a link to research with adults. Of course, an adult would be well able to ignore a prior game in such a task as this, and always respond in accord with the lexical item. To Donaldson (1978), this would be an example of the adult's ability to 'dis-embed' language from its context of use. However, recent pragmatics research suggests that language may remain firmly rooted in context. Glucksberg, Hay and Danks (1976) had an experimenter leave the room to do a job with a screwdriver and then return and ask undergraduates for a 'different' tool to complete the repair. Very often *another screwdriver* was proffered, demonstrating that situational cues which implicity signal the intentions of the experimenter can affect an adult's interpretation of the word. More remotely, Bransford and McCarrell (1975) have shown adults' recall of confusing stories to be enhanced if, during the telling of the story, a disambiguating picture context is present. But the most interesting adult parallel to the work reported here is the neglected research of the 1940s and 1950s where adults were confronted with tricky problems. These 'open-ended' tasks were usually to construct something of specified function using a limited range of materials. Duncker (1945) required subjects to fix three small candles at eye-level to a smooth door. The candles were on the table with a few drawing pins and three small boxes (resembling matchboxes), and many other 'distractor' objects. The solution was, of course, to fasten the boxes to the wall with the drawing pins so as to form a support for the candles. Half the subjects found the boxes to be empty and half found them filled with matches and drawing pins. Those who found the boxes filled had more difficulty solving the problem, they seemed to have fixed it in their minds that these boxes were containers rather than potential supports. Similar 'functional fixedness' effects have been reported by Maier (1930, 1933). Birch and Rabinowitz (1951) even went as far as playing a prior game with the subjects. The solution to the problem involved tying a heavy object to a string to form a pendulum. Two objects were available, an electrical relay and an electrical switch. Just prior to the problem half the subjects had used the relay to complete a circuit and half had used the switch. Those that had used the relay preferred to use the switch as a pendulum bob but those that had used the switch chose the relay to solve the problem. It is interesting that when asked to justify their choice, the relay-primed group asserted that the switch was obviously the better bob yet the switch-group were equally sure that the relay was superior. All these experiments thus produced effects similar to those that we have labelled 'context-sensitivity' in children. It seems as if children may not lose the tendency to be aware of the context of tasks as they grow up. We suggest that they learn to inhibit these strategies in simpler situations, but their errors may well be the precursor of a more generalised cognitive strategy which is employed in more symbolically taxing situations.

Acknowledgements

The research was supported by grants from the Social Science Research Council for work on Language and Representation in Normal and Mentally Handicapped Children. The help of Bob Carabine and Barbara Parry was very valuable.

References

Birch, H. G. and Rabinowitz, H. S. (1951). The negative effect of previous experience on productive thinking. *Journal of Experimental Psychology* 4, 121–125

Bransford, J. D. and McCarrell, N. S. (1975). A sketch of a cognitive approach to comprehension: some thoughts about understanding what it means to comprehend. *In* "Cognition and the Symbolic Processes" (W. B. Weimar and D. S. Palermo, Eds). Erlbaum, Hillsdale, New Jersey

Brown, R. (1973). "A First Language." Allen and Unwin, London

Bruner, J. S. (1975). From communication to language - a psychological perspective. *Cognition* 3, 225–287

Clark, E. V. (1973). Non-linguistic strategies and the acquisition of word meaning. *Cognition* 2, 161–182

Donaldson, M. (1978). "Children Minds". Fontana, Glasgow

Duncker, K. (1945). On problem solving. *Psychological Monographs* 58, No. 5

Glucksberg, S., Hay, A. and Danks, J. (1976). Words in utterance contexts: young children do not confuse the meaning of 'same' and 'different'. *Child Development* 47, 737–741

Goodwin, R. (1980). Two decades of research into early language. *In* "Developmental Psychology and Society" (H. J. Sants, Ed.). MacMillan, London

Grieve, R., Hoogenraad, R. and Murray, D. (1977). On the young child's use of lexis and syntax in understanding locative instructions. *Cognition* 5, 235–250

Halliday, M. A. K. (1975). "Learning How to Mean". Edward Arnold, London

Hoogenraad, R., Grieve, R., Baldwin, P. and Campbell, R. (1976). Comprehension as an interactive process. *In* "Recent Advances in the Psychology of

Language: Language Development and Mother-Child Interaction" (P. O. Campbell and P. T. Smith, Eds). Plenum Press, New York

Maier, N. R. F. (1930). Reasoning in humans. I. On direction. *Journal of Comparative Psychology* 10, 115-124

Maier, N. R. F. (1933). An aspect of human reasoning. *British Journal of Psychology* 24, 144-155

McGarrigle, J. and Donaldson, M. (1974). Conservation accidents. *Cognition* 3, 341-350

Nelson, K. (1973). Structure and strategy in learning to talk. *Monographs of the Society for Research in Child Development* 38, 1-2

Wilcox, S. and Palermo, D. S. (1974). In, on and under revisited. *Cognition* 3, 235-250

4

From Interaction Strategies to Social Representation of Adults in a Day Nursery

F. Emiliani, B. Zani and F. Carugati

Introduction

Much of the research conducted up to now on early social development has focused attention on adult-child interaction observed in
the laboratory; only more rarely have observations been made in
home or in nurseries. Since in Italy day nurseries have offered them-
selve, alongside the family, as suitable places for the care and bringing
up of small children, we thought it of interest to concentrate our
study on the characteristics of the most frequently observed interaction situation in one of these nurseries, that is, on the interaction
between one adult and a small group of children.

Our preliminary observations showed that the nursery is organised
in such a way as to divide the children according to age[1]. A consequence of this division is that during most of the day's activities (in
particular during play sessions and time spent on personal hygiene)
certain adults concern themselves with the children under 2-years-
old (the 'little ones') whilst others look after those aged between 2
and 3 (the 'big ones'). However, the criterion of division according
to age does not simply have organisational significance for the adults;
they also see it in relation to the different needs which they attribute
to the two different age groups.

We chose to analyse the techniques of verbal control, the educative
behaviour, the empathetic behaviour and the linguistic style of each
adult[2] with the aim of studying in detail some of the characteristics
of the verbal behaviour of the adults when they are playing with a
group of children.

We decided to study the play situation, since all the staff consider
play very important for the psychological development of the chil-

dren, and the play activity is often organised by the adults in small groups in which the two age-groups are separated.

In particular we hypothesise the existence of differential uses of controls as a function of the age of the interlocutors. One of the aims of our research (which is similar to that undertaken by Schaffer and Crook, 1978, with regard to mothers) is to understand what the adults on the staff do when they wish to direct the behaviour of children into particular channels. On the basis of the definition utilised by the above-mentioned writers, by 'control techniques' we mean all those methods employed by the adult which have the aim of changing the course of the children's behaviour. Our hypothesis is that in their interactions with the younger children, adults make use of a wide range of control techniques, which is found less necessary when the children are older and possess greater interactive ability.

Moreover, given the particular educational orientation of the adults with regard to the activities of the nursery, we expect that those utterances spoken by the adults in the play sessions (which are not classifiable as controls) will be like those forms of verbal behaviour known in the literature as *Teacher Specific Behaviour* (TSB) (Tizard, Philps and Plewis, 1976), and as *Empathetic Behaviour*. By the latter term we mean what was at least in part suggested by Gelman and Shatz (1977), that is the use of verbal forms expressing confirmations and comments on the interaction. Our hypothesis is that the adults use TSB and Empathetic Behaviour more frequently with older children, as they consider them more able to learn than the younger ones. In other words, adults offer a greater amount of information to the older ones, and are more ready to give verbal support to their actions.

Finally, given that verbal communication constitutes a very important instrument in every relationship, especially when the interlocutor is learning to speak, we proposed to analyse the type of language used by the adults when addressing the infants. In fact, it has now been amply demonstrated that such language is not an undifferentiated and casual corpus but a special code, which has the aim of establishing successful communication and, according to some authors, of teaching grammatical and syntactic rules (Snow, 1972; Newport, 1976; Snow and Ferguson, 1977). The age of the interlocutor is one of the basic characteristics which serve to modify the language of the speaker. Our hypothesis is that the language of the adults has the same characteristics as 'motherese' and is therefore less complex, more simplified grammatically and syntactically, and has a higher level of redundancy with younger than with older children.

The significance of these various aspects of the verbal behaviour of the adults may be better understood if an interpretative model is used which considers social behaviour as self-controlled and self-directed behaviour, that is, which considers it as consciously following rules in order to produce plans of action and to pursue explicit goals (Harré and Secord, 1972).

Thus, we assign central importance to the rules which are produced and applied with the aim of guiding the action of the individuals and of determining their expectations of the behaviour of the other participants in interaction. From an objective point of view, the rules are realised when actions are carried out regularly; from a subjective point of view they allow the individual to evaluate the extent of conformity between his own actions and social expectations.

It seems reasonable to consider that the rules are not simply juxtaposed to one another, but that they constitute an elaborate system in the course of the daily life of the adults in the nursery. The validity of this system may not be limited to one situation only, but may extend to other situations which are considered as psychologically equivalent on account of a common goal attributed to them by the adults.

Considering that the organisation of the nursery observed is inspired by a few basic principles elaborated by the local authorities (Emiliani, 1976), and that these principles by now constitute a common background for these adults, we can expect that the adults of the nursery will possess a shared system of rules of general validity. We can also expect that they will not apply these rules in a rigid manner, but will take into account the particular circumstances which present themselves in the course of everyday life in the nursery.

Moreover, we consider that the analysis of these rules and of the reasons which the adults give in order to justify their existence and possible changes in them, highlights the beliefs and convictions of these adults, that is, aspects of their social representation (Moscovici, 1961). In fact, a representation is an individual's or a group's 'universe of opinions and beliefs' about a significant object.

As a general postulate it is stated that the behaviour of an individual or a group in any given situation will actually be determined by the social representation maintained by the individual or group with respect to the relevant part of the surrounding social reality. The social representation as a system of values, notions and practices has a double function:

to create an orderly social environment for the individual, and to allow for communication between members of a community.

We think that by the analysis of rules, elements of subjects' social representation with regard to the child in the nursery and to the social significance of the nursery itself become evident.

Method

The research was carried out in a day nursery in Bologna and involved all seven members of the staff. Each adult was observed in two semi-structured play sessions: in the first, with a group of three young children (aged 22 months ± 15 days); in the second, with a group of three older children (aged 32 months ± 15 days). Each adult was told that we were interested in the way the children play at various ages: they were therefore asked to play with the children as they would do normally during their daily activities. During the play sessions the staff used the toys already provided in the day nursery (e.g. constructions in plastic material or wood, and 'nail' game and dough).

Each observation lasted 10 minutes and was video-recorded. Adults' speech was divided into separate utterances by means of both transcripts and video-recording; the utterances were coded into Controls, Teacher Specific Behaviour, and Empathetic Behaviour. For control techniques all sentences were analysed on the basis of the code manual of Schaffer and Crook (1978, 1979). First, we identified verbal controls, utterances whose potential function was to modify the child's behaviour. Subsequently a classification was made of the controls on the basis of the following categories: (*i*) action or attention, (*ii*) directive or prohibitive, (*iii*) grammatical structure (imperatives, interrogatives, declaratives and moodless utterances). All the utterances of the adults which were intended to ask for information and to give explanations to the children were included in the scoring of TSB (see the definitions by Tizard *et al.*, 1976).

We introduced the further category called Empathetic Behaviour, which is realised in two kinds of items: (*i*) confirmations to the child; (*ii*) comments about the current action or object of the child's activity. With regard to the first kind of item, we summed all the adults' utterances of explicit confirmation (as in statements of the type: 'How clever, that's very good', 'You see, you have managed after all') and those expressions by means of which the adult shows she has appreciated her interlocutor's initiative, for example, by praising the introduction of the modification in the ongoing play. The second kind of item embraces all the comments that the adult makes about the action of the child, or about the object that he is constructing or designing ('What a lovely colour', 'How well it turns!', 'Ah, it's moving!').

The agreement between two of the experimenters with regard to the identification and the classification of the utterances was calculated by using the following formula

$$\frac{\text{Number of agreements}}{\text{Number of agreements} + \text{disagreements}}$$

A reliability check, based on four randomly selected transcripts, produced coefficients ranging from 0.94 to 0.97 for utterance segmentation; for identification of controls between 0.80 and 0.82; for classification of the controls between 0.84 and 0.87; for the TSB the agreement was between 0.84 and 0.89; for confirmations between 0.83 and 0.86; for comments between 0.84 and 0.88.

In order to analyse the linguistic style, the entire sample of adult language was considered and the following measures were scored as defined by Snow (1972); (*i*) mean length of utterance; (*ii*) sentence complexity; (*iii*) incidence of utterances without verbs; (*iv*) incidence of complete repetitions; (*v*) incidence of partial repetitions (*vi*) incidence of semantic repetitions. The first three are measures of the grammatical complexity of speech, so that the higher the score the more complex the language; the last three are measures of redundancy. Measures (*i*)-(*iii*) are simple counting procedures and were scored in all cases by just one of the experimenters. Since the last three measures involve subjective judgments a second independent observer was also called on to score these. The reliability coefficients for them were found to range from 0.70 to 0.90.

In the second part of the research, related to the analysis of the system of rules and of social representation elaborated by the adults, we interviewed each of the adults, concentrating our attention above all on the play situation, but we also asked questions about other moments of daily life: arrival of the children at the nursery, lunch, rest-time after lunch, and time spent on personal hygiene. With regard to each of these moments we chose some 'problematical events' which sometimes arise in the nursery and asked the adults to specify how and why they behave as they do in such circumstances.[3]

Subsequently each adult was asked to enlarge on the significance they attributed to the subdivision of the children into 'little ones' and 'big ones', and to comment about the capacities acquired by the child in the nursery, the instruments by which he acquires them, and the functions of the nursery.

Results: Adults' behaviour in a play situation

Our observations largely confirmed the hypotheses we made (see Table 1).

With regard to the total number of controls, there was a statistically significant difference between the two age groups: the younger children did in fact, on the whole, receive a greater number of controls.

TABLE 1

Mean numbers of types of staff speech as a function of the age of children

Type of utterance	Age in months		t (1-tail) (p)
	22	32	
Control	61.23	49.57	2.12 (< 0.05)
Teacher Specific Behaviour	53.43	58.28	1.20
Confirmations	10.57	21.57	2.42 (< 0.03)
Comments	27.29	37.57	1.98 (< 0.05)
Total verbal utternaces	200.00[a]	224.57	1.15

[a]These totals can exceed the sum of the four categories; utterances may contain two verb phrases, treated as a single category

A more detailed analysis of all the control utterances showed that action controls were more numerous than attention controls. It also emerged that younger children received more demands to pay attention than older children (see Table 2).

Most control utterances, both for action and attention were expressed by the adults in a directive rather than a prohibitive form (see Table 2); the directive form was much more common than the prohibitive. The directive form was more frequently used with younger than with older children (see Table 2).

In the distribution of the four grammatical forms used to classify the sentences (imperative, interrogative, declarative and moodless), we found 78.35% of all the controls were expressed in the imperative form: this contrasts with the 50% found by Schaffer and Crook (1979) (see Table 2). The adults utilised this form of command, more frequently with the younger children.

This form may be used to express either a directive or a prohibitive

TABLE 2

Mean numbers of control utterances and distribution of grammatical forms as a function of age of children

Type or form of utterance	Age in months		t (1-tail) (p)
	22	32	
Control: action	49.86	42.71	1.59
Control: attention	11.43	6.86	2.20 (<0.05)
Control: directive	57.86	45.43	2.32 (<0.04)
Control: prohibitive	3.43	4.14	0.43
Form: imperative	49.14	37.71	2.05 (<0.05)
Form: interrogative	7.57	7.00	0.17
Form: declarative	2.43	3.14	1.51
Form: moodless	2.14	1.71	0.29

control, relating to either action or attention; in this study more imperatives were used to express controls direction action. We wondered about the significance of such a high percentage of commands (60.6% of all the controls), and we subjected them to a further analysis: our aim was to explore the quality of these controls. We regrouped the imperative controls directing action into four categories:

(i) teaching the use of the play material (TUPM)
(ii) promotion of interaction among the children (PIC)
(iii) suggestion of an opportunity for action (SOA)
(iv) maintenance of an unchanging situation (MUS)

There were however no statistically significant differences between the age groups in the use of any of these categories (see Table 3).

However, from a quantitative point of view, we can observe that most of these controls are in the category TUPM. In the situation

TABLE 3

Mean numbers of imperative directive controls of action as a function of age of children

Directive controls	Age in months		t (1-tail) (p)
	22	32	
TUPM[a]	24.00	18.57	0.77
PIC	0.86	3.57	1.57
SOA	2.71	1.71	0.73
MUS	4.14	3.28	0.90

[a]See text for explanations of these acronyms

observed by us, the staff were not satisfied simply to urge the children to play and to interest them in the attractions of one or other plaything, as was the case with the mothers observed by Schaffer and Crook: they busied themselves with teaching the children 'what to do' to utilise the material available.

As regards the category PIC we found this kind of directive to be rare despite the fact the adults stressed that this is an especially important objective to aim for in the education of the children. In fact appears evident from our observations that the most frequent interactions in the play situations were dyadic; that is, the adult from time to time addressed each child in order to interact singly with him. Moreover we observed that when the adult addressed the three children, she included herself and used the plural: 'Let's make a lovely cottage'; the use of the plural, as in this example, was reserved almost exclusively for those forms of directive control labelled SOA.

In the last category (MUS) we included all the adult's interventions designed to control the child's activity in a restrictive sense by means of sentences of the type 'Stand still', 'Sit down properly'.

The analysis of educative behaviour (TSB), that is the giving and receiving of information and the supplying of further information, did not show any statistically significant differences between the two groups of children, contrary to what we expected, although it was used slightly more often with the older children (see Table 1).

On the other hand, for Empathetic Behaviour, the item 'confirmations' appeared with greater frequency with the older children. The difference is statistically significant. Although there was a relatively low incidence of this in the total of all the sentences spoken by the adults, (see Table 1) it is clear that there was a desire to support and encourage especially with respect to the activity of the older children. Also for the item 'Comments', we found the difference between the two age groups to be statistically significant; in this case too the older children received a greater number of comments. We think that this commenting on the part of the adults assumes, in the context of their relationship with the children, the same meaning of support for their activities as we have observed in the 'confirmations' category.

The analysis carried out on measures of grammatical complexity, showed that the speech of the adults was quite simplified; they used simple grammatical constructions without syntactic elaborations. Since no work has been done on the language used by Italian mothers or teachers in the situation which we have been examining, we took the data of some research conducted by Snow (1972) on the language addressed to their children by mothers of 2-year-olds as the best available basis of comparision. The fact clearly emerged that the adults in the day nursery expressed themselves in very brief sentences in which few compound verbs and subordinate clauses appear (see Table 4). Contrary to what we expected, no statistically significance differences appeared in morpheme length per utterance, sentence complexity or in fragments between the two age groups: in these respects the adults spoke similarly to the children independently of their age.

On the measures of redundancy the adults used more redundant speech when they were speaking to the younger children, repeating entire sentences or parts of them more frequently. There were no significant differences in semantic repetitions, that is paraphrases (see Table 4).

TABLE 4
Mean incidence of complexity and redundancy as a
function of age

Complexity	Age in months		t (1-tail) (p)
	22	32	
Length of utterances	3.90	4.08	0.64
Sentence complexity	0.08	0.10	0.96
Fragments	0.15	0.14	0.22
Redundancy - repetitions			
Complete	0.16	0.09	3.14 (< 0.01)
Partial	0.05	0.04	2.19 (< 0.05)
Semantic	0.03	0.02	0.00

If our data are compared with those of Snow (1972), it can be noted that the distribution of the types of repetitions is very different: in our case, the speech of the adult revealed a much higher proportion of complete repetitions, few partial repetitions, and hardly any semantic repetitions. This means that the adults tended to repeat the entire sentence already spoken (e.g. 'Shall we make the car? . . . Shall we make the car?') rather than attempt to amplify the meaning or the context of a topic.

DISCUSSION

It is now possible to delineate some characteristics of the interventions of the day nursery staff whom we observed. In the first place the adults rarely have recourse to punitive methods or to actions which prohibit activities of the children; they prefer more subtle and diversified forms of controls. In particular we have seen that with the younger children they use a larger number of attention controls. This datum is in agreement with the speech adjustments in language addressed to small children; in fact because 2-year-old children are easily distracted, the adults probably produce this kind of linguistic device in order to gain their attention and cooperation (Shatz and Gelman, 1973).

Moreover, the high number of controls directive of action and expressed in the imperative form, assumes a special meaning in the context of the play situation: for the adults the utilisation of the toys serves not merely for the amusement of the children but also for their social and cognitive development. In this day nursery playing constitutes a highly structured situation in which there is prevalence of educative quality in the behaviour of the adults: they control the activities of the children very closely in order to assure themselves that the objective they have in mind (building a tower, a collage, etc.) is achieved. The high percentage of 'Put it there', 'Put it here', 'Push', 'Stick', that we encountered can be explained in this manner.

This is highlighted not only by the analysis of the control utterances, but also by the results in the Teacher Specific Behaviour category: the staff tend to give and to ask for information from the children thereby quite clearly characterising the quality of their interventions as educative. ('Educative' is to be understood in the sense of designed to teach the children something regarded as useful for their cognitive development). This concern is contextualised within a relationship which is warm and affectionate, as the results in the Empathetic Behaviour category demonstrate.

The analysis of the speech of the adults shows a tendency toward a levelling down in the language adopted by all the adults: they use a language which is simplified and not very elaborated. This is found to be suitable for the younger children who are learning to speak, since it enables them to decode the utterances they hear more easily and to identify more precisely the principal units and the rules for the construction of sentences.

In fact the adults realise the necessity of utilising repetitions in order to assure themselves that the children have understood, but perhaps they do not take sufficient account of the helpfulness of varying their speech, of finding different ways of expressing what they want to say, so as to offer the children already capable of speaking (as were the olders ones) a greater wealth of vocabulary and a wider range of grammatical forms.

The fact that the adults are almost constantly addressing a group of children (as opposed to single individuals) favours a 'standardisation of the interlocutor', who is probably no longer represented by any single child present in the day nursery.

Results: Adults' system of rules and social representation

THE RULES

The rules are elaborated within the day nursery through discussion among the members of the staff: 'We decided everything within the working group'. The adults choose the rule on the basis of a common evaluation of the appropriateness of their behaviour with respect to a specific situation. The behaviour considered by all to be the 'most suitable' becomes the rule which, once defined, determines reciprocal expectations, in the sense that everybody expects the others to behave in the manner indicated. It also becomes an instrument of social control, especially in respect of those aspects which are thought important for the purposes of achieving the objectives that the group has set itself: 'We try to behave in the same manner so that there is no distinction between the 'good' nanny and the 'bad' one . . .'.

The rules to which the adults refer in their reports on the play of the infants are basically concerned with two factors: the organisation of play and teaching by means of play.

As regards the former we find more general rules like, 'Play activities are planned within the group of adults', and other rules which lay down how the infants are to play such as 'The infants are divided into two groups', 'A child who wishes to change group is to be free to do so', 'The child who does not participate in the playing of the group is encouraged to do so'. These rules, which are fully approved by the adults, since they all express them in the same terms and claim to follow them, are in part an expression of the 'directive' style, which, as we have seen, characterises the verbal behaviour of the adults.

With regard to the educative component, we find rules that indicate the importance attributed to play by the adults, and the fact that they see the play as a priviledged time for the development of cognitive and linguistic skills: 'We plan the games on the basis of what we most want to develop or expand in the infants'. Consequently, rules are found such as: 'We must insist that all the children take part in play', which do not assume a simply restrictive meaning with respect to the initiative of the individual child, but arise out of the conviction that through planned play numerous opportunities occur for learning. Thus, for example, a child can freely explore the inside of the nursery buildings and utilise the available materials, but not during organised activities because in this case 'He is recalled to play with the others'. This does not mean that the adults do not consider the solitary and spontaneous activity of the child as play, but it'is the specially planned play which is regarded as 'educative'.

Also with regard to other periods during the day that were considered, such as the time spent on personal hygiene, lunchtime, the rest period, and the arrival of the infants at the day nursery, the rules that the staff have formulated are concerned both with the organisational aspect and the educative purpose of their actions. For each situation in fact we find rules such as: 'We are all present at lunchtime', 'Each adult supervises the meal of a small group of infants', 'We take the children to the bathroom in two groups according to age', 'We insist that all go to sleep', 'An adult remains in the dormitory until the infants fall asleep', etc. All these rules specifically concern the organisation of the different moments in daily life and show the tendency of the adults to direct the activities of the infants.

Further for the educative component, we find a series of rules that shows up the educative meaning attributed by the adults to the daily routines. Rules such as: 'We insist that the older children use cutlery when eating', 'We insist that the infants take off their own clothes in the bathroom and when they go to bed', reveal the aim of teaching the infants behaviour regarded as suitable for each specific situation, that is, how to behave at table or how one behaves in the bathroom.

At table, in the bathroom, and in bed, however, it is insisted that 'The infants must not take toys with them'. They are urged to play and use the objects natural to the context in which they find themselves. Thus the adults strive to get the infants to play while helping each other and exchanging objects, in the conviction that this is the most suitable way of learning the appropriate function and use of the object in question.

THE RULES IN THEIR CONTEXT

At the moment when the rule is defined as such, it is also set in its context by the adults: that is, they explain the reasons that justify its existence and that might influence possible modifications in it. For example, all agree on the fact that 'The infants should be divided into two age-groups during play activities' but at the same time they affirm: 'It depends on the type of activity', 'It depends on the time of the year – that is to say how long the children have been at the day nursery', 'It depends on how many of us there are on duty that morning'. The rules are drawn up within the group of staff, agreed upon, and then applied with the degree of elasticity that is modified in relation to the adult, the infant, and to the type of rule. Analysing the reasons given by the adults to justify the existence of the rules and modifications in them, we found that they refer to three classes of factors:

(a) factors of a structural and organisational kind: for example, the availability of space and of green open areas, the location of the rooms, the organisation of the staff, the timetable and the work rota;

(b) objective characteristics inherent in the infants, such as age, how long they have been attending the day nursery, biological rhythms, the child's family, etc. and idiosyncratic characteristics that the adults attribute to themselves at a given time such as 'He irritates me', 'He disturbs me', etc.;

(c) factors attributed to the system of beliefs and of values: that body of assertions of an ideological or, more strictly speaking, psycho-pedagogic nature related to the day nursery both as a social service and as a place where children are brought up, to the social significance of the fundamental moments in daily life (lunchtime, play, etc.) and finally, to the needs of the infants from 3 months to 3 years of age and to their learning processes. Examples of this are: *'We divide the infants during play* (rule), because the little ones have greater need of quiet and security, of identifying themselves in the group'.

It emerges from the reports collected that the factors determining the rule arise more often than not out of a combination of structural organisational needs and legitimisations of a psychopedagogic nature, while the factors modifying the rule are concerned with the individual and idiosyncratic characteristics.

This means that the elements which can render the application of a rule elastic are concerned directly with the personal characteristics of those who interact: 'It depends on the child concerned', 'It depends on how long he has been coming to the day nursery', 'It depends on the age of the child', 'It depends on how I happen to be feeling at that moment'. The degree of elasticity with which the rule is applied is therefore connected with the ability of the adults to take account of the needs, feelings and wishes of each single infant in relation also to their own emotions: that is to say, with their ability to empathise within the interaction.

We have thus seen that directive style and educative orientation are aspects of the behaviour of the adults that are translated into the system of rules; in contrast, empathy is a characteristic which is expressed through the elastic application of the rules themselves.

THE INFANT IN THE DAY NURSERY

The analysis of the system of rules and of their justification allows us – as we have said before – to expose aspects of social representation of the adults concerning the child in the nursery and the nursery itself.

The two characteristics of infants which are most frequently utilised by the adults when referring to them are: their age (they speak of 'the little ones' and 'the big ones'); and the length of time that the child has attended the nursery (they are seen as being 'settled in' or 'not settled in').

The division of the infants on the basis of age is a pre-established criterion of an institutional type, since the local authority recommends this separation in all nurseries. This is seen as being useful organisationally, but it is usually justified by psychopedagogic reasons.

What emerges in fact is a body of principles, convictions and beliefs related to the needs and to the utilities of the 'little' child and of the 'old' one. If this on the one hand constructs and objectifies two different images of the child, on the other hand it constitutes a system of legitimisation for the behaviour of the adults. In their opinion, indeed, the 'little ones' demand and require greater attention and are therefore more closely guided and controlled, even though less is expected of them and they are more readily exempted from certain activities. They are more helpless and consequently require more protection; they cannot yet speak and are therefore regarded as less capable and often less gratifying interlocutors in interaction. The 'older' children on the other hand are able to take more direct initiatives in their interactions with the adults, and this makes it possible to classify them as direct interlocutors to whom clear requests can be made, and to whom at the same time more confirmations and greater encouragement can be given. Given the more frequent and exhaustive explanations of the adults and their greater concentration on teaching, the older children both become capable of learning rules of behaviour and acquire cognitive and linguistic skills suitable for the carrying out of scholastic tasks (such as being able to identify colours, draw within outlines, etc.). Thus they become ready for the next stage of 'schooling'.

All the adults believe that it is simpler to carry out activities with a small group of infants if they are of the same age: they think that children of the same age have similar interests and capacities of concentration. This makes it possible to help and control them better. At the same time, as was repeatedly emphasised in the reports, it is more likely that stable interpersonal relations will be established both among the children and between the children and the adults.

Moreover, the adults frequently refer to the image of the 'child who has settled in', of the child who is 'well socialised' and who has realised the objectives of the socialisation of the day nursery. The 'veteran of the nursery', as one adult described him, is a child who begins his day leaving his parents calmly, because he has learnt that this is a temporary separation, who freely explores his surroundings in the nursery, who can utilise the toys available either alone or with companions, who accepts the adults' proposals and is capable of taking personal initiatives, who addresses the adult in order to receive explanations or protection, but plays mainly with his contemporaries, and who, finally, knows and accepts the rhythms of the institution.

According to the adults, the acquisition of these capacities depends on different learning processes, in particular on imitation, habitual repetition, and the direct explanation that the adults give. The adults report that children of this age watch and imitate one another. Often, expecially if there is a favourable relationship between two children, the adults observe that they imitate each other a lot. For this reason, the importance of being together is firmly underlined as an effective means of acquiring social and interactive abilities: 'the most indicative finding that we observe among the older children (those already settled in and grown up, so as to speak, in the day nursery) is that there is continual exchange between them and the adults.

The other aspect highlighted is related to the conviction of the adults that the child learns suitable behaviour (for example, toilet training) through habit: 'I try to accustom the child to sit on his pot a little every day, at least for a short time; thus, little by little, he acquires the habit'. This method, is related essentially to the daily routines: 'In this sense it is mainly the group that shapes the behaviour of the individual'.

As regards direct teaching, the adults think they provide the children with much information during the daily activities: the explanation of what interests, attracts, frightens or arouses curiosity constitutes a fundamental tool of knowledge.

THE SOCIAL SIGNIFICANCE OF THE DAY NURSERY

It clearly emerges from what has been stated above, that the predominant image the adults have of the day nursery is that of an educational community for early childhood.

The entire organisation of the daily life of the children is directed towards the realisation of this principle, as was made clear in the analysis of the rules. Another aspect that is mentioned in the reports refers to the day nursery as a 'social service' which helps the family, and especially women who have to go out to work. However, the adults aim to ensure that it is not treated simply as a centre of public assistance or for 'parking the little ones', but as a place of development and stimulation. The day nursery is therefore regarded as a 'first school' and as such offers certain characteristics typical of every scholastic institution: for example the preoccupation of providing the children with suitable knowledge that will favour their entry into the pre-school centres (from 3- to 6-year-olds). In order to attain this goal, the adults underline the necessity of possessing an 'interactive capacity', defined explicity as the fundamental prerequisite of their professional role.

Providing knowledge and educating are certainly the salient objectives of socialisation at the day nursery, and are mentioned several times in the reports of the staff. Besides this, other objectives are indicated such as: favouring the autonomy of the infants, giving them a sense of security and tranquility, stimulating their collaboration and *desire to help one another.*

As regards this last aspect, it emerges as one of the most ideological elements in the social representations of the adults: being together in a group of peers is believed to stimulate the possibility of establishing richer and more effective and communicative relationships as opposed to those typical of the interaction between two or three people. The 'group', that is, has positive connotations for the adults, because they think that it favours the development of cooperative forms of behaviour in the children, putting concrete and realistic limits on individual liberty.

Briefly, what emerges from the reports of the adults is the idea of a continuous effort to reconcile the needs of the 'group', that is of the institution, with their desire to make the nursery a place which is suitable for the child, where he may learn and where his fundamental needs are respected.

Conclusion

In summary we would like to underline those aspects of our research which we consider particularly interesting.

In the first place it is important to remember that the adults see the nursery above all as a place in which the children learn and are educated, that is, as a 'first school'. This has the effect both of encouraging the elaboration of a series of rules aiming to create conditions which facilitate the realisation of this kind of educative goal, and of giving rise to definite forms of verbal behaviour, observed during the play sessions and categorised as TSB or as kinds of controls.

Given this, it is easier to see why our initial hypothesis that educative behaviour would be more accentuated with the older children, was not explicitly confirmed; the adults' commitment to teaching is general, in as much as it is expressed in all the daily activities we considered, and is directed towards all the children in the same degree. However, the adults do take account of the different ages of the children, using more attention controls with the younger ones in order to assure themselves that their message has been properly received. This also links in with the adults' idea of the 'little child', that is of the child who has a greater need for attention and protection, and therefore of being controlled and guided.

On the other hand, it was seen that the adults express this tendency to direct and orientate the children's activities not only by means of the controls, but also by means of the elaboration of rules of an organisational nature by which the whole of daily life is ordered.

Another interesting aspect of our research is related to empathetic behaviour. We find, in fact, that the adults consider their interactional capacity as one of the fundamental aspects of their professional role, and take into account the needs of the single child by means of a flexible application of the established rules. Moreover, this kind of behaviour is more usually found with the older children who are seen as more capable interlocutors in the context of the interaction.

The last aspect we would like to emphasise is related to the importance which the adults attribute to the group; they see this as a factor which encourages the development of the children, even when it limits individual liberty. One of the most important functions of the nursery is thus seen to be that it offers the children the chance of being together and of interacting with one another.

In contrast to these considerations, we also found that the adults rarely favour the interaction between the children (see the results of the PIC category) and that, on the other hand, the necessity of usually dealing with a group of children has an effect on their language which we defined as 'standardisation of the interlocutor': it results not only in a simplification of the language, but also in a failure to modulate it according to the different ages of the interlocutors.

Acknowledgements

The authors wish to thank the staff of S. Donato Day Nursery in Bologna for their help and collaboration. A preliminary version of the first part of this research appeared in Zani, Emiliani and Carugati (1980).

Notes

[1] In the larger day nurseries there are three sections that receive respectively children from 3 months to one year, from 1 to 2 years and from 2 to 3 years. In the small day nurseries, such as the one we considered, there is no section for the smaller children.

[2] There is also a formal distinction between the adults, educators and nannies, on the basis of the roles they play in the nursery. Given, however, that in the day nursery we examined, all the adults normally agree to follow certain patterns of behaviour with the children, and all take a full part in play activities, we have not discriminated among these statuses for present purposes. This decision was influenced by the small number of adults (four educators and three nannies) who worked in the particular day nursery observed.

[3] **Outline of the interview**

Play

How is play organised?

If the child proposed to play a different game from the one planned, what do you do?

If a child does not want to participate in a game, what do you do?

Are there times when the child may use the facilities of the nursery as he wishes?

If he begins to do this during a planned activity, what do you do?

If a child from one group wishes to join another what do you do?

If two children quarrel and interrupt the game, what do you do?

Arrival

How is the arrival of the children in the nursery organised?

If a child cries when his parents leaves, what do you do?

If a mother does not have time to take the child's coat off, what do you do?

Lavatory

How are things organised when children have to go to the lavatory?

If a child does not want to sit on the lavatory, what do you do?

If a child who has refused to sit on the lavatory subsequently wets himself, what do you do?

If a child plays with his faeces, what do you do?

If a child plays with the water, what do you do?

Lunch

How is lunch organised?

If a child gets down from the table before he has finished eating what do you do?

If a child does not wish to eat or will not finish what is on his plate, what do you do?

If a child plays with his food and spoils it what do you do?

If one of the older children wishes to be spoon-fed, what do you do?

Rest period

How is the rest time organised?

If a child will not go to bed what do you do?

If a child whom you are putting to bed, wants another of the staff to do so instead what do you do?

If one child wakes up while the others are still asleep, what do you do?

Do the children go through the same routines as they do when they go to sleep at home?

References

Emiliani, F. (1976). Problemi del processo di socializzazione in un asilo nido di Bologna. *Psicoterapia e scienze umane* **4**, 8-20

Gelman, R. and Shatz, M. (1977). Appropriate speech adjustments: the operation of conversational constraints on talk to two-year-olds. *In* "Interaction, Conversation and the Development of Language" (M. Lewis and L. Rosenblum, Eds). Wiley, New York

Harré, R. and Secord, P. F. (1972). "The Explanation of Social Behaviour". Blackwell, Oxford

Moscovici, S. (1961). "La Psychoanalyses, son Image, son Public". P.U.F., Paris

Newport, E. (1976). Motherese: the speech of mothers to young children. *In* "Cognitive Theory." (N. Castellan, D. Pisoni and G. Potts, Eds) Vol. II. Lawrence Erlbaum Associates, Hillsdale, New Jersey

Schaffer, R. and Crook, C. K. (1978). The role of the mother in early social development. *In* "Issues in Childhood Social Development" (H. McGurk, Ed.). Methuen, London

Schaffer, R. and Crook, C. K. (1979). Maternal control technques in a directed play situation. *Child Development* **50**, 989-996

Shatz, M. and Gelman, R. (1973). The development of communication skills: modification in the speech of young children as a function of listener. *Monographs of the Society for Research in Child Development* No. 152, **38**, 1-37

Snow, C. (1972). Mothers' speech to children learning language. *Child Development* **43**, 549-565

Snow, C. and Ferguson, C. (Eds) (1977). "Talking to Children". Cambridge University Press, Cambridge

Tizard, B., Philps, S. and Plewis, J. (1976). Staff behaviour in pre-school centres. *Journal of Child Psychology and Psychiatry* **17**, 21-23

Zani, B., Emiliani, F. and Carugati, F. (1980). Staff control techniques and linguistic style in a day-nursery. *Italian Journal of Psychology* **7**, 149-162

5

Language Performance of Disadvantaged Children at 30 Months: Interpersonal and other Environmental Influences

A. McGlaughlin, M. Morrissey, J. M. Empson and J. Sever

Introduction

The objective of this chapter is to explain some of the variance in language performance assessed at 30 months of age within a group of 60 homogeneously deprived infants. The focus of our explanation will be on the interactions taking place between each child and (usually) its mother, observed from the child's first birthday onwards. The conceptual basis of the analysis is directly influenced by the earlier work of Macnamara (1972) which forcefully argues the view that the infant uses meaning as the key to phonology. The historical development and antecedents of this view have been most clearly expressed by Lock (1980), who concludes that the usefulness of the pragmatic approach to language development will be limited, unless greater emphasis is placed upon social factors. The study to be reported here examines social as well as linguistic influences on the child's language development. It appears to us that this approach has gained considerable currency and increasing momentum in the last few years. Bruner in particular has been concerned with the relationship of developing language to earlier interpersonal behaviour. He argues 'that the mastery of procedures for joint action provides the precursor for the child's grasp of initial grammatical forms' (Bruner, 1977, p. 274). This rejects the traditional view, that certain sounds or words are understood by the child to have a meaning, for which he must search and instead views the process as one in which 'children develop certain conceptual representations of regularly recurring experiences, and then learn whatever words conveniently code such conceptual notions' (Bloom, 1973, p. 113). The argument is thus a simple reversal of the traditional view: language can be acquired because the child has a stock of 'meanings' to which he must apply appropriate labels if his communicative competence is to progress. A number of important issues, the subject of this chapter, arise from this argument. Do children differ in the rate and degree of acquisition of 'meanings' and if so, does this result from observed differences in their participation in social interactions? And finally, does this underpin measured differences in language performance? Bruner neatly focuses the issue: 'speech makes its ontogenetic progress in highly familiar contexts that have already been well conventionalised by the infant and his mother' (Bruner, 1974/5, p. 261). Our contention is that infants and children have markedly different experiences of exposure to, and participation in, social contexts, even when they are all drawn from a narrow social status band. We shall also argue that these differences of experience persist through the second and third years and can be clearly related to language performance as measured in the third year. The relative contributions of speech, activity and wider contextual factors will also be examined.

Method

SUBJECTS, MATERIALS AND PROCEDURE

The sample was first observed when each child was 12 months of age, at which stage most children are beginning a rapid development of language and are becoming increasingly mobile. It is also the age at which joint action patterns begin to appear, the infant having grasped the concept of reciprocity and having some understanding of intentionality (c.f. Schaffer and Crook, 1978). The observations deliberately emphasise the mother's role, rather than that of her child, because we expect the performance of young children to be largely a function of mother variables. This view has received recent support from other authors, e.g. Schaffer (1979) concludes, 'Development of interactive skills cannot take place without interactive experience; it is the mother's task to ensure that such experience occurs' (p. 301).

The sample comprised two groups of 30 mothers, each with an infant under 1 year of age. The first group are highly disadvantaged. All are on low incomes, of low social class and neither parent has more than the minimum statutory education. The second group consists of one sister of each mother in the first group plus her infant, also under 1 year of age. This feature of the sample is important for future comparison of within and between family influence. But for this paper the 60 mothers and their infants are dealt with as

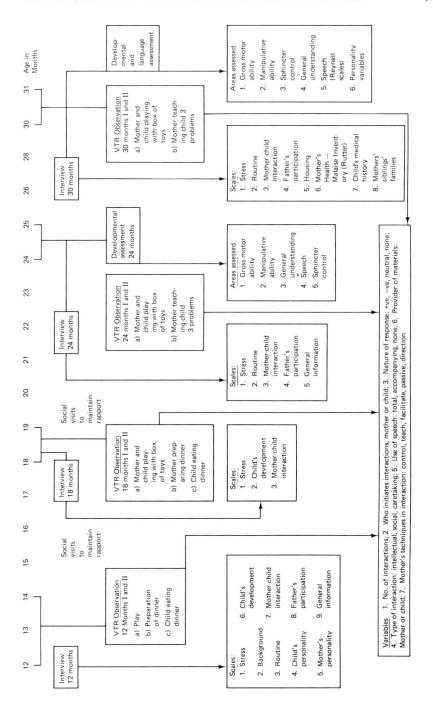

FIG. 1   Schedule and sources of variables

Variables 1. No. of interactions; 2. Who initiates interactions, mother or child; 3. Nature of response: +ve, −ve, neutral, none; 4. Type of interaction: intellectual, social, caretaking; 5. Use of speech: total, accompanying, none; 6. Provider of materials: Mother or child; 7. Mother's techniques in interaction: control, teach, facilitate, passive, direction one group. In fact, the second group proved to be just as highly disadvantaged as the first. The Osborn Social Index (Osborn and Morris, 1979) is a sensitive measure of social status which takes into account such factors as parents' education, crowding and accommodation, as well as social class. The mean scores on this index for the two groups were 50.93 and 50.83 respectively, both having a range from 48 to 54. These means place both groups clearly in the bottom 20% of the general population and justify their treatment here as one combined group.

Four methods of investigation were employed (see Fig. 1). They were:

1   *Interviews*, to determine individual differences between mothers' child care attitudes.

2   Individual *assessments* of each child's development.

3   Video-tape-recorded *observations* of each mother and child pair interacting in their own home.

4   Antecedent and concurrent *history taking* to monitor the influence of broader environmental influences.

The observations of each mother and her child playing together were recorded when each child was 12, 18, 24 and 30 months of age. At 12 months this was simply a free play session, but for the later three ages a box of toys was provided to introduce a degree of situational similarity across the families.

For present purposes it is only the play sequence that will be considered. For each family, this comprised a 9-minute video-recorded sequence of interaction. A time sampling technique was adopted, with 30 units of 18 seconds in each sequence. The maximum possible number of interactions which could be considered for each dyad at each age was therefore 30, as only the first interaction to occur (if any) in each unit was considered. This gives the simple quantitative measure of *Total Interactions*. Types and styles of interaction were determined within a detailed framework of categories defined prior to analysis. Briefly, *Intellectual* interactions were those suggesting cognitive gain, e.g. symbolic and verbal learning; concrete reasoning; age appropriate labelling; exploring properties of objects. Activities categorised as *Intellectual* included counting and colour matching; explanation with the form board, e.g. 'wrong size' or 'other way round'; naming animals and providing their 'noise'; comparisons e.g. 'it's like a giraffe'; demonstration e.g. of the powers of a magnet. *Socio-affective* interactions were those in which the focus was on either emotional content or convention. These included such activities as hugging teddy, shared amusement and routine exchanges e.g.

pat-a-cake or giving and receiving of an object. The style of inter-action was judged to be *Teach* if the mother's objective was to instruct her child in some way. Entry in this category was only made for demonstration, labelling, reading, imparting specific knowledge, e.g. new vocabulary; juxtaposing experiences, explaining, trying to determine the child's level of knowledge and imaginative play. For every interaction a *Talk* rating was given. Thus *Talk 1* if the mother used both talk and action; *Talk 2* if she used speech alone; and *Talk 0* if she used action without speech. In the subsequent analysis *Talk* refers simply to the toal number of interactions rated as *Talk 1 or 2*, although some final reference is made to the sub-categories.

A score for *Stress* and difficulties was compiled separately at each age from the interviews and informal discussion with each mother. These scales were based on the Holmes and Rahe (1967) Schedule of Recent Experiences and included information on health, housing, family, work and money. An estimate of each mother's state of men-tal health (*Malaise*) was made once only when each child was 30 months of age. The estimates comprised a simple measure of anxiety derived from the Cornell Medical Index Questionnaire (Rutter, Tizard and Whitmore, 1970).

An assessment of performance on The Reynell Language Develop-ment Scale (Reynell, 1969) was obtained when each child was 30 months of age. This provided a dependent variable to which observed interactions, attitudes and social status could be related.

Details on the reliability of measures and their consistency at and between each age are reported in McGlaughlin, Empson, Morrissey and Sever (1980).

Results and discussion

The results to be presented are derived from a much larger body of data, gathered by a variety of methods and relating to a very broad spectrum of behaviours and circumstances (see Fig. 1). In analysing these data we have used a number of different approaches. Our objective is to understand the processes which explain the different levels of performance achieved by our children on the Reynell at 30 months of age. The focus has been within the home, observing the verbal and non-verbal interactions occurring between our children and their mothers. But we have never believed that these interactions would alone account for all the observed variance. Further, the processes of interaction may themselves be amplified, suppressed or distorted by other circumstances. Accordingly, the analyses include both macro and micro approaches, the purely descriptive and the statistically analytical. The choice of approach has been made simply on the basis of what seemed most likely to add to our understanding. We have for example, included both regression analysis and broad descriptions of the changing circumstances within two sample families; even though the results of the former may be ambiguous and the latter mainly serve to point out our inability to specify and measure further important variables. We believe this is the best approach to adopt if we are to make the best use of the data and determine how far our hypotheses are supported by the evidence.

We shall begin with a detailed examination of the relationship between our Home Environment Variables measured when each child was 12, 18, 24 and 30 months of age, and performance on the Reynell at 30 months. This will be followed by consideration of the influence of socio-economic variables; a brief examination of the relationship between the mothers' opinions on child development and Reynell performance; and finally, a description of the changes in circumstances affecting two of our families, chosen to represent the highest and lowest quartiles of the sample, with examples of their interactions.

The seven main interpersonal environmental variables and their correlations at each age with the Reynell are shown in Table 1. Four simple scores each show, at all four ages, a strong and statistically significant correlation with the child's Reynell performance. These are: (*i*) total number of interactions occurring, (*ii*) total number of interactions in which mother spoke to her child, (*iii*) the total number of interactions which were of an intellectual type; and (*iv*) the

TABLE 1

Pearson Product Moment Correlations between Home Environment Variables and child's Reynell score at 30 months ($N = 60$)

Home Environment	Age (in months)			
	12	18	24	30
Intellectual	0.53^c	0.55^c	0.37^b	0.40^b
Talk	0.42^c	0.53^c	0.40^b	0.37^b
Total interactions	0.39^b	0.50^c	0.28^a	0.32^a
Teach	0.46^c	0.48^c	0.40^b	0.35^b
Stress	-0.33^b	-0.46^c	-0.28^a	-0.30^a
Socio-affective	0.06	-0.23	-0.17	-0.02
Malaise (anxiety)	-0.18	-0.20	-0.18	-0.18

$^a p < 0.05$; $^b p < 0.01$; $^c p < 0.001$

total number of interactions in which the mother employed a teaching technique. The fifth variable, a measure of stress in the home, shows a consistently significant and negative relationship with Reynell performance at all ages. The sixth and seventh variables are both mainly negatively associated with the Reynell but fail to

TABLE 2

Stepwise multiple regression analyses: full sample ($N = 60$) (Reynell score at 30 months as the dependent variable)

Age (in months)		Independent variables	R^2	F
12	1	Intellectual	0.28	22.2^c
	2	Intellectual + Teach	0.28	10.9^c
	3	Intellectual + Teach + Talk	0.30	8.8^c
		No further steps		
18	1	Intellectual	0.30	24.7^c
	2	Intellectual + Talk	0.32	13.4^c
	3	Intellectual + Talk + Total Interactions	0.32	8.8^c
	4	Intellectual + Talk + Total Interactions + Teach	0.33	6.6^c
	5	Intellectual + Talk + Total Interactions + Teach + Stress	0.39	6.7^c
	6	Intellectual + Talk + Total Interactions + Teach + Stress + Socio-affective	0.39	5.5^c
	7	Intellectual Removed	0.39	6.7^c
	8	Talk + Total Interactions + Teach + Stress + Socio-affective + Malaise	0.39	5.5^c
	9	Talk Removed	0.39	6.8^c
24	1	Talk	0.16	10.92^b
	2	Talk + Teach	0.18	6.05^b
		No further steps		
30	1	Intellectual	0.16	11.42^c
	2	Intellectual + Talk	0.18	6.2^c
	3	Intellectual + Talk + Teach	0.19	4.3^b
	4	Intellectual + Talk + Teach + Total Interactions	0.19	3.2^a
	5	Intellectual + Talk + Teach + Total Interactions + Stress	0.24	3.3^b
	6	Intellectual + Talk + Teach + Total Interactions + Stress + Malaise	0.23	2.77^a
	7	Intellectual + Talk + Teach + Total Interactions + Stress + Malaise + Socio-affective	0.24	2.36^a

$^a p < 0.05$; $^b p < 0.01$; $^c p < 0.001$

reach statistical significance at any age. It is notable that the correlations at the first two ages appear to be larger and more significant than those at the last two ages.

Next, we examined the same data by means of a stepwise multiple regression analyses to gain some insight into the relative importance of our home environment variables in accounting for the variable performance of our children on the Reynell. The results of this analysis must be treated with caution. The sample size is 60, and we are using seven independent variables in some of the regression equations. A conservative estimate is that minimum sample size should be 30 subjects per independent variable, Kerlinger and Pedhazur (1973, p. 282), if the multiple correlation is not to be unduly overestimated. This problem is exacerbated by any variable selection procedure, such as the use of a stepwise solution. In addition, where the independent variables overlap, as they do here, it becomes exceedingly difficult to attribute portions of the variance accounted for in the dependent variable, to individual independent variables. Despite these constraints, it would still seem reasonable to undertake the analysis, provided it is within an explanatory framework and the results are interpreted with caution. The squared multiple correlations appearing in the tables should therefore be regarded only as a reasonable description of our sample.

The outcome of the first regression analysis, shown in Table 2, is not impressive. Combining variables enables us at most to account for 39 percent of the variance on the Reynell. The major portion of the variance thus remains attributable to other variables. Further, by combining variables we have hardly increased the amount of variance which can be accounted for by a single variable. However, the analysis does suggest that our variables are of more importance at the 12 and 18 month stages than at the 24 and 30 month stages. At the first two stages they accounted for 30 and 39 percent of the variance respectively, whereas they account for only 18 and 24 percent of the variance at the later ages. The fact that talk can be removed at step 9 in the 18 month analysis suggests that at least at this age the quality of talk may be more important than simple quantity. In sum, it would appear that our home environment variables in combination add little explanatory power to their use in isolation; that they are more helpful at earlier ages than later; and that the talk variable shows considerable overlap with other variables. But far stronger conclusions can be reached from the next regression analyses.

Previous studies, notably Bayley and Schaefer (1964) and more recently Pawlby and Hall (1978), have reported substantial sex-differences in the relationship between variables of mother-child interaction and the development of mental and linguistic abilities. So far the analysis has paid no attention to the sex of children in our sample. When this is done, a much clearer picture emerges. Examining the means for boys and girls separately on each of our home environment variables showed hardly any differences between them at any age. The only exceptions were at 12 months for intellectual interactions, teaching technique and stress in the home. At that age only 15 percent of all interactions are coded as intellectual and a similar proportion of techniques are coded as of the teach type. But where they do occur, boys are likely to be involved in a far greater proportion of intellectual interactions ($\overline{X}$ = 3.0 for girls and 5.03 for boys) and subject more often to a teaching technique ($\overline{X}$ = 2.2 for girls and 4.0 for boys). Accordingly, in the remaining analyses the data on male and female infants are treated separately and we have entered the variables in the order in which they most interest us: talk first, then intellectual, teach, total interactions, stress, socio-affective and malaise. The results are shown in Tables 3(a), (b) and 4(a), (b), treating boys (N = 29) and girls (N = 31) separately. For boys we have a reasonably clear picture. Talk alone accounts for a decreasing proportion of the Reynell variance as we move from 12 to 30 months. This is also true when variables are combined. But now, at 30 months variables in combination account for 29 percent of the variance and at 12 months they account for an impressive 63 percent. Thus combining variables has enabled us to account for substantially more of the variance than is the case with single variables, while separating the sexes shows the considerable

TABLE 3(a)

Correlations between Home Environment Variables and Reynell score at 30 months: males only (N = 29)

Home Environment	Age (in months)			
	12	18	24	30
Talk	0.62^c	0.59^c	0.48^b	0.39^a
Intellectual	0.66^c	0.65^c	0.43^a	0.36^a
Teach	0.55^b	0.64^c	0.47^b	0.30
Total Interactions	0.54^b	0.51^b	0.37^a	0.32
Stress and difficulties	-0.51^b	-0.44^a	-0.29	-0.44^a
Socio-affective	0.06	-0.28	-0.09	-0.03
Malaise	-0.25	-0.25	-0.25	-0.25

$^a p < 0.05$; $^b p < 0.01$; $^c p < 0.001$

TABLE 3(*b*)
Stepwise multiple regression: males only (N = 29) (Reynell score at 30 months as the dependent variable)

Age (in months)		Independent variables	R^2	F
12	1	Talk	0.38	16.72[c]
	2	Talk + Intellectual	0.50	12.82[c]
	3	Talk + Intellectual + Teach	0.53	9.41[c]
	4	Talk + Intellectual + Teach + Total Interactions	0.53	6.82[c]
	5	Talk + Intellectual + Teach + Total Interactions + Stress	0.57	6.07[c]
	6	Talk + Intellectual + Teach + Total Interactions + Stress + Socio-affective	0.63	6.12[c]
	7	Talk + Intellecutal + Teach + Total Interactions + Stress + Socio-affective + Malaise	0.63	5.11[c]
18	1	Talk	0.34	14.07[c]
	2	Talk + Intellectual	0.42	9.35[c]
	3	Talk + Intellectual + Teach	0.46	7.10[c]
	4	Talk + Intellectual + Teach + Total Interactions	0.46	5.12[b]
	5	Talk + Intellectual + Teach + Total Interactions + Stress	0.47	4.10[b]
	6	**Talk Removed**	0.47	5.35[c]
24	1	Talk	0.23	8.29[b]
	2	Talk + Intellectual	0.24	4.09[a]
	3	Talk + Intellectual + Teach	0.26	2.93[a]
	4	Talk + Intellectual + Teach + Total Interactions	0.29	2.47 N.S.
	5	Talk + Intellectual + Teach + Total Interactions + Stress	0.30	1.93 N.S.
	6	Talk + Intellectual + Teach + Total Interactions + Stress + Socio-affective	0.35	1.97 N.S.
	7	Talk + Intellectual + Teach + Total Interactions + Stress + Socio-affective + Malaise	0.35	1.62 N.S.
	8	**Stress Removed**	0.35	1.98 N.S.
30	1	Talk	0.15	4.83[a]
	2	Talk + Intellectual	0.17	2.63 N.S.
	3	Talk + Intellectual + Teach	0.18	1.89 N.S.
	4	Talk + Intellectual + Teach + Total Interactions	0.19	1.39 N.S.
	5	Talk + Intellectual + Teach + Total Interactions + Stress	0.28	1.81 N.S.
	6	Talk + Intellectual + Teach + Total Interactions + Stress + Socio-affective	0.28	1.46 N.S.
	7	Talk + Intellectual + Teach + Total Interactions + Stress + Socio-affective + Malaise	0.29	1.22 N.S.

[a]$p < 0.05$;   [b]$p < 0.01$;   [c]$p < 0.001$

TABLE 4(a)

Correlations between Home Environment Variables and Reynell score at 30 months: females only ($N = 31$)

Home Environment	Age (in months)			
	12	18	24	30
Talk	0.14	0.46^b	0.26	0.39^a
Intellectual	0.36^a	0.46^b	0.32	0.48^b
Teach	0.40^a	0.34	0.30	0.41^a
Total Interactions	0.18	0.48^b	0.13	0.38^a
Stress and difficulties	0.01	-0.47^b	-0.25	-0.14
Socio-affective	0.01	-0.20	-0.30	0.02
Malaise	-0.11	-0.15	-0.11	-0.11

$^a p < 0.05$; $^b p < 0.01$; $^c p < 0.001$

TABLE 4(b)

Stepwise multiple regression: females only ($N = 31$) (Reynell Score at 30 months as the dependent variable)

Age (in months)		Independent variables	R^2	F
12	1	Talk	0.02	0.57 N.S.
	2	Talk + Intellectual	0.13	2.16 N.S.
	3	Talk + Intellectual + Teach	0.18	2.02 N.S.
		No further steps		
18	1	Talk	0.21	7.64^b
	2	Talk + Intellectual	0.24	4.27^a
	3	Talk + Intellectual + Teach	0.24	2.81^a
	4	Talk + Intellectual + Teach + Total Interactions	0.26	2.19 N.S.
	5	Talk + Intellectual + Teach + Total Interactions + Stress	0.37	2.83^a
	6	Teach Removed	0.37	3.68^b
		No further steps		
24	1	Talk	0.07	2.12 N.S.
	2	Talk + Intellectual	0.10	1.54 N.S.
	3	Talk Removed	0.10	3.20 N.S.
		No further steps		
30	1	Talk	0.15	5.10^a
	2	Talk + Intellectual	0.23	4.24^a
	3	Talk + Intellectual + Teach	0.26	3.08^a
		No further steps		

$^a p < 0.05$; $^b p < 0.01$; $^c p < 0.001$

influence our home environment variables are exerting on boys, especially at the 12 months stage. It is also notable, that at 18 months talk can be removed from the equation without loss.

For girls rather less variance on the Reynell can be explained by the home environment variables. Indeed at 12 and 24 months they explain respectively only 18 and 10 percent of the variance. At 18 and 30 months rather more of the variance is explained (37 and 26 percent) although still less than is the case for boys.

These findings are largely in agreement with those of Bayley and Schaefer (1964). They concluded that the data on the girls showed 'fewer and usually different predictive criteria available than for boys' (p. 68). But the recent study by Pawlby and Hall (1978) reached a different conclusion. In their study, variables of mother-child interaction at twenty weeks were significantly associated with Reynell performance at 27 months for girls only. The crucial difference between that study and ours is the age at which observational measures are used. This suggests that for girls, home environment variables may have their maximum effect before one year of age, whereas for boys, their greatest influence is at one year of age. Our data lend some support to this view. Talk, the variable of greatest interest to us at 12 months explains more of the boys' variance on the Reynell than at any other age and decreasing proportions of that variance as we move from 12 through 18 and 24 to 30 months. There is no equivalent trend for girls, suggesting that if talk is an influential variable for them, then it exerts its effect either before 12 months or after 30 months. If talk is important for girls earlier than 12 months, we might expect to find some differences between boys and girls at 12 months. We have already noted that boys of 12 months are more likely than girls to take part in intellectual types of interaction and receive a teaching technqiue. They also have a lower mean score than do girls for providing the activity which is the focus of any interaction, although the difference is not statistically significant. On this latter variable, a child rather than adult characteristic, the girls are precocious.

Clearly then, the mother's use of talk during interaction at 12 months is of particular significance for a male child's language performance at 30 months. Such performance is also affected by other of our home environment variables, which together explain over 60 percent of the variation on the Reynell.

We shall now turn our attention to other methods used to examine our data.

Our sample was chosen to score low for parents' education, income and social class. Yet there are considerable variations within such a group. Some of these are measured by our home environment variables. But we shall now directly examine the relationship between the Reynell performance and each family's standing on the Osborn and Morris (1979) Social Index. The latter index is more discriminating than allocation to a particular class on the basis of employment alone. The Spearman Rank Correlation between the Osborn Social Index scores at 12 months and Reynell performance at 30 months was insignificant, $(rho = -0.0422)$. Thus for our sample there is no relationship between these two measures. The range of the Social Index for our sample is of course relatively narrow and this will in part explain the lack of relationship found. The age of the children when the Reynell was used is also against finding such a relationship. But there are considerable differences between our families, which we would expect to influence family dynamics and child development. For example, between our first contact at 12 months and our latest contact at 30 months, 15 of our 60 mothers either became pregnant or gave birth to another child (two of them did both). Seven of our mothers were separated or divorced during this time, and the husband of one mother was murdered in a family feud. Such factors must influence the behaviour of our mothers and children, but as yet have only entered into consideration indirectly through their contribution to the stress variable. However, we have now begun to examine the relationship between the attitudes and views our mothers have on child development and their children's performance on the the Reynell. The mothers' views on child development were rated in three areas, from answers to 15 of the questions asked during the interview when the child was 30-months-old. Three of these questions were concerned with the quantity, quality and initiation of speech during their daily exchanges with their child (Speech). Seven questions sought the mother's view of how her child learnt and the relative importance she placed on her own influence and that of other people and experiences (Learn). The final five questions concerned the mother's use of explanations, teaching of words and functions and the estimation of the child's understanding, during daily activity (Instructs). Comparisons were made between the Reynell scores at 30 months, for approximately the top and bottom thirds of the sample, as rated for Speech, Learn and Instructs, separately and in combination. It can be seen in Table 5 that the mean ratings are in all four cases higher for the children performing in the top strata on the Reynell. The differences are only statistically significant however when the ratings on Speech,

Learn and Instructs are combined ($U = 80, n_1 = 18, n_2 = 19, p < 0.01$, one-tailed).

TABLE 5

Differences in performance on the Reynell at 30 months by rating on Speech, Learn, Instructs and all three combined

Ratings	Mean Reynell score		$U\,(p)$
	Top stratum	Bottom stratum	
Speech	66.33	60.63	93.5
Learn	63.83	57.11	114.5
Instructs	65.35	59.72	200
Combined	69.78	56.21	80 ($p < 0.01$)

The results presented so far provide evidence on the influence of both home environment variables and mothers' attitude on early child development. Yet to us there still appear to be considerable qualitative differences between our families which have not been taken into consideration. The nature of these differences can be gauged from the remainder of this section. What follows is a description of the changing life events and circumstances of two of our sample families, together with examples of the interactions we observed between each mother and her child. The examples given refer to 'Zachary' and 'Albert', who respectively represent children performing in the lower and upper quartiles on the Reynell. The two families are, however, similar in that both are at the lower end of the income scale for the sample, live in Council housing and have three children of which the target child is the youngest and male.

Two case studies: Zachary and Albert

TWELVE MONTHS

At the beginning of the project, Zachary's mother had separated from her husband. Her three children each had a different father and she was at this time cohabiting with the target child's father. She had been in hospital suffering from depression, during which time the children had been fostered; the family had recently moved house. Albert's family, by comparison, were leading a fairly uneventful life. The only thing in their past worthy of note being the fact that the eldest child had been born before the mother's marriage and later legally adopted by her present husband, who was not the father.

The interactions observed within these two mother-child pairs were markedly different in quantity and quality. Zachary and his mother were below the sample mean on nearly all of our variables. His mother left him largely to his own devices, directing him from a distance to do things which he was usually doing already. When present, his mother told his two older sisters to 'Get out of the way' and, when the eldest commented to her mother, 'You're supposed to be playing with him', she was firmly told 'He is playing'. In fact at that point Zachary was crawling aimlessly around the floor. Zachary's mother frequently talked at him without any accompanying activity and used a directive approach, e.g. 'Build the bricks', with no attempt to demonstrate or assist. When her speech was accompanied by action, it was usually in a caretaking context, e.g. 'Come on droopy drawers', as she pulled his pants up.

Albert and his mother were above the sample mean on most of our variables. His mother was involved in the maximum number of interactions and directed him appropriately to new activities. She also labelled objects, played games such as peek-a-boo and recited nursery rhymes. When the two older children were present, Albert's mother continued to focus her attention on him, whilst ensuring that his brothers were also involved in some activity. Albert's mother invariably accompanied her speech with actions. She showed Albert how to build a tower of bricks, took turns in knocking it down and handed stray bricks to him when directing him to 'put the bricks away for Mummy'. She also praised him when he did so, 'Good boy. Oh he is clever!'

At this age neither Zachary nor Albert were capable of speech beyond single words such as 'Mama' and 'Geegee'.

EIGHTEEN MONTHS

Zachary's family had again moved house. His mother was now engaged to be married to a new partner, who was living with them, his father remaining in the household nonetheless.

Albert's family were pleased to learn that their house was to be modernised by the Council, although they were slightly anxious about the probable increase in rent.

At this and subsequent sessions, a box of toys was provided for the use of each mother-child pair during play. Zachary's mother chose to label the animals in the picture book and read out the brief descriptive passage beneath each picture. She encouraged Zachary 'to bake' as he stirred some bricks in the saucepan, but, as at the previous age, her approach was largely directive and appeared to be rather frantic.

Albert's mother also labelled the animals in the picture book, distinguishing between a horse and a donkey, and imitated the noises made by each, to Albert's great amusement. When Albert chose to play with the saucepan and bricks, his mother suggested that he 'make believe dinner', and the rest of the family joined in having imaginary tastes.

TWENTY-FOUR MONTHS

Zachary's mother had now divorced his father in order to marry her new fiancé. In fact the marriage never took place, as the fiancé moved out when Zachary's mother's sister and her young child moved in with them, following a dispute with her own husband. Throughout, Zachary's father remained within the household. But at this time he lost his job 'because of my nerves' and, together with Zachary's mother, was placed on probation for stealing from the gas meter. Zachary had been in hospital following an accident(?).

Albert's family reported few changes of circumstance. His mother had been employed temporarily as a play-centre assistant, for two hours each evening for one month, to earn extra money before Christmas. The house had not yet been modernised.

Zachary and his mother still participated in relatively few interactions. Even fewer were of an intellectual nature, although his mother did label objects and demonstrate how to play a skittles game. Zachary's speech was still restricted to single word utterances. In contrast, the interactions between Albert and his mother were now of a predominantly intellectual nature. The skittles game was enjoyed and also used to practise counting. The picture book was again used for naming activities and additionally for explaining the use of things, e.g. 'I cut your hair with scissors like that', and 'Wellingtons – for going out in the mud and snow'. The picture of a cake led to a discussion of Albert's birthday, which was the next day. What would he like for tea and how many candles would be on the cake? Albert's understanding and speech were clearly well developed. He understood that he would have a cake because it was his birthday, that it would have candles on it, that he would be two-years-old and that he would be given presents.

THIRTY MONTHS

Zachary and his sisters had again been in the care of the local authority, during a period when his mother was readmitted to hospital suffering from depression. As the result of a fractured skull, Zachary had also spent some time in hospital.

During play, Zachary's mother still persisted with her directive approach, providing little guidance other than exhortations to 'do it, you do it', and exaggerated praise for his efforts.

Albert and his mother took turns with another game, magnetic fishing. Again the game was used for naming and also for colour matching and counting. It was also related to Daddy's fishing expeditions.

Summary

The home environment variables, on which Zachary and Albert so clearly differ, have been analysed in detail earlier. Some account will also have been taken of the stresses within the homes. But the examples of Zachary and Albert also indicate changes which are bound to affect the children, yet cannot readily be included in the analysis. Some comment was also made on the association between mothers' views on child development and the performance of the children. Zachary's and Albert's mothers have highly contrasting views. Albert's mother thought he learnt through a combination of his own effort, imitation and positive teaching. She also considered her present actions would influence his later level of performance. Zachary's mother, however, did not believe his performance at school was at all related to his previous experiences. Nor did she believe in trying to teach him. Her attitude is clearly conveyed by her statement, 'He knows what to do. He isn't daft'.

General conclusions

The evidence presented here gives substantial support to our hypotheses where male children are concerned, but rather less in the case of girls. Interactive experience is strongly associated with later language performance. But as the child grows older, the strength of this relationship declines. This suggests that mother and child variables are changing in relative importance. Freedle and Lewis (1977), reach a similar conclusion from studies of mother-child communication between 3 and 24 months. Their study also reports sex differences, which they attribute to differential socialisation rules in the mother's responsivity to her infant. As yet, we cannot comment on the responsivity of our mothers, although we do have evidence that they behave differently with their male and female children. Interactions can be divided between three categories, according to whether the mother employs both talk and action, talk only, or action only. When this is done, we find that talk and action is strongly and significantly related to Reynell performance for boys at both 12 and 24 months but not later. For girls it is significant only at 12 months. Conversely, talk without action becomes significant for girls by 24 months, but not until 30 months for boys. In addition, action without talk is a significant adverse influence on boys but not girls. This is in keeping with the Freedle and Lewis findings on sex differences, and with the evidence of Pawlby and Hall (1978), that differences between girls in language performance on the Reynell can be partially explained by patterns of interaction before 12 months. It is also entirely consistent with the view expressed by Bruner (1974/5, p.284),

If there is one point that deserves emphasis, . . . it is that language acquisition occurs in the context of an 'action dialogue' in which joint action is being undertaken by infant and adult.

However, it should be remembered that at 12 months our observations were based on free play interaction, whereas at all other ages a box of toys was provided by us. Individual variation might therefore be expected to be greater at 12 months. This may in part account for the higher association with the Reynell found for observations at that age. The mean number of interactions between 12 and 18 months shows very little difference but there are substantial changes in type of interaction which may be the result of this change in procedure. There is available a tempting analogue for this situation. Robinson (1965) demonstrated that working-class children would use elaborated speech codes given appropriate contexts, even though it remained true that they were customarily less likely to do so than were middle-class children. Perhaps some of our mothers and their children are more likely to interact in the slightly artificial context with the toy box, than they are customarily. If so, then our observations at 12 months are likely to be the best indicator of how each mother and her child usually interact, whilst the later observations indicate how they would interact if a box of toys were normally available. This has important implications, particularly if we accept Schaffer's view, that it is the mother's task to ensure that interactive experience occurs. Some of our mothers would appear to have both competence and performance, despite their generally disadvantaged circumstances and background; others appear to have the competence but only demonstrate this in certain contexts; whilst a final group perhaps simply lack the competence and skills necessary for performance. Zachary's mother is an example of the last group and Albert's an example of the first. Zachary's mother expressed views which were largely negative and demonstrated a fatalistic attitude towards her child's development. She also exhibited a directive style of interaction with little evidence of sensitivity to her child's needs in relation to his current level of performance. In contrast, Albert's mother believed she was an important influence on her child and acted appropriately. These marked differences in mothering behaviours must in part relate to the sometimes colourful changes of circumstances described earlier. Yet we have so far been unable to give them sufficient representation in our analyses. The Osborn Social Index in fact proved to have no relationship with Reynell performances. The measure of Stress and Difficulties looks more promising. At least for boys, the correlation with Reynell performance is high and negative at all ages and there is a noticeable contribution to the squared multiple correlation even though entry was not allowed until step five. Of equal importance, the analyses presented take little account of child variables. Other data show that as we observe interaction at later ages, so there is an increasing contribution from the child, both in terms of who initiates the interactions and who provides the activity on which they focus. We would expect these child variables to have an increasing importance with age, unlike the mother variables we have discussed, which appear to be of decreasing importance for our children's language performance, as they grow older.

References

Bayley, N. and Schaefer, E. S. (1964). Correlations of maternal and child behaviours with the development of mental abilities: Data from the Berkeley growth study. *Monographs of the Society for Research in Child Development* No. 97, Vol. 29, No. 6

Bloom, L. (1973). "One Word at a Time: The Use of Single Word Utterances before Syntax". Mouton, The Hague

Bruner, J. (1974/5). From communication to Language – a psychological perspective. *Cognition* 3, 255-287

Bruner, J. (1977). Early social interaction and language acquisition. *In* "Studies in Mother-Infant Interaction" (H. R. Schaffer, Ed.). Academic Press, London

Freedle, R. and Lewis, M. (1977). Prelinguistic conversations. *In* "Interaction, conversation and the Development of Language" (M. Lewis and L. A. Rosenblum, Eds), Wiley, New York

Holmes, T. H. and Rahe, R. H. (1967). The social readjustment rating scale. *Journal of Psychosomatic Research* 11, 213-218

Kerlinger, F. N. and Pedhazur, E. J. (1973). "Multiple Regression in Behavioural Research". Holt, Rinehart and Winston Inc., New York

Lock, A. (1980). Language development – past, present and future. *Bulletin of the British Psychological Society* 33, 5-8

Macnamara, J. (1972). Cognitive basis of language learning in infants. *Psychological Review* 79, 1-13

McGlaughlin, A., Empson, J. M., Morrissey, M. and Sever, J. (1980). Early child development and the home environment: consistencies at and between four pre-school stages. *International Journal of Behavioural Development* 3, 299-309

Osborn, A. F. and Morris, A. C. (1979). The rationale for a composite index of social class and its evaluation. *British Journal of Sociology* 30, 39-60

Pawlby, S. J. and Hall, F. (1978). Evidence from an observational study of transmitted deprivation among the children of women from broken homes. *Proceedings of the Second International Congress on Child Abuse and Neglect*, September, London. *See also*: Hall, F., Pawlby, S. J. and Wolkind, S. (1979). Early life experiences and later mothering behaviour: a study of mothers and their 20-week old babies, *In* "The First Year of Life" (H. Schaffer and J. Dunn, Eds). Wiley, New York, *and* Pawlby, S. J. and Hall, F. Early interactions and later language development in children whose mothers come from disrupted families of origin *In* "High-Risk Infants and Children: Adult and Peer Interactions (T. Field, S. Goldberg, D. Stern and A. Sostek, Eds). Academic Press, New York (in press)

Reynell, J. (1969). "Reynell Developmental Language Scales". National Foundation for Educational Research, Slough

Robinson, W. P. (1965). The elaborated code in working-class language, *Language and Speech* 8, 243-252

Rutter, M., Tizard, J. and Whitmore, K. (Eds) (1970). "Education, Health and Behaviour". Longman, London

Schaffer, H. R. (1979). Acquiring the concept of the dialogue. *In* "Psychological Development from Infancy: Image to Intention" (M. H. Bornstein and W. Kessen, Eds) pp. 279-305. Lawrence Erlbaum Associates, New Jersey

Schaffer, H. R. and Crook, C. K. (1978). The role of the mother in early social development. *In* "Issues in Childhood Social Development" (H. McGurk, Ed.). Methuen, London

6

Mothers as Teachers and their Children as Learners: A Study of the Influence of Social Interaction upon Cognitive Development

E. Hartmann and H. Haavind

Cognitive development and social mediation

The present study is based on the argument that social interaction and communication influence cognitive development. In accordance with the theory of Piaget (1950), Piaget and Inhelder (1969) cognitive developmental change is seen as a gradually increasing degree of decentration. A cognitive structure is more decentred when it has changed in ways that make possible simultaneous consideration of relatively more aspects or views when forming an impression, a judgement or another cognitive result. Developmentally more advanced structures contain more knowledge and are better adapted to reality. Through the process of assimilation the individual incorporates experiences according to already existing structures. Through the process of accommodation, structures change according to the demands of reality. This makes possible assimilation of new impressions. The interactive process of assimilation and accomodation together form an equilibration of inner and outer change.

Piaget's theory of how equilibration leads and organises development is very abstract. He admits that the social milieu plays a role, but does not concern himself with a more detailed analysis of the social factors which may stimulate or inhibit the development of the child. Further, his main focus of interest has been the child's understanding of physical events.

Hunt (1961), Smedslund (1966) and others have pointed out how the environment constantly produces imbalances to which the child tries to assimilate and accommodate. Hunt says that the environment evokes discrepancies between outer influence and inner structuring, which the child tends to reduce. Smedslund asserts that communication conflicts may force the child out of his ordinary way of thinking.

The events the child will attend to and which thereby may initiate growth are determined by motivation inherent in the child. If the discrepancies or conflicts between external influences and inner structure are too great, the child will not be able to grasp it. No modification of schemata will occur. The situation will either be irrelevant or perhaps anxiety provoking. If there is no or too little a discrepancy, there also will be no change. The situation will be well known and perhaps boring. This is what Hunt (1971) has called 'the problem of the match'.

Environmental influences on cognitive development thus can only be understood in relation to the capacities and learning styles the child already has established. Hunt's and Smedslund's ideas give us no exact answer to the question of how to find the stimulating circumstances, but they give the important advice to use the child's own interests as a guide. It seems sound to suppose that while physical objects must be actively selected by the child, social communication in addition can be adjusted to the child's level of functioning. This mediating process is the main focus of this study.

In recent years many studies have been based on the assumption that parents, particularly mothers, are the main mediators between the child and the outer world. According to Vygotsky's and Luria's theoretical analysis intellectual development advances through dialogues between parent and child. The way parents demarcate the relevant and important dimensions of experience plays an important role in promoting the child's cognitive development (Luria and Yudovich, 1959; Vygotsky, 1962).

Bernstein (1961, 1970, 1972, 1973) points to social class differences in speech in his socio-linguistic theory of socialisation. He distinguishes two kinds of linguistic codes or modes of communication, 'restricted' and 'elaborated' codes. Restricted codes give rise to speech which is stereotyped, limited, condensed and is neither very exact or differentiated, nor discriminative. Elaborated codes are more precise and more differentiated, permitting more complex and flexible expressions through linguistic means. Bernstein (1972) suggests that in the middle-class elaborated codes are used together with restricted ones. In the lower-class, however, a high proportion of families are expected predominantly to use restricted codes. When children are limited to a restricted code, they learn a code where the extra-verbal tends to become a major channel for the qualification and elaboration of individual experience. An elaborated code orients its speakers to the possibilities which inhere in a complex conceptual hierarchy for the organisation of an expression of inner experience. What is made available for learning through elaborated and restricted codes are then supposed to be radically different. Children who have access to different linguistic codes thus are suggested to adopt quite different social and intellectual procedures despite common potentials. Cook-Gumperz (1973) has given empirical support to some aspects of Bernstein's theory. She finds social class differences in maternal modes of social control and language codes and in maternal replies to hypothetical questions about how they would deal with certain misbehaviour of their children. In general the middle-class mothers take up strategies within the personal mode, the mixed-class within the positional mode and the working-class within the imperative mode of control. Further the middle-class mothers are more likely to use an elaborated code, the working-class mothers a restricted code. The results for the children, however, show very few differences between social class position and the children's forms of control. There is a relation between differences in maternal speech and control strategies and the children's performance on standardised IQ-tests, especially between maternal use of an elaborated code and high scores on verbal intelligence tests, but the relation is not very strong.

Turner (1973) has further explored the data of Cook-Gumperz using Halliday's (1973) concept of meaning potential which suggests that the same sentence may have different meanings for speakers from different social groups. He then finds that working-class children were more likely to take up options within the imperative mode and middle-class children within the positional mode of control.

Hess, together with his collaborators (Hess and Shipman, 1965, 1967, 1968; Hess, Shipman, Bear and Brophy, 1968) have further developed and empirically tested their own and Bernstein's ideas. They distinguish three types of maternal control which should lead to complementary orientations of their children. Their results show that imperative – norm – centred mothers tend to have children who have learned to attend to and obey authority. Personal-subjective mothers tend to have children who are directed towards expressive, internal reactions and to personal and individual considerations. Cognitive-rational mothers tend to have children who are oriented towards tasks and logical principles. The relation they find between teaching strategies and children's cognitive performance are, however, not so strong. Robinson (1973), Robinson and Arnold (1977) and Robinson and Rackstraw (1972) have demonstrated convincing social class differences in question-answer exchange between mothers and their children. The class differences to some extent differed according to how familiar the tasks were expected to be to middle-class and working-class families. The mothers' provision of cognitive meaning and of feedback correlated highly with their children's rates of questioning and knowledge revealed both within and across classes.

In our opinion the Cook-Gumperz study and the studies of the Hess-tradition have methodological deficiencies which may explain why they did not find stronger relations between mother and child. A possibly relatively sound theory of social mediation is tested empirically with methods insufficiently related to the theoretical concepts.

Our main objection is that the maternal communication is often analysed in a situation where the mother is talking about the child or about how she will behave towards the child and not in a situation where she is interacting with the child. The data obtained make it difficult to know whether the mother's in actual situations would use similar speech-patterns or strategies of control (Cook-Gumperz, 1973; Hess and Shipman, 1968).

Secondly, Cook-Gumperz, the Hess-tradition, as well as several other studies devoted to cognitive socialisation have used 'social class' as an independent variable. This variable is used wholly or partly to replace a direct method for studying social interaction or the cognition of the child (Bayley, 1965; Bee, van Egeren, Streissguth, Nyman and Leckie, 1969; Brophy, 1970; Hertzig, Birch, Thomas and Mendez, 1968; Hess and Shipman, 1965; Klaus and Gray, 1968; Milner, 1951; Olim, 1970). The categories of social class are too gross for the necessary detailed description of the mediating process. The overlap between the results may be great even if the social class differences are significant (Cook-Gumperz, 1973; Hess and Shipman, 1965; Ginsburg, 1972). It is necessary to separate the problem of how social mediation influence cognitive development from the problem of how differences in social structure produce different forms of social mediation.

The estimation of the child's intellectual performance often are made from the same situation where a mother teaches the child a certain task. The measure of the mother's and the child's behaviour thus are interdependent. In other cases IQ tests are used as independent measure, without any discussion of the relation between the process studied by IQ tests and those involved in the maternal tasks, e.g. teaching of logical concepts. Ordinarily the correlation between scores on general intelligence tests and those on tests of logical concepts are fairly small (Dudek, Lester, Goldberg and Dyer, 1969).

Hess gives no rationale for how the selected tasks, object sorting and Etch-a-Sketch (cooperation in copying designs), are supposed to elicit relevant behaviour. These tasks seem to be rather unnatural to both mother and child. It is not likely that a mother from her daily life has any experience in or idea of how one teaches children to sort objects according to two characteristics simultaneously. Thus one may question the generality of data obtained in these situations. Instead of giving the mothers an opportunity to use activities from their daily repertoire of behaviour, they are forced to explain logical principles to small children. That most mothers do not find this relevant, is best shown by the fact that many of them totally ignore the instruction of explaining the task to the child (Hess and Shipman, 1967, pp. 77–79). The mother ought to be given a chance to direct and assist the child in her own manner and in a task which she could probably have chosen herself.

In addition the tasks selected by the researchers are too difficult for the children to solve. This may hinder representative and smooth communication between mother and child. Further it gives little chance of really teaching the child anything. Hess and Shipman report for example (1967, p. 57) that over fifty percent of the mothers failed to teach the children to verbalise any part of the principle in a double-sorting task.

Probably the children are also too young for testing of the theory. Hess and Shipman (1967) point to mechanisms of exchange that mediate between the child and his environment. They focus on a linguistic presentation of alternatives for thought and action which may promote the child in reflection, considering, comparisons and anticipation about actual events. According to a theory for cognitive development, these could be relevant ways of mediation when the child is about to acquire concrete operations. Ordinarily this will not take place before the child is about 6 years of age, and will go on intensively to at least the age of 8 and even longer (Hunt, 1961; Smedslund, 1964).

Reliable measures of children's cognitive capacity imply that the children are motivated to do their best. According to Zigler and Butterfield (1968) and Hertzig et al. (1968) children's motivation varies greatly. Most children also find tests boring and meaningless (Smedslund, 1966). This probably also holds for the tests of the Hess-tradition.

Method

RATIONALE FOR THE APPROACH ADOPTED

Due to the above criticism, two methods were devised, one for observing the mother and another for observing the child. In order to evoke social and cognitive processes which are theoretically related to the present theory of cognitive development and social mediation, mother and child were observed in the same kind of learning situation, the mother as teacher, the child as learner.

To get a lifelike, but still structured, situation where mother and child could get a chance to draw from their ordinary repertoire of behaviour and also become meaningfully involved in the situation so that their behaviour would be representative, the selected task was a game similar to other games of the culture, but with unknown rules.

The game, called 'Running Horses', was devised for the present study. It is a board game of the race type similar to Ludo. There are two players. Each one has two horses. Chance – throws of four chips – determine how far one can go in a move. Different rules decide where one is allowed to move. Two horses give the players constant possibilities to decide which horse is the most profitable to move in order to avoid obstacles and gain advantages. Winning thus depends both on luck and on skill.

Attention to the causal structure of the game may vary. There exists a hierarchy of possible cognitive awareness beginning with the more stimulus bound recognition of facts and going deeper into the underlying causes of the facts. According to Heider (1958) the causal structure may consist of a certain composition of personal and impersonal factors. The analysis of the social events created by the game, corresponds very well to Heider's 'naive analysis of action'. This allows the participants in the research-situation to use their ordinary modes of perceiving events and persons.

Running Horses can be played with success independent of awareness of the opportunity to influence the run of the game. Thus most children, even those who have a very restricted understanding of the rules, find the game interesting.

The game creates opportunities to see actual outcomes from many different legal perspectives, to anticipate supposed consequences and to choose among alternatives. According to how many rules are taken into account, an event can be viewed as favourable or unfavourable. The conflicting aspects of one state can lead to more decentred combinations. Varying degrees of decentred understanding of the child can be diagnosed, and maternal behaviour can be judged according to its decentring effect.

The social matrix created by playing this game is thus well suited for generalisation to social conditions of daily life and for eliciting cognitive processes relevant for acquisition of concrete operations.

The children were aged 6 to 7 years. This is an age characterised by extensive and fast change in cognitive functioning during the transition to concrete operation, good mastery of language and lack of formal education.[1] At this point of the child's history family influences on socialisation and thus effects of differences in social environment are still fairly important.

RESEARCH DESIGN

To prevent interdependency between the measures of mother and child, the following procedure was used: The experimenter taught each child the game. The child's way of receiving instructions, that is his *learning style* was observed, and his *capacity in changing cognitive concepts* was diagnosed. The concept *educability* is used to include both. The mother was then taught the game, and later she taught it to another child of the same age, and her *maternal teaching strategy* was observed.

In a control study it was demonstrated that the mother's way of teaching does not differ when teaching her own child or another child of the same age (Haavind and Hartmann, 1977).

The research was carried out in the home of the families where mother and child were supposed to feel safer and act more natually. The conversation was recorded and relevant non-verbal behaviour was noted.

The instruction of the child was based on what Hunt (1971) calls 'intrinsic motivation'. The quantity of new information was always balanced against the child's receptivity. The rules were presented during the game, but ahead of the child's need for them. Opportunities to plan and choose was regularly explained though adjusted to the child's understanding.

To obtain smooth communication and cooperation with the child the training was not standardised in the strictest sense of the word, but continuously adapted to the child's level of motivation and need for feedback and new information. The essential element was to get the child to understand that he should try to do his best, play as cleverly as possible, win the race, answer questions, listen to explana-

[1] In Norway children start elementary school at the age of 7.

tions and be task-oriented. Contrary to the case in projective testing, it was important to stop the child from following his own whims and fantasies.

To get the mother to cooperate well, care was taken to explain the purpose of the research. The mother was taught the game twice, once some days before her own teaching and once just before she was going to play. Training was never stopped before the mother mastered the game, which is rather easy for adults. Opportunities to plan and to choose were constantly demonstrated during the training. Questions about the rules were always answered. Questions about how to behave, however, were met by suggestions to act in the way the mothers found most natural.

To test the reliability of the results and validity of the methods the study was done twice, with two samples.

SUBJECTS

To get equivalent samples in the primary study and the re-test study each mother-child pair in the primary study was compared with a pair in the re-test-study in a way that made the compared pair similar on the following dimensions: Socio-economic status, civil status of the mother, age of the child, and whether or not the child had been to kindergarten.

In both studies 34 mother-child pairs and 34 surrogate children took part. In each sample one third of the subjects came from the upper-middle-class, one third from the lower-middle-class and one third from the lower-class. The classification is based on income, standard of housing and education of both parents. In all the families the mother was the chief caretaker of the children.

The children studied were aged 6;5 to 7;4 in both samples. Within each compared pair in the two samples, the age of the child never varied more than 3 months. The average variation was 1 month. In each sample 14 of the children had been to kindergarten. The surrogate-children were aged 5;3 to 7;1. The age-difference between own and surrogate-child varied somewhat more than was considered desirable in both samples. It was found more important that the surrogate-children were well known to the mothers than that they were of the most desirable age.

The main impression was that both mother and child in the two samples found this research unthreatening and rather amusing. None of the children lost interest in the game. One reason might be that the children were asked to solve problems which require cognitive processes that emerge during the transition to concrete operations. This creates intrinsic motivation and lasting interest, conditions necessary to obtain reliable data about the cognition of children.

Two mothers in the primary study dropped out after the first visit to their homes; none in the re-test-study. The dropouts were the most insecure of all the mothers. They belonged to the lowest socio-economic class in the sample. Their children were among the slowest learners; they were the only ones who found the game boring. The loss of these mothers deprived the research of two representative of a social and intellectual milieu that otherwise does not exist in the sample.

CLASSIFICATION OF BEHAVIOUR

Coding: maternal behaviour   The intention behind the classification system of maternal teaching strategy was to classify a great variety of aspects of maternal behaviour in ways that relate her teaching to theoretical considerations of how cognition is stimulated or inhibited. The general hypothesis was that pointing to relevant aspects and taking them into account simultaneously could promote decentration. The same holds for the invitation to act independently of the other person and the perceptual appearance. On the other hand cognitive development may be delayed when the mother's behaviour restricts the child's possibility to reflect, choose, anticipate or act on account of his own understanding of the rules. Maternal behaviour was classified when the mother on her own initiative explained things, discerned alternatives or pointed to future consequences. In addition the child's behaviour could be interpreted as demanding certain social reactions. In such instances maternal behaviour was judged and classified according to the mother's ability to take the role of the child and to take account of what he needed to know in order to play correctly.

The training situation had emotional as well as intellectual elements. Support and encouragement are necessary for maintenance of the child's self-confidence and thus for his ability to be problem-oriented and motivated for new learning. The game included competition, and a moderate degree of focus on this may also direct and motivate the child for relevant learning. These aspects of maternal behaviour was also classified.

Maternal behaviour was interpreted according to what sort of understanding logically followed from her presentation, not according to what she might have intended to explain, nor what the child understood or reacted to.

The following nine variables for describing maternal teaching strategies were developed:

1 *Informing* includes statements where mother gives information about the rules of the game. Information is coded once for each new item of information. When the same information is repeated later in the game, it is not coded. A certain criterion of efficiency has to be passed. Only instructions which are complete and specific enough to make correct understanding of the rules possible, belong to this category.

2 *Anticipation* is coded every time mother talks about what may or might have happened in the game according to the possibilities the rules create.

3 *Demonstration of alternatives* includes statements about the player's possibilities to choose which horse to move and where to move it. The demonstration of alternatives must include explicit focusing on the possibilities of choice. At least two alternatives must be mentioned.

4 *Seeking feedback* is coded every time the mother overtly tries to check how the child understands the game and/or her teaching.

5 *Imperative feedback* is coded every time the child expresses uncertainty, does not remember things or acts against the rules, and the mother responds to this with an order without any explanations. The scores, however, are calculated as a percentage of all situations that requre feedback, thus eliminating differences due to the functioning of the surrogate child.

6 *Ordering* includes instances where the mother spontaneously direct the child about what he should or should not do. Ordering is coded when directions are given without explanation and when she acts on the child's behalf.

7 *Restriction* consist of different types of maternal behaviour that are supposed to confuse the child. Separately these kinds of behaviour do not differentiate well among mothers. Put together into one category, the dispersal becomes good. Restriction is coded whenever the mother explains the rules in such a vague and unintelligble way that the communication becomes meaningless, every time her instructions or behaviour are discordant to previous given information and whenever the situation requires feedback, but this is ignored by the mother.

8 *Competition* is coded whenever the mother speaks about who has the best chances to win or about other competitive elements.

9 *Emotional support* is coded every time the mother gives overt support and encouragement to the child.

Coding: child behaviour   The intention behind the classification system of educability was both to diagnose cognitive processes and to record the child's way of receiving teaching. Behaviour indicating the emergence of concrete operations were the main basis for diagnosing the child's capacity in changing cognitive concepts. Behaviour indicating the child's reaction to cognitive demands from grown-ups were the basis for registration of his learning style.

The degree of decentration in the child was most clearly indicated by his mastery of the rules when playing, and by his ability to take several present and non-present aspects into consideration to form decisions and plans.

The social reactions of the child were judged as appropriate or inappropriate for the learning process. For example sometimes his behaviour is not in accordance with trying to win the game, but has to be understood in relation to other wishes and needs of the child. If the child's discerning of consequences often is led by personal symbolism and irrelevant emotional engagement which are not task-oriented, it might hamper steady cognitive development. Thus it was found informative to obtain a measure of plans and decisions which are not task-oriented. Further stability in attention as well as fluctuations according to personal or social conditions may influence cognitive functioning. Both the child's manner of accepting or rejecting instructions from the adult and the way he presents his own uncertainty and insufficient understanding, will probably influence the possibilities for change through further assimilation and accommodation.

The training aims at giving the child opportunities to become an active learner. He is guided towards becoming intellectually and emotionally involved without losing a task-oriented attitude to the game. He is animated to ask questions and to express his thoughts and doubts aloud. Children who are able to meet such a challenge, have a favourable kind of educability. The training is experienced as motivating, not as dangerous or humiliating.

Several such sub-categories describing the child's reactions would, if used as variables, give a skewed distribution. For instance one way of rejecting corrections is to start talking about something else. This strategy was typical of some children, but most of the children never reacted in this way. However, many of them presented other types of inadequate behaviour. The classification system was therefore simplified to include two main categories, coding respectively reactions judged as creating an adequate or an inadequate social relation between grown-up and child. In addition passivity as a way of showing uncertainty was separated as one main category.

Behaviour indicating emotional engagement was also separated as one main category. But the emotional involvement had to be in accordance with a realistic apprehension of the course of the game to be coded. The use of magic comfort or positive enthusiasm of irrelevant aspects or unfavourable events was not coded in this category. The game includes competition. Interest in this aspects was coded as a variable. A certain emotional involvement in the playing and a spontaneous interest in the competition aspect may create a social relation to the adult which gives good opportunities to focus on other relevant aspects which the child can understand.

The following nine variables for describing educability were developed:

1   *Rule-mastery* is coded when the child spontaneously is capable of using the rules or combinations of them in a correct as well as efficient way. The child must be able to judge the results of the rules in action as favourable or unfavourable. Rule-mastery is coded separately for the main rules in every move throughout the playing. The scores are calculated as the percentage of the moves where the rule-mastery exceeds a certain criterion for advanced apprehension.

2   *Decision-making* is coded every time the child spontaneously manages to set up a choice where two or more alternatives are clearly discriminated, or where one of the consequences is properly discerned.

3   *Planning* is coded every time the child spontaneously puts forward adequate plans which demand liberation from the strict here-and-now-situation.

4   *Task-irrelevant discerning* is coded every time the child makes or sticks to plans and decisions that are clearly not task-oriented. The scores are calculated as a percentage of the number of relevant decisions and plans made by the child.

5   *Adequate interest* is coded every time the child shows behaviour which indicates interest or shows alert understanding, like verbal extensions of the grown-up's information, questions, comments or corrections to the grown-up's plans, developing new rules etc.

6   *Inadequate reactions* is coded when the child expresses negative, irrelevant or over-excited reactions, like experiencing questions and comments as corrections, ignoring new information, keep to persistent patterns of response failure, seeking refuge with magic, trickery or other idiosyncratic behaviour.

7   *Passivity* is coded when the child sits passively waiting for instructions, is unresponsive to questions or in other ways expresses uncertainty by just doing nothing.

8   *Competing* is coded every time the child spontaneously focuses on the competetive aspects of the game.

9   *Adequate emotion* is coded when the child expresses emotional involvment that is relevant to the events occurring during the game.

INTER-RATER RELIABILITY

The inter-rater reliability for the variables was tested on tape-recordings of 31 of the mothers and 15 of the children. The reliability was calculated both in relation to every single assignment of coding and as the correlations between total scores for each variable. The agreement between two raters for every single assignment for the maternal variables and for the child variables varied from 73 percent to 91 percent, and the correlation between the total scores varied between 0.86 to 0.99, indicating that the rules for classification are explicit enough to guarantee satisfactory agreement among raters. The remaining tape-recordings were scored by one rater and checked for mistakes by another.

HYPOTHESES

The maternal teaching strategy variables *informing, anticipation, demonstration of alternatives* and, to a lesser extent, *competition* and *emotional support* count behaviour which is supposed to instigate decentration in the child. Strong positive interrelations were expected among these promoting variables.

Imperative feedback, ordering and *restriction* count behaviour supposed to hamper decentration. Strong positive relations were expected among these restraining variables. Between the variables counting promoting and those counting restraining teaching, significant negative correlations are expected.

The child educability variables *rule-mastering, decision-making, planning* and *adequate interest* count behaviour indicating high educability. Strong positive interrelations were expected among these variables. *Passivity, task-irrelevant discerning,* and *inadequate reactions* indicate low educability. Strong negative relations were expected between the variables counting high educability and those counting low. High educability is supposed to be the result of promoting cognitive socialisation and low educability the results of cognitive socialisation that has been restraining or that has lacked promoting conditions.

Thus, the variables which measured promoting maternal teaching were expected to be positively related to the child variables indicating high educability and negatively related to the variables indicating

TABLE 1

Spearman Rank correlations between the nine variables of maternal teaching strategy:
The primary study ($N = 34$)

Variable	Informing	Anticipation	Demonstration of alternatives	Competition	Seeking feedback	Emotional support	Restriction	Ordering	Imperative feedback
Informing	1.000								
Anticipation	0.8667^c	1.000							
Demonstration of alternatives	0.7111^c	0.8150^c	1.000						
Competition	0.5630^c	0.5189^b	0.5816^b	1.000					
Seeking feedback	0.4700^b	0.5694^b	0.5386^b	0.3624^a	1.000				
Emotional support	0.5170^b	0.3712^a	0.3650^a	0.6625^c	0.2982^a	1.000			
Restriction	-0.7501^c	-0.5700^b	-0.4143^a	-0.2057	-0.3206^a	-0.3540^a	1.000		
Ordering	-0.7453^c	-0.5360^b	-0.4555^b	-0.3262^a	-0.4638^b	-0.4557^b	0.6707^c	1.000	
Imperative feedback	-0.8208^c	-0.7376^c	-0.6118^c	-0.4979^b	-0.5338^b	-0.5047^b	0.6663^c	0.6382^c	1.000

$^a p < 0.05$; $^b p < 0.01$; $^c p < 0.001$

low educability. Inverse relations were predicted between the restraining maternal teaching variables and the educability variables.

The data of the primary and the re-test study were analysed in exactly the same way. The results of the two studies are presented side-by-side.

Results: Mother as teacher

Tables 1 and 2 summarise the intercorrelations among the nine maternal teaching strategy variables in the two samples.

The patterns of correlation in the two matrices are very similar. In both samples all the correlations are in the expected direction, and most of the coefficients are statistically significant. The correlations of the primary study are generally a little higher than in the re-test.

To obtain a description of the differences between the mothers in terms of a relatively few composite variables, principal component analysis was used.

The analysis showed that in both samples most of the variables are related to the first component, which accounts for 60% of the total variance in the primary and 57% in the re-test study. The second component accounts for 12% in the primary and 18% in the retest study. Table 3 shows the first and the second principal component loadings of the nine maternal variables of the two samples. The differences between the results are slight. In both samples the first principal component seems to be a bipolar dimension. The second component in both cases seems to be rather unipolar.

In both samples it makes considerable sense to describe the main variation in teaching strategy among the mothers as reflecting their degree of decentered presentation of the game. The variables having the highest positive loadings on the first principal component in both studies all include behaviour supposed to instigate decentration, the variables having the highest negative loadings include behaviour supposed to hamper decentration.

Interpretation of the second component is more difficult in both studies. This component only accounts for a small amount of the total variance. Still, it makes sense to interpret this component as a dimension of different kinds of involvement in the playing and in the presentation of the game. It seems to range from a pure task-oriented attempt to make the child understand the game to an attitude where competitiveness and feelings dominate at the expense of instructing the child.

Thus, the main dimension of the material in both studies dis-

TABLE 2

Spearman Rank correlations between the nine variables of maternal teaching strategy:
The re-test study ($N = 34$)

Variable	Informing	Anticipation	Demonstration of alternatives	Competition	Seeking feedback	Emotional support	Restriction	Ordering	Imperative feedback
Informing	1.000								
Anticipation	0.7586[c]	1.000							
Demonstration of alternatives	0.8231[c]	0.8776[c]	1.000						
Competition	0.4242[b]	0.4919[b]	0.4658[b]	1.000					
Seeking feedback	0.4743[b]	0.4823[b]	0.5706[b]	0.4825[b]	1.000				
Emotional support	0.5800[b]	0.4568[b]	0.5194[b]	0.7023[c]	0.6841[c]	1.000			
Restriction	−0.6761[c]	−0.5647[b]	−0.5647[b]	−0.1387	−0.1408	−0.1371	1.000		
Ordering	−0.7557[c]	−0.5566[b]	−0.5843[b]	−0.1398	−0.1873	−0.3320[a]	0.7539[c]	1.0	
Imperative feedback	−0.7365[c]	−0.5886[b]	−0.5886[b]	−0.2456	−0.2812[a]	−0.2756	0.5582[b]	0.6977[c]	1.000

[a] $p < 0.05$; [b] $p < 0.01$; [c] $p < 0.001$

TABLE 3
Loadings on the first and second principal component of the
maternal teaching strategy variables[a]
The primary study ($N = 34$)

Variable	Component vector	
	I	II
Informing	0.9415	−0.1337
Anticipation	0.8779	−0.0373
Demonstration of alternatives	0.7987	0.1611
Competition	0.6637	0.6603
Seeking feedback	0.6444	0.0212
Emotional support	0.6298	0.4670
Restriction	−0.7235	0.5105
Ordering	−0.7644	0.3237
Imperative feedback	−0.8756	0.1135

The re-test study ($N = 34$)

Variable	Component vector	
	I	II
Informing	0.9363	−0.1274
Demonstration of alternatives	0.8989	0.0320
Anticipation	0.8672	−0.0107
Emotional support	0.6628	0.6041
Seeking feedback	0.6095	0.5657
Competition	0.5699	0.6076
Restriction	−0.7017	0.5373
Imperative feedback	−0.7366	0.3397
Ordering	−0.7620	0.4782

[a]Programme library developed by Tom B. Johnsen, Department of
Psychometry, University of Bergen, Norway

tinguishes two types of teaching strategy, the informing and the
imperative. In addition there are indications of a third type of
teaching strategy, the competitive expressive.

The psychological description of the three strategies appears as
follows:

1 *The informing teaching strategy* involves justification of
behaviour based on consideration of common rules. Information
about the rules are presented in a well elaborated manner. Rational
explanations about how one can anticipate the run of the game,
make plans and choose among alternatives are frequently given.

Initiative is often left to the child who is also given much overt encouragement. Uncertainty is usually met by offering new information and not by giving orders. Competitive elements are focused on, but to a moderate degree. Restraining behaviour like giving unintelligible or contradictory information, ignoring uncertainty or direct ordering of the child occurs seldom. This strategy is not perfect, by ideal standards, but can still be characterised as a rather decentered way of presenting the game and as teaching which may have a promoting effect. The child is invited to explore and debate possibilities. He is led to take the role of another and see his own behaviour from different perspectives.

2   *The imperative teaching strategy* involves a minimum of rationale and justification with reference to reciprocal rules. Incomplete and partly contradictory information is typical. Opportunities to explain how to choose and make plans are ignored, or the explanations are very vague. There is little sensitivity for the process of learning and understanding of the child. Supportive behaviour is seldom offered, and the competitive aspect of the game is often omitted. This strategy can be characterised as a rather centred way of presenting the game and as teaching likely to have a hampering effect. The child is prevented from reflecting, considering, questioning and searching for rational principles. He is trained to obey to authority without knowing or asking why.

3   *The competitive-expressive teaching strategy* involves much focusing on competitive and interpersonal aspects. Considerations about who will win, what can be done in order to win etc., seem to play a more important role than how to teach the child to play correctly and wisely. To some extent this mother fails to take account of the child's need for intelligible information. On the other hand this strategy is likely to include orientation towards the feelings of the child. Much praise, encouragement and other kinds of emotional support is common. It is difficult to say what degree of decentration a presentation according to this strategy will have. Likewise it is difficult to decide what impact such a strategy may have on the child.

The maternal strategies described above, are in many ways similar to the three strategies for maternal control described by Hess and Shipman (1967). In the present study, however, the general description of the strategies are more closely related to observed maternal behaviour and more directly based on the relation between different variables.

Results: The child as learner

In Tables 4 and 5 the intercorrelations among the nine child educability variables in the two samples are summarised. The patterns of correlations in the two matrixes are very similar.

All the correlations, except for the variable 'inadequate reaction' in the primary study are consistent with the hypothesis, and most of the coefficients are statistically significant. As for the maternal variables, the correlations are generally a little higher in the primary than in the re-test sample.

Principal component analysis showed that in both samples most of the variables were related to the first component, which accounts for 57% in the primary and 61% re-test study. The second component accounts for 23% in the primary and 19% in the re-test study. Table 6 shows the first and the second principle component loadings of the nine child educability variables. The differences between the results are slight.

In both samples the first principal component and the second component seem to be bipolar dimensions.

In both samples the main variation among the children can be interpreted as reflecting their degree of decentred cognition and decentred manner of receiving learning. The variables having highest positive loadings on the first principal component all include behaviour associated with relatively decentred cognition. The variables having highest negative loadings on the first principal component all include behaviour associated with relatively centred cognition.

The second component can be interpreted as a dimension of different kinds of involvement, ranging from a mainly task- and learning-oriented attitude toward the game to an attitude where emotions and competitiveness dominate at the expense of understanding other elements of the game. This emotional involvement can be both adequate and inadequate.

Thus, the main dimension of the material in both studies distinguishes two types of educability, one of high and one of low educability. In addition there are indications of a third type of educability, the expressive.

The psychological description of the three types of educability appears as follows:

The active mastering educability implies an assertive, rather verbal approach to learning, and an orientation towards logical principles as a guide for behaviour. The rules are handled at an

TABLE 4

Spearman Rank correlations between the nine child educability variables:
The primary study ($N = 34$)

Variable	Planning	Decision-making	Rule-mastery	Adequate interest	Adequate emotion	Competing	Inadequate reaction	Task irrelevant discerning	Passivity
Planning	1.000								
Decision-making	0.7315^c	1.000							
Rule-mastery	0.8350^c	0.8495^c	1.000						
Adequate interest	0.6532^c	0.5773^c	0.5046^b	1.000					
Adequate emotion	0.4656^b	0.4516^b	0.3550^a	0.7436^c	1.000				
Competing	0.4676^b	0.3143^a	0.2342	0.5872^c	0.6561^c	1.000			
Inadequate reaction	-0.1347	-0.2431	-0.3281^a	0.3399^a	0.4385^b	0.2598	1.000		
Task irrelevant discerning	-0.6954^c	-0.8481^c	-0.8576^b	-0.5009^b	-0.3588^a	-0.2010	0.3454^a	1.000	
Passivity	-0.7320^c	-0.7176^c	-0.7509^b	-0.6241^c	-0.4313^b	-0.3619^a	0.1107	0.6579^c	1.000

$^a p < 0.05$; $^b p < 0.01$; $^c p < 0.001$

TABLE 5

Spearman Rank correlations between the nine child educability variables:
The re-test study ($N = 34$)

Variable	Planning	Decision-making	Rule-mastery	Adequate interest	Adequate emotion	Competing	Inadequate reaction	Task irrelevant discerning	Passivity
Planning	1.000								
Decision-making	0.7277[c]	1.000							
Rule-mastery	0.7517[c]	0.7970[c]	1.000						
Adequate interest	0.8102[c]	0.5443[b]	0.6485[c]	1.000					
Adequate emotion	0.4962[b]	0.2725	0.2733	0.4929[b]	1.000				
Competing	0.6371[c]	0.3025[a]	0.4175[c]	0.6044[c]	0.7796[c]	1.000			
Inadequate reaction	-0.5094[b]	-0.6079[c]	-0.6795[c]	-0.3309[a]	-0.0271	-0.1046	1.000		
Task irrelevant discerning	-0.6899[c]	-0.7691[c]	-0.7392[c]	-0.4967[b]	-0.1955	-0.2762	0.7112[c]	1.000	
Passivity	-0.7215[c]	-0.7136[c]	-0.7108[c]	-0.5821[b]	-0.3019[c]	-0.3544[a]	0.7382[c]	0.7676[c]	1.000

[a] $p < 0.05$; [b] $p < 0.01$; [c] $p < 0.001$

TABLE 6

Loadings on the first and second principal component of the
child educability variables[a]

The primary study (N = 34)

Variable	Component vector	
	I	II
Planning	0.8899	−0.0829
Decision-making	0.8865	−0.2454
Rule-mastery	0.8805	−0.3667
Adequate interest	0.7917	0.4508
Adequate emotion	0.6559	0.6192
Competing	0.5456	0.5695
Inadequate reaction	−0.0747	0.8769
Task-irrelevant discerning	−0.8360	0.3733
Passivity	−0.8441	0.0972

The re-test study (N = 34)

Variable	Component vector	
	I	II
Planning	0.9123	0.1703
Rule-mastery	0.8827	−0.1661
Decision-making	0.8537	−0.2476
Adequate interest	0.7848	0.3173
Competing	0.5951	0.7129
Adequate emotion	0.4934	0.7469
Inadequate reaction	−0.7112	0.5323
Task-irrelevant discerning	−0.8349	0.3300
Passivity	−0.8618	0.2147

[a] Programme library developed by Tom B. Johnsen, Department of
Psychometry, University of Bergen, Norway

advanced level. Considerations about planning and decisions are
common and are based on fairly elaborated judgements and comparisons between different alternatives, and seldom guided by
irrational or personal factors. Emotional and competitive involvement is present to a moderate degree. Uncertainty is not typical
and does not result in passivity, but in an active claiming of more
information. This style of educability is not perfect by ideal standards, but can still be characterised as rather decentred cognitive
functioning combined with adequate responsiveness to instruction.

The passive educability implies a fundamental passive approach to
learning. Solutions to problems are reached by superficial imitation
or impulsive guessing rather than by reflection. The rules are mastered

on a low level of differentation and complexity. Generalisation to rational principles is lacking. Decisions and plans are vague and determined by fortuitous factors. To some extent interest in the competitive elements and adequate emotions may still be present. This style of educability can be characterised as rather centred cognition combined with little or inadequate responsiveness to instruction.

The expressive educability is oriented toward emotional, interpersonal and competitive elements; affections are easily stimulated. Excitement and disappointment frequently interfere with the general cognitive functioning. The expressive child is seldom passive, and the degree of decentration vary.

The classification made by Hess and Shipman (1965, 1968) of orientation in children have much in common to our types of educability. We think that our methods for describing maternal teaching strategies and child educability have improved the empirical foundation of their general descriptions.

Results: Mother-child relationships

The correlation between the mothers' and their children's scores on the first principal component is 0.55 ($p < 0.01$) in the primary and 0.51 ($p < 0.01$) in the re-test study. The results indicate a strong correspondence in degree of decentred maternal teaching and decentred educability of their children.

The correlation between the scores and the second component is 0.34 ($p < 0.05$) in the primary and 0.14 in the re-test study. Thus there are indications of a relationship in degree of expressive and competitive involvement in the primary study, but not in the re-test study.

The correlations between the variables of maternal teaching strategy and child educability are presented in Table 7 for the primary sample and in Table 8 for the re-test sample.

The pattern of interrelations in the two samples are very similar . In the primary sample all the maternal variables, except seeking feedback, correlate in the predicted direction with all the variables of educability, except inadequate reactions, and most of the coefficients are statistically significant. Thus both samples demonstrate a close relationship between maternal teaching strategy and child educability.

This relationship between teaching and educability becomes even clearer when mother-child pairs are classified according to the distinguished types of maternal teaching strategy and child educability.

TABLE 7

Spearman Rank correlations among nine maternal teaching strategy and nine child educability variables:
The primary study ($N = 34$)

Teaching strategy	Planning	Decision-making	Rule-mastery	Adequate interest	Adequate emotion	Competing reactions	Inadequate reactions	Task-irrelevant discerning	Passivity
					Educability variables				
Informing	0.3466^a	0.4254^b	0.3683^a	0.5084^b	0.3453^a	0.1474	0.0049	-0.3524^a	-0.3735^a
Anticipation	0.2842^a	0.4192^a	0.3012^a	0.6634^c	0.6147^c	0.2390	0.3410^a	-0.3681^a	-0.4329^b
Demonstration of alternatives	0.3209^a	0.3828^a	0.3099^a	0.4843^b	0.3606^a	0.0516	0.1115	-0.2979^a	-0.4463^b
Competition	0.1897	0.4385^b	0.2163	0.4445^b	0.3810^a	0.2765	0.1890	-0.2712	-0.2657
Seeking feedback	0.0218	0.3513^a	0.1223	0.1387	0.2217	-0.1269	0.0796	-0.1961	-0.1759
Emotional support	0.2787	0.4800^b	0.2471	0.4804^b	0.4118^a	0.3698^a	-0.0044	-0.2594	-0.3094^a
Restriction	-0.3094^a	-0.4923^b	-0.4071^a	-0.3209^a	-0.1977	-0.1255	0.1930	0.3865^a	0.4618^b
Ordering	-0.3036^a	-0.3928^a	-0.3122^a	-0.4833^b	-0.2888^a	-0.1341	-0.0779	0.3450^a	0.3946^a
Imperative feedback	-0.3639^a	-0.4288^b	-0.4203^b	-0.3929^a	-0.2327	$-0;0560$	0.3079^a	0.4388^b	0.3133^a

$^a p < 0.05$; $^b p < 0.01$; $^c p < 0.001$

TABLE 8

Spearman Rank correlations among nine maternal teaching strategy and nine child educability variables:
The re-test study ($N = 34$)

Teaching strategy		Educability variables							
	Planning	Decision-making	Rule-mastery	Adequate interest	Adequate emotion	Competing	Inadequate reactions	Task-irrelevant discerning	Passivity
Informing	0.3761^a	0.4756^b	0.3578^a	0.4763^b	0.3351^a	0.1581	-0.3117^a	-0.3516^a	-0.3648^a
Anticipation	0.3915^a	0.4173^a	0.3071^a	0.5843^b	0.4719^b	0.2871^a	-0.2935^a	-0.3729^a	-0.4259^b
Demonstration of alternatives	0.3627^a	0.3736^a	0.3186^a	0.4758^b	0.3512^a	0.0819	-0.3062^a	-0.2918^a	-0.4537^b
Competition	0.1820	0.4263^b	0.2058	0.3271^a	0.2771	0.2156	-0.1736	-0.2673	-0.2716
Seeking feedback	0.0413	0.3115^a	0.0417	0.1175	0.0138	0.0163	-0.0571	-0.0162	-0.1094
Emotional support	0.2871^a	0.4716^b	0.2065	-0.4612^b	0.3260^a	0.2563	-0.2836^a	-0.2384	-0.3178^a
Restriction	-0.3194^a	-0.5162^b	-0.4163^a	-0.3317^a	-0.3877^a	-0.2016	0.3141^a	0.3751^a	0.4725^b
Ordering	-0.3225^a	-0.3826^a	-0.3019^a	-0.4725^b	-0.2951^a	-0.0251	0.3279^a	0.4063^b	0.3617^a
Imperative feedback	-0.3548^a	-0.4375^b	-0.4117^a	-0.3758^a	-0.3162^a	-0.0731	0.3162^a	0.4273^a	0.3228^a

$^a p < 0.05$; $^b p < 0.01$; $^c p < 0.001$

According to the general descriptions of teaching strategy and educability, about half of the mothers in both samples could be classified as respectively informing and imperative, and about half of the children in both samples could be classified as respectively active mastering and passive. Just a few of the mothers were judged as competitive expressive, and just a few of the children were certainly expressive. The mothers' and the children's scores on the first principal component were used as criteria for dividing the mothers into either the informing or the imperative type of strategy and the children into either the active mastering or passive educability. In addition the few mothers and the few children with high scores on the second component were classifed as belonging to respectively the competitive expressive teaching strategy and the expressive educability.

TABLE 9

Mothers and children classified according to teaching strategy and educability: The primary study ($N = 34$)

Maternal teaching strategy	Educability of child		
	Active mastering	Expressive	Passive
Informing	11	2	1
Competitive expressive	0	3	0
Imperative	2	0	15

TABLE 10

Mothers and children classified according to teaching strategy and educability: The re-test study ($N = 34$)

Maternal teaching strategy	Educability of child		
	Active mastering	Expressive	Passive
Informing	12	2	2
Competitive expressive	1	1	0
Imperative	3	0	13

Tables 9 and 10 show the results of such a classification for the primary and re-test sample. In both samples there is very strong relationship between informing teaching and active mastering educability and between imperative teaching and passive educability.

In the primary study there is also a moderate relationship between competitive expressive teaching and expressive educability. This relationship was not found in the re-test study.

Discussion

The strong interrelations among the variables describing maternal teaching strategy and child educability are congruent with the hypothesis. The strength of the relations exceeds what is ordinarily found (Wandersman, 1973).

The results are in agreement with the description of maternal strategies given by other researchers (Bee *et al.*, 1969; Brophy, 1970; Hess, 1970; Wren, 1970; Jacobs, 1971; Bernstein, 1972; Cook-Gumperz, 1973; M. Steward and D. Steward, 1973). Child educability has not been correspondingly elaborated.

There has long been a growing awareness of the influence of parent-child communication on cognitive development, with particular respect to language functions (e.g. Bernstein, 1972; Hess and Shipman, 1967; Lawton, 1968). However, so far, little has been known about how and in what ways different parent-child communication influence cognitive development. What is needed, is a more precise delineation of the different aspects of parental influences together with an analysis of their separate effects.

Our study, with its weight on detailed description of behaviour and quantitative analysis, and on relating both maternal and child variables to a common theory of social mediation, is a step towards more informative studies of the mechanisms of exchange between adults and children.

The research by Robinson and Rackstraw (1972), Robinson (1973) and Robinson and Arnold (1977) on question-answer exchange between mothers and children and the study of Wood and Middleton (1975) of assisted problem-solving also pay more attention to specific psychological variables affecting cognitive development.

The social mechanisms of exchange described by our results do not characterise all interaction between mother and child. Both mother and child have a wider spectrum of interaction. In ordinary life the frequency of teaching/learning situations similar to the ones established in our study vary. By giving the mother a teaching task, she is forced to adopt a teaching rationale for the ensuing interaction with the child. Mothers differ according to how accustomed they are to the demands of such a social setting. The impera-

tive mothers are probably more unaccustomed than the informing
ones to using a teaching rationale. Imperative and restrictive behaviour may reflect the mothers' ordinary interaction with their children.
Such behaviour may, however, also be specific for the test situation
and reflect unsureness in an unknown situation.

Our goal has not been to devise methods which make it possible
to predict the intelligence of the individual child from the behaviour
of his mother. The social influence takes place within certain biological limits. The mother is not the only socialiser. In our culture,
however, her work as the main caretaker implies such a considerable
amount of interaction that her special strategy will have some effect
on the child. But the influence from other adults, siblings and peers
may alter these effects.

Lastly, our intention has not been to show that the child has no
effect on maternal behaviour. We do not believe that the direction of
influence is exclusively from mother to child. The study focuses on
differences between the mothers in their capacity to create a social
interaction adapted to the child's needs, and in our opinion this adaptation is more determined by individual characteristics of the mother
than of the child.

Acknowledgement

The research was partially supported by a grant from The Norwegian
Research Council for Science and the Humanities.

References

Bayley, N. (1965). Comparisons of mental and motor test scores for ages 1–15
    months by sex, birth order, race, geographical location, and education of
    parents. *Child Development* **36**, 379–411
Bee, H. L., van Egeren, L. F., Streissguth, A. P., Nyman, B. A. and Leckie, M. S.
    (1969). Social class differences in maternal teaching strategies and speech
    patterns. *Developmental Psychology* **1**, 727–734
Bernstein, B. (1961). Social class and linguistic development. *In* "Education,
    Economy and Society" (A. H. Halsey, J. Floud and C. A. Anderson Eds).
    Free Press, Glencoe, Illinois
Bernstein, B. (1970). A sociolinguistic approach to socialization. *In* "Language
    and Poverty" (F. W. Williams, Ed.). Markham, Chicago
Bernstein, B. (1972). A critique of the concept of compensatory education. *In*
    "Functions of Language in the Classroom" (C. B. Cazden, V. P. John and
    D. Hymes, Eds). Teachers College Press, New York

Bernstein, B. (1973). "Class, Codes and Control" Vol. 3, Routledge, London

Brophy, J. E. (1970). Mothers as teachers of their own pre-school children. *Child Development* **41**, 79–94

Cook-Gumperz, J. (1973). "Social Control and Socialization". Routledge, London

Dudek, S. Z., Lester, E. P., Goldberg, J. S. and Dyer, G. B. (1969). Relationship of Piaget measures to standard intelligence test scales. *Perceptual and Motor Skills* **28**, 351–363

Ginsburg, H. (1972). "The Myth of the Deprived Child". Prentice Hall, New Jersey

Halliday, M. A. K. (1973). "Explorations in the Functions of Language". Edward Arnold, London

Haavind, H. and Hartmann, E. (1977). Mothers as teachers and their children as learners. Report No. 1, Institute of Psychology, University of Bergen

Heider, F. (1958). "The Psychology of Interpersonal Relations". Wiley, New York

Herzig, M. E., Birch, H. G., Thomas, A. and Mendez, O. A. (1968). Class and ethnic differences in the responsiveness of pre-school children to cognitive demands. *Monographs of the Society for Research in Child Development* **33**, Serial No. 117

Hess, R. D. (1970). Social class and ethnic influences on socialization. *In* "Carmichael's Manual of Child Psychology" (P. H. Mussen, Ed.). Wiley, New York

Hess, R. D. and Shipman, V. C. (1965). Early experience and the socialization of cognitive modes in children. *Child Development* **36**, 869–886

Hess, R. D. and Shipman, V. C. (1967). Cognitive elements in maternal behavior. *In Minnesota Symposium on Child Development* (J. P. Hill, Ed.). **1**, University of Minnesota Press, Minneapolis

Hess, R. D. and Shipman, V. C. (1968). Maternal influences upon early learning. *In* "Early Education" (R. D. Hess and R. M. Bear, Eds). Aldine Press, Chicago

Hess, R. D., Shipman, V. C., Bear, R. M. and Brophy, J. E. (1968). "The Cognitive Environments of Urban Pre-school Children". University of Chicago Press, Chicago

Hunt, J. McV. (1961). "Intelligence and Experience". Ronald Press, New York

Hunt, J. McV. (1971). Using intrinsic motivation to teach young children. *Educational Technology* **2**, 78–80

Jacobs, J. C. (1971). Evaluation of mother teaching styles in high ability families. *The Gifted Child Quarterly* **15**, 32–35

Klaus, R. and Gray, S. (1968). The early training project for disadvantaged children: a report after five years. *Monographs of the Society for Research in Child Development* **33**, Serial No. 120

Lawton, D. (1968). "Social Class, Language and Education". Routledge, London

Luria, A. R. and Yudovich, F. (1959). "Speech and the Development of Mental Processes in the Child". Staples Press, London

Milner, E. (1951). A study of the relationship between reading readiness in grade one school children and patterns of parent child interaction. *Child Development* **2**, 95–112

Olim, E. G. (1970). Maternal language styles and children's cognitive behavior. *Journal of Special Education* **1**, 53–67

Piaget, J. (1950). "The Psychology of Intelligence". Routledge, London (Originally published, 1947)

Piaget, J. and Inhelder, B. (1969). "The Psychology of the Child". Routledge, London (Originally published, 1966)

Robinson, W. P. (1973). Where do children's answers come from? *In* "Class, Codes and Control" (B. Bernstein, Ed.) Vol. 2. Routledge, London

Robinson, W. P. and Arnold, J. (1977). The question-answer exchange between mothers and children. *European Journal of Social Psychology* 7, 151–163

Robinson, W. P. and Rackstraw, S. J. (1972). "A Question of Answers". Routledge, London

Smedslund, J. (1964). Concrete reasoning: a study of intellectual development. *Monographs of the Society for Research in Child Development* 29, Serial No. 93

Smedslund, J. (1966). Les origins sociales de la décentration. *In* "Psychologie et Epistemologie Genetique" (F. Bresson and G. de Montmollin, Eds). Dunod, Paris

Steward, M. and Steward, D. (1973). The observation of Anglo, Mexican, and Chinese-American mothers teaching their sons. *Child Development* 44, 329–337

Turner, G. J. (1973). Social class and children's language of control at ages five and seven. *In* "Class, Codes and Control" (B. Bernstein, Ed.) Vol. 2. Routledge, London

Vygotsky, L. (1962). "Thought and Language". Wiley, New York

Wandersman, L. P. (1973). Stylistic differences in mother-child interaction: a review and re-evaluation of the social class and socialization research. *Cornell Journal of Social Relations* 8, 197–218

Wood, D. and Middleton, W. (1975). A study of assisted problem-solving. *British Journal of Psychology* 66, 181–191

Wren, K. T. (1970). Two familial antecedents of cognitive styles in young children. *Dissertation Abstracts International* 31, 1526B–1527B

Zigler, E. and Butterfield, E. C. (1968). Motivational aspects of changes in IQ test performance of culturally deprived nursery school children. *Child Development* 39, 1–14

7

Mothers' Answers to Children's Questions: From Socio-Economic Status to Individual Differences

W. P. Robinson

Introduction

In this chapter we trace the history of a project that began by testing whether or not mothers of different social classes reported different ways of answering their children's questions in line with Bernstein's thesis (1961, 1971) of a sociological differentiation in the distribution of restricted and elaborated codes of language use.

In the original study (see Robinson and Rackstraw, 1972) mothers were asked to imagine what they would say if their child asked certain questions; this was criticised as being doubly hazardous. It was suggested that the mothers' replies were contaminated by the interview situation: problems of differential anxiety and susceptibility to give socially desirable answers were cited as confounding influences. Was the requirement to imagine rather than report a more difficult act of role-playing for mothers of one social group? Were the questions themselves representative of those typically asked by 5-year-olds?

Complementary to these social psychological issues were objections made by socio-linguists that the speech was not 'natural' – the mothers' answers had not arisen in reaction to questions occurring in conversation in everyday activities. No attention could be paid to the context of utterance in terms of what preceded or succeeded the question-answer exchange in the discourse. The categories of analysis employed were not linguistically respectable, and they were certainly not complete.

There was a murmur from sociologists that the population sampled was not representative of the general population of the United Kingdom either geographically or socially. Since the objective of the work was to test a thesis that was formulated quite precisely in terms of the two social groups studied, and there was no sense in which the investigation was intended to be a sample survey of mothers' answers to children's questions, this murmur faded quickly.

As well as the social psychological possibilities of the instruments of measurement giving a distorted view of reality, we had also to consider the psychological significance of such differences as were found. If mothers' answering does indeed differ in the ways inferred, what are the consequences for the children? Perhaps the differences are so small or of such kind that they are irrelevant to the development of the children. To begin to answer that question required at least two activities: empirical investigations of appropriate children and the integration of the results into theories of child development and learning. Bernstein's ideas about socialisation were a bald and simple assumption of reproduction: 'Like father, like son'. He was interested in the kinds of socialisation practices and educational experiences that would be associated with the intergenerational transmission of the codes, but he never seriously confronted the question of the psychology of the child as learner. How does the child learn? Are we to turn to Piaget, Pavlov, Skinner or whom? If the sociological thesis is valid, it still requires psychological mechanisms of learning for its mediation. This is in no sense 'reducing' sociology to psychology; it is merely stating that sociology works with and through people.

The series of studies initiated were attempts to examine the validity of objections raised to this first investigation and to transpose the consequential socialisation issues to a psychological level of analysis. While this work has been reported in detail elsewhere (Arnold and Robinson, 1971; Robinson and Rackstraw, 1972; Robinson, 1973; Robinson and Arnold, 1977), it has not been brought together as a single story. Also, as sometimes happens with long journeys, purposes change en route. The increasing concern with the psychology of what makes for differences between children and how they might arise was accompanied by a decrease in concern with 'restricted' and 'elaborated' codes. These concepts in fact offered too stark a contrast for the data as found. The status of the codes themselves is still problematic. It is ironic in view of the salience of the Bernstein thesis as an issue of contention that such important empirical evidence is still lacking, even some twenty years after the matter first commanded academic attention. What we still lack are studies of the orientation to speech of members of different social groups in everyday life. We still do not know to what in speech people are disposed to attend. According to the original hypothesis of Bernstein (1961) those confined to a restricted code attended to the social significance of utterances – that is, the components of meanings relevant to role relations. By contrast, in appropriate contexts, those who were oriented to elaborated code would be predisposed to attend to the representational content of utterances in terms of the semantic relations between the propositions and the extra-linguistic world to which the utterances were referring. On a strong interpretation of the hypothesis, the restricted code user be unaware of those relations; on a weak interpretation he would at the least be disposed to ignore them. Differential attention to the various components of utterances has yet to be studied in relations to social class. Almost all the empirical work has been concerned with the encoding rather than the decoding of speech and writing.

Neither do we know how mothers of different social groups view the problems of child-rearing: what their theories of child development are, what objectives they have, what means they employ, and what the relationships between these objectives and means are in practice? A final part to this edited collection was to have been devoted to this issue, but the contributor invited felt that the state of the art was too inchoate for such a chapter to be a feasible proposition at this point in time. The last chapter will attempt to comment briefly on these two issues.

Although most of the work relevant to Bernstein's thesis has been couched in terms of 'social class', the term 'socio-economic status' (SES) will be used here. Bernstein's thesis was and is about social class in the sense in which this technical term has been used by sociologists in the traditions of Marx or Weber. However what has been measured in empirical studies has not been 'class', but status. The scales used to assign families to categories have been derived from ratings of occupational prestige and not from indices of economic power. The Bernstein work, including our own initial studies included additional information about parental education, but in an academically important sense it remains misleading to call the scales measures of 'social class'. The cost of replacing the phrase is to suffer the more cumbersome phrases 'middle SES' (MSES) and 'low SES' (LSES) – the latter will be divided into LSES (Sk) where the occupations of parents have been skilled manual and LSES (U) where they have been unskilled or semi-skilled.

SES differences in the ways mothers' reported ways of answering children's questions

The questions to which the mothers were invited to respond were questions actually asked by 5-year-old children. They were not intended to be representative or typical, but they were real. They were also appropriate for children of the age studied. In a study of naturally occurring questions Arnold and Robinson (1971) found that 49% of them arose out of the immediate context, and in the main these were triggered either by an object, person or action (41%) or by the utterance of another person (41%); 91% of the questions were coded as 'seeking information' rather than seeking advice, action, opinions, or reassurance, testing, or protesting. Given that these results are valid, at this age at least, the most common reason for children to ask questions is because they want to know the answers. In fact, in the interview, a distinct minority of the mothers mentioned that one or more of the questions posed to them by the interviewer had been asked recently by their child. These results suggest that the choice of questions was not ill-judged.

The interviewer introduced the task by saying, 'I wonder if we could talk a little about everyday questions children often ask. What do you think you might say if X asked one of these?'

(1) (Children sometimes ask) why people have to do things. (Imagine X asking) Why does Daddy shave every morning? (What would you say?) The words in brackets were repeated for each question.

(2) . . . how things work . . . Where does the water in the tap come from? . . .

(3) . . . why things happen . . . Why do leaves fall off the trees? . . .

(4) . . . why people act as they do . . . Why did Mrs Jones cry when Johnny went into hospital? . . .

(5) . . . where things go or come from . . . Where do I come from? . . .

(6) . . . who people are . . . Who is the man who brings the milk? . . .

(7) . . . why they have to do things . . . Why do I have to go to school in September? . . .

If Bernstein's (1961) thesis is correct, under appropriate conditions, and this setting should constitute such a situation, elaborated code users, *viz.* MSES mothers relative to LSES (U) mothers should:

1   Evade answering fewer questions.

2   Give answers which are more contextually accurate, that is correspond more closely to the extra-linguistic realities at issue.

3   Supply more information in their answers.

4   Show less linguistic 'disorganisation' in their answers, that is maintain syntactic cohesion.

5   Have fewer 'noisy'-linguistic items, that is syntactically acceptable, but semantically empty additions to their utterances.

6   Use fewer social psychological checks, e.g. 'You know', 'Doesn't it?'

7 For modes of answer to 'why' questions, they should prefer: categorisations raised to a higher level of generality (and not just classify behaviour as 'naughty' for example), arguments appealing to analogies, causes, and consequences; they should eschew denials of oddity, transformations of questions as their own answers, appeals to essence, appeals to simple regularity and simple appeals to authority.

RESULTS AND COMMENTS

SES differences were found in all the predicted respects bar one: the LSES (U) mothers did not exhibit more 'disorganisation' in their answers. While the original report of these results emphasised the differences between mothers, which were indeed substantial, it is also important to point out that the differences were not total. I have argued elsewhere (Robinson, 1980, p. 29) that current methodology in psychology encourages us to look for and think in terms of differences *per se* rather than differences and similarities together – partly because our statistical techniques and experimental designs are not couched in ways which enable us to answer the question, 'In what ways alike and in what ways different?'

In this situation mothers of both SES groups appeared to interpret question-asking by children as an expected activity. Their behaviour suggested that they saw themselves as under an immediate obligation to provide the child with informative truthful answers if they could, and that this is what they generally did. Both SES groups interpreted the situation as one calling for the use of an elaborated code; the child was seen as using speech to find out about gaps in his knowledge. LSES (U) mothers did not appear to interpret the questions as focusing on the state of the mother-child role relation as such, although they were in fact more disposed to make simple appeals to tradition and authority in response to moral questions, and in effect their higher use of categories such as restatements of the questions as an answer might be said implicitly to deny the semantic validity of the question. Such behaviour is perhaps more easily interpreted, however, as a greater degree of personal acceptance of things as they are than as an exercise in defining and regulating role relations. Some of the child's questions may be dismissed because they refer to what are obviously unproblematic matters as far as the mothers are concerned.

Hence it would have been misleading on this evidence to assert that the LSES (U) mothers were confined to uses of language which are concerned solely to define and express the general nature and present state of role relationships: the tendency for their answers to realise that function was no more than a weak tendency. However the opportunities they reported they were making available for their children to learn were not the same as those offered by MSES mothers.

Were their reports a valid representation of their actual behaviour? Two main empirical avenues were open to check this. One would have been to observe, in an unobtrusive manner, the everyday behaviour of mothers who reported that they would answer differently to see whether they did so. This was not done, but Wootton (1974) did examine recorded interactions between mothers and their 4-year-old children in the home, and his data yielded SES differences similar to those found in our study. The second possibility was to make predictions about SES differences in children and to see whether these were supported; the results are reported below.

Additional evidence linking socially based and individual differences in maternal and child behaviour can be adduced from observations of mother-child interaction, as reported below and elsewhere in this volume (Hartmann and Haavind, chapter 6; McGlaughlin, Morrissey, Empson and Sever, chapter 5), and as pursued formerly by Hess and Shipman (1965) and latterly by Wood (D. Wood, H. Wood and Middleton, 1978).

It is also worth noting some evidence from the context of the data collection itself. One index of anxiety about social situations is an unwillingness to participate in them: all mothers of both SES groups not only agreed to be interviewed, but did so with enthusiasm; they enjoyed them. We were not asking them to do something strange or threatening, either in terms of the manner in which the interviews were conducted or in terms of the task itself, and the tapes themselves showed no symptoms of anxiety that might be linked with SES. Even if there had been, for the criticism to be sustained it would be necessary at least to offer the steps of an argument to show how extra anxiety in either social group would have generated the *particular* set of differences actually observed. These interviews bore no obvious similarity to Labov's (1969) caricature of a small Negro boy being intimidated into silence by an overpowering (and most unscientific and inhumane) tester. It has also been suggested that MSES mothers were exaggerating their behaviour to give 'socially desirable' responses, but two worries at least surround the force of this criticism. Why should MSES mothers be more likely to put on a front than their LSES (U) counterparts? And why, other things being equal, would one not expect mothers actually to do what they think is socially desirable? Logical possibilities are no more than logical possibilities; they have to be translated into psychological arguments whose correspondence to reality can be empirically tested. While exercised by such concerns, we had no grounds for believing them to have distorted the data, and our eventual strategy was to proceed to examine SES differences in the children themselves.

SES differences in the ways children answer questions

When the children were 7-years-old, that is two years after the maternal interviews, a sample (70 girls and 33 boys) drawn from the same population was asked 29 'Wh' questions by a familiar female interviewer in an informal and friendly setting.

The 29 questions were again not a representative or random sample; they were drawn up to provide representation of each of 'Wh' interrogatives. They were questions asked by children of the appropriate age. The data were coded according to a systematic taxonomy of possible variations in answers to questions (Robinson and Rackstraw, 1972, pp. 25–70) that paid attention to appropriateness, completeness, and presupposition at grammatical, lexical and contextual (semantic) levels of analysis, as well as to modes of answering. Without yet committing ourselves to a particular psychological theory of learning we predicted that SES differences in children's answers would reflect the differences in their mothers; that the differential opportunities to learn afforded by the mothers would give rise to corresponding differences in what was learned.

RESULTS AND COMMENTS

The results were unequivocal. For the girls, of 32 variables examined 23 gave differences in the predicted directions, most of them at the 1% level of significance. [It is noteworthy that LSES (U) girls who had experienced a Use of Language Programme designed by D. M. Gahagan and G. A. Gahagan (1970) were more like their MSES peers than control group girls, as were also LSES (U) girls whose speech as sampled at age 5 had been more relatively complex in respect of the number of subordinate clauses, rank-shifted clauses, verb tenses, and adverbial groups]. For the smaller sample of boys contrasted (the main comparison was 11 *versus* 11 only) just over half the variables discriminated significantly between the SES groups.

As with the mothers however, there was no suggestion of a qualitatively different orientation to the task by the two SES groups. LSES (U) children appeared to treat the questions as requiring answers realising the representational function of language; they did not interpret the questions as being concerned with role relations, and neither did their answers express a primary concern with this function.

What kind of explanation is to be offered then for the differences found in non-responses, grammatical and lexical inappropriateness and incompleteness, contextual completeness (amount of information in questions answered) and unjustified presupposition and the numerous differences in mode preferences for answering 'when', 'where', and 'who' as well as 'why' questions? Differential exposure to quantities and qualities of verbally mediated experience has to be the prime candidate for consideration. This demonstrated covariation of SES differences in both mothers' reports and children's answering of comparable questions could however be supplemented by a direct analysis of mother-child pairs from the same sample.

Associations between mothers' reports of ways they answer their children's questions and children's answers: mother-child pairs

Too few boys existed for whom both mother and child data were available, but a sub-sample (N = 55) of girls was extracted from the two previously used samples (Robinson, 1973). To eliminate more general effects of SES itself, analyses of relationships were conducted within SES groups. The first step was to check whether SES differences for mothers and girls were like those already reported; this was so. Variables in mothers' answering were then collapsed into five clusters: strategies of answering, linguistic style, amount of information, use of 'strong' modes, and use of 'weak' modes. 'Strong' modes were those ways of answering 'why' questions already mentioned as being more common among MSES mothers and children, supplemented by nominal as contrasted with relative modes of answering 'when', 'where' and 'who' questions. 'Weak' modes were statements, appeals to simple regularity, unspecified authority, and simple categorisation.

RESULTS AND COMMENTS

Although mothers' use of strong modes had one apparently anomalous association with children's answering behaviour, in the LSES (U) group two conclusions seemed to be warranted. There seemed to be a weak general factor at work such that mothers who showed a semantically rich strategy, absence of linguistic noise, high information content, the presence of strong modes and the absence of weak ones (which were in fact positively associated with each other) did have a significant but weak general predictive power in relation to the general quality of their children's answers. Specific predictability also existed: for maternal strategies of answering and amount of information there were direct associations with the corresponding categories in the children's answers and maternal use of weak modes predicted weak modes in daughters. Maternal use of strong modes predicted both weak and strong modes. Style had no corresponding features in child speech. This pattern of specificity was much attenuated in the MSES sub-sample; only maternal weak modes predicted the corresponding use by daughters. In fact there was very little variance in either mothers or children to become associated as covariance for strategies of answering. This was not so for either amount of information or strong modes.

To be able to show there are within-class mother-child linkages like the between-class differences further weakens the feasibility of any hypothesis that asserts a strong generalised confinement to a restricted code of language use by members of the LSES (U) group. That such mothers may be more oriented to attend to the social than the representational components of speech in many situations remains an open possibility, but there is no evidence that this kind of selective attention has excluded the possibility of learning representational forms and content to be used as such.

That linkages can be made for individual differences within SES groups further weakens criticisms that the original investigation was distorted by strong SES-linked biases of differential anxiety or concern to say the right thing. That both between and within SES differences in mothers' answering behaviour could be used to predict characteristics of answering in children *two years* later points to the power of the variables investigated.

Having moved to the psychological level of analysis and successfully discovered mother-child association in spite of the two year delay in asking the children questions, it became timely to consider which models of child development and learning were most compatible with the evidence and to pursue the origins of the answering competencies and preferences of children in the light of that analysis.

Models of child development and learning

Models of child development are discussed in the final chapter, and here it will suffice to summarise some main points. Associative principles of learning were somewhat cavalierly discarded in the 1960s and 1970s, but we have seen no reason to dismiss them as influences which determine what is initially connected with what, at the point at which the child is *collecting* raw data about language. The equally well-established cognitive developmental concepts of a self-organising active child *collecting* and *processing* data had to be articulated with the associative principles that emphasise the child as a passive reactor to his environment. Observational learning can be seen to be a particular case of these two perspectives. While this articulation puts together two components of child learning and development, and both views include motivational principles to give impetus to development, the more recent demands that we recognise the child as a *social* being from birth also need to be integrated. Communion with other people, particular caretakers, is relevant both to states of well-being of infants and to the development of some of the earliest actions and interactions in which they engage. The 1980s are likely to witness an acceleration of the re-assembly of the component parts of the child into a whole creature.

Our theoretical position on learning had been eclectic from the start. We saw both associative and cognitive developmental principles as valid but partial accounts of development, in competition with each other only in respect of their appropriate domains of application. It is not a case of either/or; it is a problem of ascertaining when which set of principles is relevant.

In terms of verbally mediable knowledge realised through a proficiency to answer questions and a disposition to prefer some modes of answering these to others what can be managed by the child will be limited by what has been made available for him to learn – as a *reductio ad absurdum*, no opportunity, no learning. However, we cannot then proceed simply to argue that the more opportunities for learning XRY (X in a specified relation to Y), the greater the probability that XRY will be learned – except in a trivial sense. We have to take into account the child's contemporary information processing capacity. We also need to know under what conditions XRY is presented to the child. We might reasonably expect that if a child has actually asked its mother about X, R, or Y, then he is both motivated to learn an answer and is attending to the focus of his question. Whether the mother's answer will be learned will depend on more than her successful filling of the apparent gap in the child's knowledge. Does she set her answer in the experience of the child so that he can readily assimilate it to knowledge already controlled ('associate' could substitute for 'assimilate')? Does she anchor her answer to currently observable or recallable features of the environment? Is her answer within the child's limits of comprehension? If the answer has to be semantically compound or complex, does she break it into assimilable chunks? Is her primary verbal formulation clear, simple, and precise? Does she then extend the topic, not to such an extent that the child becomes overloaded or confused, but at least sufficiently for rehearsal and further exploration of the matter in hand? Does her answer subsequently check out with the child's experience?

It was expectations of these kinds that guided our last study in the series. The earlier studies implied that differential opportunities to learn answers to questions were linked to SES and to individual differences within SES, at the crude level of the amount and kind of knowledge made available to the child. There were also suggestions that the verbal packaging of the information was relevant. In the first study for example, although the answers of MSES mothers were not syntactically more cohesive, they were less likely to have semantically irrelevant words and phrases added to them.

Their answers were less likely to include uninformative adjuncts (e.g. 'really'), simplifying adjuncts (e.g. 'just'), redundant finishers (e.g. 'and all that'), and finalising socio-centric sequences (e.g. 'you see'). While these may be trivial for an adult listener's information processing capacities, their presence is not necessarily irrelevant to a young child's capacity to extract the essential information. A high incidence of such features in maternal answers was in fact associated with certain characteristics of children's answers in the subsequent within-SES study of mother-child pairs. Additionally, in that investigation the 'maternal strategy' category (which included counts of absence of not knowing what to say, the provision of accurate facts relevant to the question, along with the enumeration of comparisons in respect of differences and similarities) could be used to predict the facility with which daughters could give more and fuller answers of relevance, particularly within the LSES (U) group. These findings and ideas established a frame of reference for an observational investigation of mother-child interaction focusing both on answering and on questioning. It would be strange if maternal reactions to questions had no consequences for questioning as well as answering, and we decided to incorporate some ideas about this activity into our investigations.

We would expect proficiency in the mastery of the propositional content of questions to be directly associated with the quantity and quality of verbally mediable knowledge. 'Wh' questions can be conceived for as specifying gaps in knowledge; the point of asking an information-seeking 'Wh' question is to have the interlocutor replace the 'Wh' with substantive content. Logically the range of questions which *could* be asked about a topic bears a positive relation to the amount of knowledge already achieved; psychologically however the empirical relations between what is known and what a person wants to know are variable. Developmental psychology has not made great headway in its study of curiosity (two brief references in the latest Carmichael Manual). On associative principles of learning we might expect a double consequence of receiving a satisfying (rewarding) answer to a question; a considerably decreased probability of asking the same question again and an increased probability of asking further questions, especially of a comparable kind, of the answerer. With our data this would lead us to expect that mothers who are providing 'good' answers will be increasing the probability of their children asking further questions. Mothers who give unsatisfying answers should not reduce the probability of the particular questions being asked, but in the longer term, if the rate of satisfying answers falls below what is unfortunately an unspecifiable level, the rate of questioning should decline. One of the advances in operant conditioning (Ferster and Skinner, 1957) was the discovery that random variable ratio positive reinforcement schedules were associated with greater resistance of habits to extinction than were full positive reinforcement schedules, and the crucial difficulty is to specify the rate of reinforcement below which extinction would begin to occur. Are the answers of LSES (U) mothers below that rate? And how do these associative principles interact with the child as an active adaptive organiser of experience? Within that perspective, cognitive conflict arising from uncertainty is accorded motivational force, and learning not to be curious is an idea which is incompatible with a basic tenet of the approach. There do not seem to be systematic investigations of the extent to which classical or operant conditioning procedures can be use to 'interfere' with intellectual processes themselves. There is evidence to show that public behaviour may well conform to the reinforcement contingencies of the environment, especially under punitive conditions. However, none of our investigations showed evidence of punishment *per se* of children by mothers for asking questions of an information-seeking kind.

Any prediction of lower rates of questioning would have to locate the lower rate among LSES rather than MSES children, but would be derived from their mothers' somewhat lower rate of supplying, satisfying and extending answers set in efficient teaching frameworks rather than in their active discouragement of questioning. MSES children should however make higher scores than LSES children on any index of more advanced questioning (e.g. proportion of syntactically complex questions).

We expected the amount of knowledge displayed by children to be positively correlated with the proportion of complex questions, but had no basis for predicting any relation between the amount of knowledge and the rate of questioning.

Children's answers and questions in relation to mothers' verbal behaviour

Mothers and their 6-year-old children examined a succession of objects and materials in the presence of an experimenter-observer (see Robinson and Arnold, 1977). As each pair of objects or other material was displayed the child was invited by the experimenter to tell her as much as he/she could about them. Following the elicitation of as much as the child could say about the item, E. suggested to the child that he/she ask his mother if there was anything he/she wanted to know about the item. When the question-answer exchange began to lag, E. brought out the next item from her bag. All children and mothers were able and willing to enter into the spirit of this activity.

As a finale to the pursuit of the nature of SES differences, three of the sets of items selected were such that they would be either equally familiar to both groups, or more familiar to MSES mothers and children. Two items were intended to be equally or more familiar in LSES homes. These were included to see whether LSES mothers and children would offer more information of a representational kind about them.

METHOD

Subjects

The final sample consisted of 32 mothers and their 6-year-old children. Sampling began by approaching the Headmistress of an Infants/Primary school located in the middle of an extensive 30-year-old estate of Council-owned houses. Armed with addresses of the 6-year-old children, the experimenter approached mothers to see if they would take part, until 20 (10 with boys and 10 with girls) had agreed to do so. Three of those approached declined. Of the 20, four were subsequently dropped because it transpired that although their husbands had not held white-collar jobs, they themselves had either held white-collar jobs or had left school beyond the minimal leaving age. After the observations had been completed, individual children were given the Raven's Coloured Progressive Matrices at school.

The experimenter then approached the Headmaster of an Infants/ Primary school in an owner-occupied housing estate to follow a similar recruiting and testing procedure; three of the mothers declined to take part.

The Hall-Jones Scale of Occupational Prestige Status (1950) located all the middle SES families in classes in 1, 2 or 3, all the low SES families in 5b (skilled manual) or 6 (semi-skilled). IQs and ages were: middle SES boys 100.7, 6.0; middle SES girls 100.0, 6.3; low SES boys 106.1, 6.5; low SES girls 99.6, 6.0. While the low SES boys are somewhat older and make somewhat higher IQ scores, this was as close a matching as could be achieved and is likely to work against rather than for most of the differences to be examined.

Materials

The materials comprised a toy cash register with the new decimal money introduced one month previous, a Bingo card, a Family Allowance book, six pairs of objects and a picture of Nursery Rhyme Land depicting characters and events from nine nursery rhymes. The six pairs of objects included one familiar and one hopefully unfamiliar item in each pair. The pairing was intended to encourage comparisons. Items were (1) pear and Avocado pear, (2) football rattle and African drum, (3) Cheddar and Emmental cheese, (4) conker and cedar cone, (5) tin of baked beans and tin of bean sprouts, and (6) sand eggtimer and pinger. In England, Bingo is a low SES rather than a middle SES game. It is a game of chance in which rows and columns of numbered squares are filled in response to randomly drawn numbers announced by a 'caller'. Family Allowance books may be more openly familiar in low SES homes; they enable all parents to draw weekly payments for their children. These two items were included to give low SES mothers more of a chance than middle SES flavoured materials may accord them; they were intended to serve as a contrasting set to see whether any differences found in performance on the other tasks were possibly merely a consequence of middle SES mothers having greater knowledge. They are labelled low SES tasks and the other three are labelled middle SES tasks, but these labels are only intended to provide a contrast in this study.

Procedure

Mothers were given a choice of home or school as a location for the interaction. All middle SES mothers elected to remain at home. All low SES mothers elected to go to a separate room in the school. Parents were regularly welcomed at the particular school, and there was no indication that the mothers were ill at ease there. The instructions differed slightly for each task, but basically they required the child to say what he/she knew about each object and then to ask his/her mother anything else he/she wanted to know. Initially, children were able to and likely to direct their questions to the experimenter, but appropriate use of eye and head movements and speech achieved natural re-directions to the mothers. Mothers were asked not to initiate events, but to respond naturally to the child's inquiries.

The sacrifice in objective structure and content was in the interests of achieving a still controlled but natural situation. We believe we were successful.

TREATMENT OF RESULTS

Maternal behaviour

The coding frame was based on categories derived and defined in an earlier analysis (Arnold and Robinson, 1971). In the mother's behaviour a broad separation was made between the quality of the answers which she gave in reply to her child's questions and the nature of other utterances she made. For the most part the functions of these latter were self-evident, at least at one level of analysis: asking the child a question, orienting the child to the task and materials, praise, ('Well done'), corroboration ('That's right'), pointing to error (of speech/fact relationships), correcting of error (also semantic). Refractive replies were those that asked the child 'What do you think?', re-assigning the speaking responsibility back to him. The possible functions of repetitions of the child's utterances are several. They could be delivered with an intonation that invited the child to elaborate his previous utterance; in fact those occurring in this situation tended to be flat repetitions, hence the label 'echo'. We cannot see that echoes have a progressive discourse function; they leave the child or mother to exercise a fresh initiative. What constituted a 'theme' is more difficult to explain verbally than to score in practice; in most cases it meant continuing to talk about a particular aspect of an object. Together these items are labelled 'Strategies of Interaction'.

Quality of answers incorporated a simple count of the number of words uttered in reply to questions. Did the mother admit she was ignorant of an answer? Did she attempt to establish her answer in the past experience of the child by reminding him of something comparable or identical already familiar? Did she provide an informative answer, that is one that was semantically coherent with the focus of the question? Did she supplement the immediately appropriate answer with additional information? Did she make explicit comparisons with other events or objects? Tokens of uncertainty (e.g. 'I think') were coded according to the criteria of Turner and Pickvance (1973).

Child speech

As well as asking questions of the mother, the child made statements about the materials provided. Most of these were syntactically simple sentences used to make single statements; these could be coded as 'units of information'. This count was conducted separately for the objects expected to be more familiar to middle SES children and for those likely to be more familiar to low SES children. Children could admit ignorance. They could echo what their mothers had said. They could make semantically appropriate reactions to maternal questions or initiating comments, elicitations of some kind.

The number of questions could be counted for the objects of presumed differential familiarity. Their word length was counted. They were classified as open ('Wh') or closed (answerable by 'Yes' or 'No'). 'Complex' was defined as any syntactic elaboration beyond a simple interrogative form (subordination or coordination).

RESULTS

Maternal Behaviour

SES differences   Data were coded separately for the two sets of materials (see Table 1). In terms of management of the interaction, MSES mothers asked more questions of their children regardless of the materials. The low SES materials yielded no other maternal differences although it must be noted that the total frequencies of occurrence of all other management items are very low. On the middle SES materials, MSES mothers were less likely to direct their child's attention to the task and less likely to echo his utterances. They were more likely to turn the responsibility for answering questions back to the child with refractive replies, and more likely to maintain any theme beyond four pairs of utterances.

MSES mothers were more likely to set her answers in the experience of the child and used more tokens of uncertainty regardless of the materials. With the middle SES materials they were more likely to extend their answers beyond the immediate question, and they made more reference to comparisons. There was a trend for MSES mothers to give more informative answers with the middle SES

TABLE 1
SES differences in speech of mothers $(N = 32)$

	Tasks					
	MSES items $(n = 3)$ Raw scores: Totals			LSES items $(n = 2)$ Raw scores: Totals		
Category	MSES	LSES	U-test z	MSES	LSES	U-test z
Strategies of interaction						
Orientation to task	13	23	$6.22^a(X^2)$	0	0	x
Question-asking	678	329	4.01^c	52	18	2.08^a
Echo of child	52	102	2.07^a	2	8	x
Refractive reply	54	37	2.10^a	3	6	x
Corroboration	275	213	0	17	19	x
Praise	5	7	x	5	7	x
Pointing to error	83	67	—	8	7	x
Correction of error	47	48	—	4	3	x
Themes held over 4 pairs of utterances	52	18	3.00^b	2	3	x
Quality of answers						
Number of words	5188	3813	—	377	566	2.65^b
Informative answers	241	172	1.51	40	87	2.45^a
Set in experience	121	62	2.59^b	21	8	2.44^a
Extension beyond question	166	105	3.29^b	0	0	x
Mention of comparisons	52	26	2.66^b	3	2	x
Use of tokens of uncertainty	115	43	4.38^c	13	1	$4.73^a(X^2)$

$^ap < 0.05$; $^bp < 0.01$; $^cp < 0.001$ x, No test sensible

materials; this result was significantly reversed on the low SES materials, about which LSES mothers also uttered more words.

Children's behaviour

SES differences Comparable reversals were present in the task-related statements offered by children: LSES children offering more units of information about Bingo and the Family Allowance book; MSES more units about the other items. Over all tasks MSES children more often admitted to not knowing something and made more appropriate responses to their mothers' elicitation utterances.

While there were no SES differences in the number of questions asked in relation to middle SES materials. LSES children asked significantly more questions about Bingo and the Family Allowance book.

MSES children asked a higher proportion of closed questions and questions of more than simple interrogative form.

TABLE 2
SES differences in speech of children ($N = 32$)

Category	SES group with higher score	U-tests z
Questions (all tasks)		
Length (words)	=	—
Incidence (MSES items)	=	—
Incidence (LSES items)	LSES	2.40^a
Proportion with complex syntax	MSES	2.62^b
Proportion closed questions	MSES	3.77^c
Statements (all tasks)		
Echo of mother's utterances	=	—
Appropriate response to elicitation from mother	MSES	2.79^b
Admission of ignorance	MSES	2.79^b
Labelling nursery rhymes	MSES	2.25^a
Task-related statements (MSES items)	MSES	2.04^a
Task-related statements (LSES items)	LSES	2.71^b

$^a p < 0.05$; $^b p < 0.01$; $^c p < 0.001$

Comment on SES differences

New results were: the higher echoic behaviour of LSES mothers; the greater tendencies of MSES mothers to be refractive (turning the child's question back to him for his opinion) and to maintain themes over four utterances each. Hess and Shipman (1965) found greater orientation by MSES mothers. We found the reverse, at least on the MSES items. They viewed orientation as attempts to direct attention. We viewed orientation as serving to direct and concentration of a child whose attention has wandered. Our category comprised mainly 'enthusiastic' imperatives, 'Look at this!'. Hess and Shipman (1965) presumably scored our question-asking 'What's this?' in their orientation category. This may account for the difference. Questions from mothers in this situation appeared to be intended to serve to arouse rather than just direct interest. This strongly MSES habit occurred on both sets of items. That LSES provided significantly more information than MSES in answer to questions about Bingo and the Family Allowance book may be taken to impy that LSES are disposed to provide information in reply to their children's questions and when they know more than their MSES peers they will relay more. They were using language to represent propositional knowledge; there is no question of their speech being confined to or even oriented towards social functions in this context.

However, as the distribution of other features of quality of answers, it was the MSES who were more likely to set their answers in the past experience of the child and to extend their answers beyond the immediate requirements of the question, both of which should be conductive to learning, as should the mentioning of similarities and differences and the longer maintenance of themes.

The LSES children showed more knowledge than the MSES children about the Family Allowance book and Bingo. Hence as with their mothers, there are situations in which they will use the representational function of speech to convey more information than their MSES peers. Further they asked more questions than MSES about these items. Is it the case that the more you know about something the easier it is to locate gaps in your knowledge and the more questions you can and do ask? There was no sign that the curiosity of the LSES children had been differentially reduced as a result of any history of negative reinforcement arising in earlier question-answer exchanges with their mothers. Although they asked more questions, relatively fewer of these were either hypothesis-testing closed questions or syntactically complex, a result consistent with other SES differences found in question posing by 9-year-old children (Robinson and Rackstraw, 1978).

RESULTS

Mother-child associations within SES groups

Two summary indices were constructed for mothers, three for children. Since question-asking had appeared to be 'pushing' rather than luring, it was treated as a variable in its own right. On the basis of the expectations cited in the previous section about factors likely to be conducive to learning and as an initial result of inspecting correlation matrices a number of other scores were summed, and two indices were constructed. Corroboration, pointing out errors (of fact) and correcting errors (of fact) appeared to form a cluster that could be labelled 'provision of feedback'. This correlated 0.44 ($p < 0.05$) with the number of children's questions. Giving informative answers, set in the past experience of the child, and going beyond the question immediately posed, were grouped and labelled 'provision of cognitive meaning'. This correlated 0.50 ($p < 0.01$) with the incidence of questioning by children. These last two were finally combined as being the best single extractable predictive index.

The three scores from the children's speech were: the total number of questions asked, the proportion of these which were complex, and the amount of verbally-mediated knowledge elicited from the children about the items.

TABLE 3
Correlations (*rho*) between behaviour of mothers and children

Mothers	Children					
	Numbers of questions			Amount of knowledge		
	MSES	LSES	All	MSES	LSES	All
Question-asking	03	15	00	−19	00	06
Provision of cognitive meaning and feedback	62[b]	77[b]	61[c]	27	49[a]	50[b]
N	16	16	32	16	16	32

[a] $p < 0.05$; [b] $p < 0.01$; [c] $p < 0.001$

As Table 3 shows the rank order correlations between the behaviour of mothers and children offered a clear pattern. Question-asking by mothers was unrelated either to the number of questions asked by children or the amount of knowledge they displayed. Provision of cognitive meaning and feedback was significantly correlated with the amount of knowledge displayed in the LSES group and overall. It was strongly correlated with the rate of asking questions by children in both SES groups and overall. The proportion of these which were complex was also positively associated with the provision of cognitive meaning and feedback, (Groups combined, *rho* = 0.43, $p < 0.01$). The amount of knowledge displayed correlated postively with rates of question-asking (*rho* = 0.44, $p < 0.01$). The variation in intelligence test scores of the children was only insignificantly associated with these measures: in the LSES group, IQ correlated with children's questions 0.28 and with the provision of cognitive meaning and feedback by the mother 0.34; in the MSES group, the correlations were 0.26 and 0.02 respectively. None of these is significant.

Comment

To claim that the results entirely support the expectations and the predictions made would be ingenuous. The amount of knowledge elicited in answer to questions from *E.* and volunteered to the mother by MSES children was not significantly correlated with the index of maternal provision of cognitive meaning and feedback, and no satisfactory explanation for this can be offered, especially since the relationship in the LSES was positive as predicted. That the correlation in the sample as a whole was positive and at a higher level of significance suggests that unreliability of estimates stemming from the smallness of the within-SES samples may have been responsible (two children contributed one third of the sum of d^2). Otherwise the correlations between this maternal index and the child variables were not only significant but high, implying that what has been learned, the impetus to learn more via asking questions, and the facility to do so with complex questions are related to specifiable tactics used by mothers in their handling of children's questions.

The decision to keep question-asking by mothers separate proved to be fortunate. *Prima facie* this activity might have been expected to be positively related to children's knowledge and inquiries. In other work we had found (Prosser, 1974) that whether questions facilitated learning was contingent upon their origin: when they were provided by the experimenter they did not; when they were the children's own they did. The conclusion would be that provided questions only acquire motivational properties for learning if they are taken over by the learner and become his questions, which may or may not happen. In the situation here, it was as though mothers' questions were interfering, potential distractions. The children already had their questions requiring answers; they had no need of provided ones. Such an interpretation is consistent with a conception of the child as an active, self-organising learner. The example illustrates the dangers of assuming that linguistic form and psychological function are always related in simple and crude ways. In this case, the paralinguistic features of the form and the occasions of occurrence pointed to the questions being 'pushing' rather than 'pulling'.

Discussion

Taken together the results on both answers and questions of children in relation to mothers' handling of children's questions present a clear picture of social group and individual differences. The individual differences found point to some of the characteristics of mothers' behaviour that are relevant to variations in answering and questioning in their children. The differences between the SES groups for both mothers and children appear to stem from quantitative differences in the frequency with which members of the groups display particular pieces of behaviour. This is a more accurate representation of the reality than any claim that a majority (or even minority) in either social group behave in a qualitatively different manner from those in the other; for the kind of context of situation examined here most members of both social groups used speech mainly to seek or relay information of a propositional nature – they used speech representationally. There was no suggestion that any child or mother in either SES group in any of the samples was confined to a 'restricted code' of language use focusing on definition and maintenance of role relations.

What tendencies there were of this kind were in the direction that Bernstein's thesis would require; some of the responses of LSES (U) mothers to children's questions were simple appeals to authority or tradition; others were of such a kind that any further question from the child would have been a threat to the status of the mother; others implicitly denied that the question was valid as an information-seeking enquiry. While these approaches discriminated between the SES groups, they were not common within the LSES (U) group, and not one mother appeared to be dominated by such modes of responding. It would also be misleading to view the answering of such mothers as elaborated code 'variants', which is one poorly defined concept invoked by Bernstein (1971) to account for some LSES people appearing to use an elaborated code in some contexts; these LSES mothers and their children were representing a non-verbal reality with verbal means; the meanings expressed were universalistic, they were realised explicitly in a context independent manner. The most common reason for them not answering questions in this way appeared to be not knowing the substantive answers. It was also true these mothers were less likely to manifest ways of setting about answering that would maximise their children's chances of learning from their answers, if the analysis of conditions of learning presented here is valid, but this again does not look to be the realisation of a deliberate policy. The data on the children were consistent with an interpretation in terms of differential learning opportunities.

In an important sense, for these question-answer exchanges it would be wrong to see the differences found as sociological; the differences are among individual mothers. It still has to be explained why these differences are linked to SES, but any explanation offered must not be too strong; it has to account for the basic similarities as well as the differences. This is not a surprising outcome. While there are cultures and sub-cultures in which question-asking by children is seen both as a special kind of activity and one to be discouraged on a variety of grounds – rudeness and lack of respect being among them – perhaps particularly in the Anglo-Saxon Protestant sub-cultures of Western industrialised societies the manifest child-rearing ideology is sympathetic to the enhancement of knowledge and curiosity in young children and would see not answering questions as being improper and this ideology is not confined to any one SES group.

In so far as mothers are trying to promote the mastery of verbally mediable knowledge of the kinds examined here, then more MSES mothers are behaving as more effective 'teachers'. Hess and Shipman (1965) found a similar differential in instructional efficacy. Hartmann and Haavind (chapter 6) find individual differences in mothers' instructional proficiency which can be linked to child learning. Wood and Middleton (1975) have argued for variation in maternal instructional efficiency and have shown (Wood *et al.*, 1978) how different teaching methods lead to differences in learning. The various investigations in this area are severally agreed on the conditions for effective learning and these are consistent with the principles mentioned here: guiding and encouraging attention but accepting the child's focus of interest, establishing a joint frame of reference for any learning, offering what is to be learned in assimilable form and quantities and maintaining the focus long enough for the initial learning to have occurred. The variation in such practices is wide enough in our society for there to be consequences in the questioning and answering proficiency and preferences of children from ages 5 to 7.

References

Arnold, J. and Robinson, W. P. (1971). "Children's Questions and the Mothers' Answers: Diary Recordings". Unpublished manuscript, University of Southampton

Bernstein, B. (1961). Social structure, language and learning. *Educational Research* 3, 163-176

Bernstein, B. (1971). "Class, Codes and Control" Vol. I. Routledge, London

Ferster, C. B. and Skinner, B. F. "Schedules of Reinforcement". Appleton-Century Crofts, New York

Gahagan, D. M. and Gahagan, G. A. (1970). "Talk Reform". Routledge, London

Hartmann, E. and Haavind, H. (1981). Mothers as teachers and their children as learners, Chapter 6, this volume

Hall, J. and Caradog-Jones, D. (1950). Social grading of occupations. *British Journal of Sociology* 1, 31-55

Hess, R. D. and Shipman, V. C. (1965). Early experience and the socialisation of cognitive modes in children. *Child Development* 36, 896-886

Labov, W. (1969). The logic of non-standard English. *Georgetown Monographs in Language and Linguistics* 23, 39-87

McGlaughlin, A., Morrissey, M., Empson, J. M. and Sever, J. (1981). Language performance of disadvantaged children at 30 months. Chapter 5, this volume

Prosser, G. V. (1974). Questions as an aid to learning. *In* "Education, Curiosity and Questioning" (W. P. Robinson, Ed.). Technical Report, Schools Council, University of Southampton

Robinson, W. P. (1973). Where do children's answers come from? *In* "Class, Codes and Control" (B. Bernstein, Ed.) Vol. 2. Routledge, London

Robinson, W. P. (1980). Language management, socio-economic status and educational progress. *In* "Language and Language Disorders in Childhood" (L. A. Hersov, M. Berger and A. R. Nicol, Eds). Pergamon, Oxford

Robinson, W. P. and Arnold, J. (1977). The question-answer exchange between mothers and young children. *European Journal of Social Psychology* 7, 151–164

Robinson, W. P. and Rackstraw, S. J. (1972). "A Question of Answers" Vols 1 and 2. Routledge, London

Robinson, W. P. and Rackstraw, S. J. (1978). Social class differences in posing questions for answers. *Sociology* 12, 265–280

Turner, G. J. and Pickvance, R. E. (1973). Social class differences in the expression of uncertainty in five-year-old children. *In* "Class, Codes and Control" (B. Bernstein, Ed.) Vol. 2. Routledge, London

Wood, D. and Middleton, D. (1975). A study of assisted problem-solving. *British Journal of Psychology* 66, 181–191

Wood, D., Wood, H. and Middleton, D. (1978). An experimental evaluation of four face-to-face teaching strategies. *International Journal of Behaviour Development* 1, 131–147

Wootton, A. J. (1974). Talk in the homes of young children. *Sociology* 8, 277–295

8

Instruction *versus* Conversation
as Opportunities for Learning

M. Heber

Introduction

OBS. 125. At 6;7 (4) J. was looking for her doll and could not find it: "You've no idea where you put it? – *No. I've no more ideas in my tummy. My mouth will have to give me a new idea.* – How? – *It's when I talk, my mouth helps me to think.* (Piaget, 1962, p. 256)

These ideas coming from a child of Piaget's appear to express an opposite view to those of her father regarding the rôle of speech in the development of thought. However her opinion is not confined to childish theory; in more sophisticated guises it is the viewpoint of many who disagree with Piaget on this issue. Indeed, what may be a very complicated relationship has been turned into a matter of practical contention in applied fields such as education without sufficient empirically-based grounds to support the opinions held.

The author took up the problem as it stood contested between Bruner (1964, 1966; Bruner, Olver and Greenfield, 1966) and Piaget's group (Inhelder and Piaget, 1964; Sinclair-de-Zwart, 1967; Piaget, 1970). Bruner had suggested that once a child has mastered speech, this then becomes the major instrument of environmental and social influences shaping thought.

Once a child has succeeded in internalizing language as a cognitive instrument, it becomes possible for him to represent and systematically transform the regularities of experience with far greater flexibility and power than before. (Bruner, 1966, p. 4)

In contrast Piaget believes that the origin of logico-mathematical ideas resides not in language but in the child's earliest activities; the child builds increasingly complex schemes and systems of action which by adaptive modifications gradually coalesce into logico-mathematical groupings and subsequently groups (Piaget, 1962, 1970;

Inhelder and Piaget, 1964). Piaget does admit social influence upon thought but this he thinks arises only indirectly as a result of the child's own self-regulating activity. Thus language of any kind is of only secondary importance in early cognitive growth.

Turning to the question of the relations between language and logical operations, we have always maintained that the origin of logical operations is both deeper than and genetically prior to language; that is, it lies in the laws of general co-ordinations of action, which control activities including language itself. (Piaget, 1970, p. 722)

This brief outline seems to suggest that one could hold one of two hypotheses about the effect that language has in the development of thought: (*i*) that it is a kind of grid acting as a selective and shaping instrument or, (*ii*) that it is purely a vehicle of developing thought systems which are generated by deeper cognitive processes. But this dichotomy is not a happy one because it overlooks different kinds and levels of thinking and possible differences in the character of developmental processes at various periods of growth. Moreover it assumes that the term 'language' is sufficiently precise to represent its processes and functions in any situation and in all its manifestations, whether written or spoken. It ignores the distinction made by de Saussure between *la langue*, *le langage* and *la parole*. In order to avoid this kind of confusion the author has chosen to study the relationship of their *speech*, (*la parole*) to the development of their understanding of ordinal relations by children of 5 and 6 years (Heber, 1978). This form of understanding is the basic logico-mathematical system of ideas which Piaget calls seriation. His studies suggest that children around 3- and 4-years-old group items into separate categories, e.g. if size is the dimension in question they put items into groups as 'big' and 'little'. These children are 'pre-operational' in his terms. They may also divide elements into 'big', 'middle-sized' and 'little'. Gradually they realise that items may be 'bigger' and 'smaller' than each other. When they order such a series albeit by trial and error he will designate them as 'intermediate'. But it is only when they finally understand that in an asymmetrical series each item is uniquely placed because it is 'bigger' than those below it *and also* 'smaller' than those above it that children are held to have grasped the concept of seriation properly. Such children are termed 'operational seriators'. This concept according to Piaget is only reached at about 6 or 7 years of age. ·

Among her other studies relating to the role of speech in cognitive development of children between 5 and 7 years, Sinclair-de-Zwart (1967) compared how they described size relations with their level of understanding seriation. She found a correlation between the type of description and the level of understanding. The early absolute descriptive terms mentioned above tied up with a similar kind of grouping of items. Older children who used comparative terms such as 'bigger' and 'smaller' were also able to construct asymmetrical series of rods correctly. It is reported that training the younger and less competent children to give comparative descriptions produced little advance in understanding the concept of seriation. Results from similar observation and training concerned with the concept of continuous quantity showed even less change. She therefore concluded that Piaget was correct in assuming that speech does *not* play a major rôle in the development of rational thought:

These Genevan results, . . . confirm Piaget's view on the role of language in the constitution of intellectual operations: language is not the source of logic, but is on the contrary structured by logic. (Sinclair-de-Zwart, 1969, p. 325)

In this chapter the author describes her own training study in seriation which was based on that of Sinclair-de-Zwart (Heber, 1977). In contrast to the conclusions of Sinclair-de-Zwart, the outcome of this work seemed to indicate that conversational inter-actions can significantly influence the growth of understanding seriation in the child. This difference is partly explained by the fact that Sinclair-de-Zwart was interested in children's advance from pre-operational or intermediate stages to complete operational seriation whereas the present study was concerned with small intervening stages of progress children made measured on a five point scale. Sinclair did remark on such changes but did not regard them as sufficient to indicate the kind of cognitive advance with which she was concerned. However the present study revealed that they occurred more system-atically and more frequently under certain conditions than others, and this suggested that they were important features of cognitive change. The outcome of this study provoked further studies which were designed to explore and define more closely the kinds of inter-active processes most conducive to development. An outline of this work will be given here, and an explanation of the results will be offered which brings together apparently disparate views on speech and thinking. This synthesis of ideas should apply to teaching and learning situations at home and in school, for it appears that the conversations a child may have with more experienced people such as mothers and teachers may help him to resolve problems. This kind of interaction gives him the best opportunities for developing his understanding of general principles, provided that such discus-sions guide him to resolve the relevant issues for himself. On the other hand, if the child has to follow instructions and to learn appropriate descriptions by rote he may have little opportunity to understand the problems being taught to him. He may acquire the terminology and techniques required of him without the insight which may be gained from thinking things through for himself. Moreover in this situation he is unlikely to grasp the need for or the value of verification based on reasoning with others simply because the teaching itself is arbitrary. Thus what he learns will be task and/ or situation specific, will not be based on general principles, and will probably be unstable.

Seriation training: Study 1

As this study has already been reported in detail elsewhere (Heber, 1977) only a brief account of it will be given here. Does learning the appropriate use of the descriptive terms 'bigger' and 'smaller' affect progress in seriation; especially among children initially incompetent in the use of these comparative descriptors? The design of the study was similar to that of Sinclair-de-Zwart (1967) and provided the pattern for all those that followed it. Children were selected and matched in groups at pre-test for their competence in seriation. Speech training was then provided, or in later studies different kinds of speech intervention on three successive days. Post-testing in seriation was conducted on the next day and again two weeks later, no further training having been given. All subjects were tested and trained individually except for one type of intervention later to be described. In the first study data were sound recorded, whilst for all subsequent studies video-recording was used to enable very detailed inspection of seriation strategies.

The first study extended Sinclair-de-Zwart's study in three respects: (*i*) comparisons were made between children who were initially at different rather than a single level of descriptive competence, (*ii*) within each of these groups control children were tested who had no speech training; and, (*iii*) tests for seriation were tightened, especially in respect of the final criterion, already mentioned, by which one may judge this concept, namely, that in an asymmetrical series each item is uniquely placed because it is less than those on one side of it and greater than those on the other, e.g. where $A > B > C$, B lies between A and C because it is $< A$ and $> C$. Thus in this study children were selected in two matched groups. There were 40 children altogether aged between 5 and 6 years. Twenty of these were from middle class (MC) homes; all could use the terms 'bigger' and 'smaller' appropriately. Twenty were from lower working class homes (LWC); these children tended to give only absolute descriptions, using the terms 'big' or 'little'. The children were drawn from schools of similar educational ethos in Southampton. They were all either pre-operational or intermediate seriators. This meant that in tests of seriation they either classed elements by size in groups of 'big' or 'little', or they could arrange them in order of size correctly but only using trial and error. None of the children selected could insert an extra item between others in an ordinal series using systematic comparison with those on either side of it, i.e. none of the children were operational seriators.

The seriation tests consisted in asking children to arrange a jumbled set of rods of different sizes into correct sequence *and also* to find the right place for one extra item in a covered series. This test was designed by Woodward (1974). A series of ten rods lies in grooves on a board with nine extra intermediate length rods of contrasting colour placed in extra grooves between the first ten. Before the child is given the task the intermediate length rods are removed and the series is covered. *One* of the extra rods is given to the child to place correctly in the existing covered series but without removing the cover. He may decide where to insert the extra rod by comparing it with any or all of the rods in the set *one at a time*. Thus if he takes a rod out to look at it he must replace it before he considers another one. Only when the child feels entirely satisfied that he has placed the extra rod in its correct position can he remove the cover. In this way it is possible to observe whether the child makes his placement by comparing the extra item systematically with those on either side of it. This he must do in three successive tasks with different sets of rods of varying dimensions, orientation, amount and regular or irregular size differences between items. If he succeeds in this he is judged to have gained the concept of seriation.

Varying degrees of success provided a graduated measure of progress children made in their understanding of seriation. This contrasts with Sinclair-de-Zwart, who although she used a variety of tests, laid the emphasis on judging children's progress on whether or not the child could place extra intermediate items into an open set correctly. This was her main criterion of the grasp of the concept of seriation. However, in such circumstances the child may easily be placing intermediate rods with reference to the general appearance of the series visible to him. There is no way of telling whether he really understands that each item has its place for the precise reasons already outlined.

After the seriation pre-tests experimental subjects in both social groups (LWC and MC) were given three training sessions concerned with learning appropriate comparative descriptions of size relationships. In particular they were led to explain the relations of intermediate items to those on either side, namely, where $A > B > C$, B is $< A$ and $> C$. This training was conducted in the form of a discussion where the observer's questions and comments were designed to help the child to formulate the appropriate descriptions for himself. It was originally assumed that if there was any influence of speech on the acquisition of seriation, this would be relative to the child's initial competence in the use of descriptions. In other words, if speech is a major influence in cognitive development it should produce progress where it is supplied to subjects who lack its proper use. Presumably children already able to describe size relations appropriately would not benefit from speech training because its effects should already have taken place. Thus because (MC) children were more likely to offer comparative descriptors at pre-test they were less likely to show cognitive advance after speech training. Comparisons were made against control groups who received no training and across time within experimental groups. However this rather simple assumption overlooked the possible *communicative functions* of speech. Perhaps talking to and with another person produces interactive influences which have less to do with the semantics and grammar of the utterances than with learning to appreciate a problem from the standpoint of another. Linguistic features may be secondary to the communicative aspects of speech in a particular context. Sinclair-de-Zwart did not specify the communicative style of her interventions. Piaget and his co-workers appear to be referring solely to the relevant linguistic features of speech when they deny its efficacy; its communicative features are not considered by them.

The results of the experiment were not as straightforward as the first assumptions suggested. Rather they indicated that speech was affecting cognitive growth through some interactive influence. The results were as follows:

1   experimental subjects in both the (MC) and the (LWC) groups performed significantly better than the controls in post-test seriation tasks;

2   the (MC) children improved in the post-test task immediately following training. They were significantly better than at pre-test and also better than the (LWC) at first post-testing although all the children had succeeded in learning the appropriate descriptions within the three training sessions;

3   the (LWC) children took longer to learn the descriptions within the three sessions but by the *second* seriation post-test they had reached the same level of competence in seriation as their (MC) counterparts;

4   the quality of progress for most children consisted in advancing very gradually by small steps which were increasingly more efficient. In other words children did not suddenly grasp the concept of seriation. Only a very few children progressed more rapidly and none of them became 'operational' by the strictest criterion which had been set. It was noticeable that the children's initial descriptive competence corresponded exactly to the kind of progress they made in seriation, i.e. the description a child gave related to the type of seriation feature in which he subsequently improved. Children who could use the comparative terms 'bigger' and 'smaller' made progress in grading rods in the loose sets. A few children who could describe the relations of an intermediate item from the start improved in the covered-sets tasks. This apparently close liaison of initial speech repertoire and apposite seriation progress suggested that speech interacts with cognitive processes at the particular point of development to which the task relates. It seems to be a closely combined communicative and referential effect.

On the basis of this interpretation later studies were designed to discover the nature of this interactive process and it was thought to be most economical to focus precisely at a clear point of conceptual transition among subjects most likely to reveal immediate effects of different styles of intervention. In this way perhaps subtle but important influences might be detected. Hence for all subsequent studies, children were selected who could explain the placement of an intermediate item if prompted e.g. where $A > B > C$, B is $< A$ and $> C$ and who were also 'intermediate' seriators. Seriation tests were confined to the covered-set tasks already described as this seemed most apposite to their descriptive and conceptual level of competence.

While Study 1 formed an experiment on its own, the four further studies to be reported are in effect sections of a single large second experiment since the method and procedures were all the same. Comparison of results between the sections was thus possible. Since the content of the intervention task was also common to all, the only differences which remained to be investigated between the matched groups of ten children aged 5–6 was the communicative or referential style of intervention. Piaget has always elicited children's judgements by means of discussion and Inhelder, Sinclair and Bovet in their 'learning studies' (1974) use the same probing question and answer routine when they observe the way children solve a variety of problems. Sinclair-de-Zwart (1967) describes her language training in seriation as four interrogative exercises leading the child from a general description of the items to a precise account of the comparative relationships, especially those concerning intermediate items. It is not clear whether the children's own judgements are drawn from them by means of a fairly flexible discussion or whether the style of questioning constrains the child to give the correct description. Her account seems to indicate that it was the latter. The author endeavoured to maintain a discussion with each child that precisely fitted his need and which it was thought might encourage him to formulate the relationships for himself. For instance, once the child had described the difference between elements in one direction and then the other in terms of 'bigger' and 'smaller', the relations of an intermediate item to its neighbours would be elicited thus:

Will that one go in between J? NO. Try it. Is it alright? YES. Why is it alright? COS THAT ONE'S BIGGER THAN THAT ONE. The middle one is . . . ? BIGGER THAN THAT ONE . . . and? SMALLER THAN THAT ONE. Yes.

If a child proffered an incorrect description or faulty judgement, he was encouraged to reconsider the matter by inspecting the differences in size between the elements of the series in question. Almost always children arrived at correct answers for themselves but there were occasions when the observer had to provide a description e.g. if absolute terms were being used by a child who apparently did not know the comparative descriptors then he would be corrected. This style of interaction did not follow a set routine but took up the child's responses in an open dialogue form. However it was not compared with any other style of intervention. Obviously comparisons with other forms were now needed in order to discern effective interactive influences.

Kinds of interaction in relation to progress in seriation: Studies 2-5

Four sections of the investigation will now be outlined in turn. These are designated Studies 2, 3, 4 and 5 respectively. Each was designed to answer a new question as it arose concerning the interactive influence of speech in cognitive growth. They will be dealt with in this order and comparisons of all conditions of intervention will be made overall. Although styles of intervention differed in each section the content of the intervention task was common to all. It consisted in asking the child to find elements which could be correctly inserted between two end-items which were of different sizes. Items to be inserted should maintain ordinal relationships. In Studies 2, 3, and 4 the items to be placed were flat squares of different sizes and in Study 5 squares which differed in size *and* shading were used for one condition. But for a second intervention condition of Study 5 serial differences were in shading alone, not size. In this condition the squares were all the same size but were 'blacker' or 'whiter' than each other. In all these studies an ordinal series was first shown to the child consisting in circular discs set out on the working surface. He was led to realise that between two different sized items of contrasting colour there were two others correctly placed in size sequence. Below this arrangement there was one disc that was too small to go between the end-items and another that was too big. In Study 5 the demonstration set differed in shading and not in size. Except in Study 5 the task consisted in placing a large and small square beside each other in front of the child. He was then asked to take other squares, one at a time, from a bag and to decide which of them should be placed between the end squares if ordinal sequence was maintained. End squares contrasted in colour from those which were to be placed in order to preserve a distinction between them. The demonstration set remained in front of the child for reference. In all the studies, including Study 5, pre- and post-testing consisted in the *size* seriation covered-set tasks which have already been described.

STUDY 2: CONVERSATION VERSUS INSTRUCTION:
COMPARISON OF FOUR INTERACTIVE CONDITIONS

In Study 1 intervention had consisted in the child learning to use descriptions of serial relations appropriately *in dialogue with the observer*. This dialogue led the child to think for himself and it seemed likely to be a major influence upon cognitive progress in itself. But alternatives were considered. These were as follows:

(*a*) *Action condition*   The child was asked to place items between the end squares without discussing his actions. He was asked to 'Find the squares that go between', but comments about size differences were not encouraged.

(*b*) *Dialogue condition*   Here discussion between the observer and child centred round the relationships which define correct placements. Decisions and actions were taken by the child himself and he was led to explore the nature of the relationships concerned and to formulate them. In *all* these conditions the observer ended the session by reversing the left/right positions of the large and small end squares and asking if the intermediate item was still correctly placed. Here the child was asked to *judge why* this was so:

If we turn those around is the middle one still alright? YES. Why? BECAUSE YOU ONLY MOVED THE OUTSIDE ONES AND THE MIDDLE ONE'S STILL THE SAME AS IT WAS WITH THE OTHER TWO. Yes, from this one it's? . . . . SMALLER and from that one it's?. . . BIGGER.

In condition (*a*) a 'Yes' or 'No' answer was sufficient, in condition (*c*), to be described, explanations were *given* to the child by the observer.

(*c*) *Didactic condition* Here the child received direct instruction and demonstration from the observer from whom he learned to recite a correct description of the relations of the items so placed.

(*d*) *Control condition* In this condition children only received the pre-and post-test seriation tasks at the appropriate times. They had no intervention tasks.

Results of Study 2 showed a significant difference in post-test seriation competence between the groups. There was no difference for any group between the first and second post-tests. For this reason results of post-tests were summed for making overall and individual comparisons between groups. Results of these comparisons showed that the difference between groups was due entirely to the superiority of the *Dialogue* condition. All the other conditions, including the *Control*, were not significantly different from each other in seriation outcome. Thus the communicative function of speech evidently plays an important role in the growth of understanding serial relations. But what kind of discussion or dialogue is likely to give the child the best opportunities for learning? What aspects of this kind of communication are most effective? These questions led to further studies being made.

STUDY 3: CONTENTION VERSUS GUIDANCE

Since the dialogue in Study 2 was between the observer and the child the communicative influence just observed could be due to the observer's guidance in eliciting appropriate descriptions from the child, but, on the other hand the reflexive nature of discussion might in itself be the operative influence. In Study 3 an attempt was made to test this question by selecting five pairs of 'intermediate' seriators on exactly the same criteria as before. These pairs of children were on a par with each other both in descriptive and cognitive competence. They were pre-and post-tested individually but did the intervention task together. This was called condition (*e*) *Pairs condition*. In the *Pairs* task the children took turns to find correct places for items and were encouraged to discuss where these should be placed. When an item was placed to mutual satisfaction, agreement having been reached between the pair, then the next one could be dealt with. In the event there was plenty of argument about where to place the squares, but this was finally resolved. However the discussion rarely contained reasoning. Rather it consisted in a sequence of simple retorts which relied heavily on demonstration e.g. 'It goes there'. 'No it doesn't. It goes there' . . . and so on. The seriation post-test results of the *Pairs* condition were no better than the *Controls*, the *Action* and *Didactic* conditions. The *Dialogue condition* (*b*) of Study 2 remained significantly more effective than all the others. This result suggested that discussion with the observer led the child to formulate an apposite and objective description of the seriation problem and that mere contention, even if it made the child realise other points of view, had little influence. An attempt was then made to discover in more detail the effective features of the guided discussion led by the observer. In other words, how does the child's formulation assist him in learning the seriation problem?

STUDY 4: EFFECTIVE FEATURES OF A GUIDED DISCUSSION

Study 4 aimed to draw the child towards an even more explicit for-mulation of the insertion problem used in the intervention task. Perhaps because the observer is obviously knowledgeable in the child's eyes there may be some degree of presupposition in his explanations to her, whereas if he is teaching the task to someone patently ignorant he will be forced to enlarge on details previously taken for granted in conversations between the child and the observer. An attempt was made to explore this area of explanation by asking children to teach the insertion task to a glove puppet represented to them as rather ignorant and stupid. This condition was labelled

(*f*) *Puppet condition*   Ten children, selected in the same way as before, first learned the task with the observer and then explained it to the puppet. Each child chose his own name for the puppet. When the child was teaching he was encouraged to rely most heavily on explanation although he was allowed to demonstrate if necessary using his *own* set of squares. The puppet had a set of its own which it selected and placed under the guidance and instruction of the child. The observer spoke for the puppet. When it made errors these were corrected by the child but in doing so he was asked not to point to or move the puppet's own squares. Children enjoyed this game, and although it was clear that the observer was in control of the puppet they entered into the make-believe and attempted to enlarge on explanations required by the puppet.

Results showed some individual differences within the group of children teaching the puppet. For instance those who scored high in post-test seriation could most easily describe the intermediate item B in relation to A and C where $A > B > C$. This might well have been expected but most interestingly the high post-test scorers were also children who could find ways of *verifying* their judgements to the puppet, although even they found this difficult to do and paused to think out their explanations. For instance, the puppet would ask how *it* could tell that a particular item was suitable to place between the end-squares. At first the child replied, 'Because its bigger than one and smaller than the other'. But when the puppet insisted, 'But how do *I* know this?', these children found ways of verifying the first explanation e.g. 'By looking', 'Put it on one and put it on the other' (referring to the end-squares). The children who were significantly less advanced at post-test would be inclined to reply 'Because I tell you'. No further explanation could be extracted from them, suggesting that they felt this was sufficient! Thus in the dialogue with the puppet there were cases where the explanation and its verification were made explicit, and this appeared to be linked with progress in understanding general principles. However these children's explanations did not fall into a set form of words, rather they were striving to express these principles in their own way. It seemed most likely therefore that it is the expression of principles as such and not the precise terminology used to formulate them which leads the child towards a better understanding of seriation.

STUDY 5: PRINCIPLES VERSUS TERMINOLOGY

Study 2 confirmed that communication in dialogue form is an important influence in cognitive progress. In Study 3 it appeared that this must involve guidance and not just disagreement. The puppet study indicates that this guidance may be concerned with expressing precisely the general principles of the problem which can be verified by consensus. It is not the exact terminology which appears to matter but the understanding of reasons which are derived from discussion and mutual verification. If the terminology were at the heart of the matter learning to use contrasting comparative terms such as smaller and blacker would be as effective in producing progress in seriation as using opposite comparatives which refer to two opposing differences in *another* dimension than size, e.g. 'blacker' and 'whiter' where size is *not* concerned but the principle of ordination *is*.

Study 5 set out to test this idea. As in all previous conditions there were ten children in each group who were selected in the same way and pre- and post-tested in the size seriation tasks. One group were given an insertion task where size *and* shading were the criteria for inserting squares between the end-items e.g. the child learned 'Because it is whiter than one and bigger than the other'. The squares provided differed in both these dimensions for this condition which was labelled condition (g). The somewhat arbitrary statements were easily learned by the children who enjoyed this task as much as they did all the others. The other group were asked to insert items between squares which were graded for blackness and whiteness but did *not* differ in size. Here insertion was determined by the general principle of seriation, namely, because the intermediate item is blacker than those on one side and whiter than those on the other, i.e. by opposite degrees of difference. This condition was labelled (h). Here, although the terms were not concerned with size differences, post-testing, as already stated, did consist in size seriation tasks. Learning the opposite relations of an intermediate item in a series had always been difficult. Sinclair-de-Zwart had also noted this. It took time for children to grasp that the item B could be *both* bigger and smaller where $A > B > C$. These opposite relations were just as difficult to learn where they referred to shading as where size was the difference in question. The outcome of comparing post-test seriation size tasks for groups (g) *Terminology* versus (h) *Principle* showed that the group who learned the principle of seriation rather than just different comparative terms *without* the principle being stated improved significantly more in the size seriation tasks. It is interesting to note that condition (g) provided children with size differences to see whereas condition (h) did not, thus the description of principle seems to over-ride both the terminology and the perceptual information. Indeed the children who learned the principle in condition (h) did as well at post-test seriation in size as those who had experienced discussion about *size* seriation differences in the *Dialogue condition* (b).

A comparison of the differences in seriation competence at post-test between all eight conditions $(a–h)$ using the Kruskal-Wallis one-way analysis of variance indicated a highly significant difference existed between them. Comparison of all conditions individually with each other using the Mann Whitney U test, revealed that conditions (*b*), (*f*) and (*h*) were associated with progress in seriation. Condition (*b*) was the original dialogue between the observer and child concerned with size relations. Here discussion between the child and observer led the child to use appropriate descriptions. Condition (*f*) extended our knowledge of the nature of this discussion by requiring the child to explain himself more fully as he tried to teach a puppet. Here, not only was the description of the seriation principle linked with progress but also the awareness and attempts to show that this can be verified by observation. Condition (*h*) indicated that even where the child was not using size descriptions e.g. 'bigger' and 'smaller', but terms simply concerned with the seriation principle in another dimension than size, namely shading e.g. 'blacker' and 'whiter' he still makes as much progress in seriation tasks concerned with the size differences as when he discusses size description. It is the principle which he determines for himself through the aegis of a guided dialogue. This kind of discussion impels him to reason out the commonly agreed and defining relationships and to recognise that they are verifiable. He is drawn to appreciate another's standpoint by conversation which guides him. His own action alone without discussion, (condition *a*), the appropriate demonstration of the descriptive terms themselves by another, (conditions *c* and *g*), and mere contention empty of reasoning, (condition *e*) do not provide better opportunities for learning than if he had no speech training at all, (condition *d*).

Interpretation of results

The findings of Study 1 indicated that speech is an effective influence in the child's learning especially if he is already primed with the appropriate descriptive uses. As speech intervention was conducted in the form of a discussion between the observer and the child it seemed likely that this form of interaction might be partly responsible for the progress that was made although the reference could naturally not be dismissed. Studies 2, 3, 4 and 5 variously analysed the nature of this communicative influence and Study 5 isolated the kind of reference which was most effective.

It is not appropriate here to write of piecemeal cause-effect relationships but the intervention procedures may be said to have highlighted conditions which coincide with cognitive change and those which do not. Conditions (*b*), (*f*) and (*h*) are those which provide the best opportunities for learning. The others appear to make no difference beyond the normal course of a child's daily experience. The *Dialogue*

(condition *b*) is common to the other two effective styles of intervention. It is a particular kind of discussion in which a more experienced
person guides the child towards formulating the definitive, general
principles of the problem he is solving. The child himself judges the
placement of an intermediate item. If he is wrong he is asked to reconsider the matter. If he is correct he is asked why and in the puppet
study he is asked to show how he himself and others can verify his
judgement. This discussion is adjusted to each child's individual
need, e.g.

Does that go between? NO. Try it. YES. Why? BECAUSE IT DOES. Well how
is it different from that one? IT'S BIGGER . . . and from that one? SMALLER.
So why does it go between? COS IT'S BIGGER THAN THAT ONE AND SMAL-
LER THAN THAT ONE.

In a previous example the child in question gave the description of
the relations of the intermediate item immediately. This child had to
be led to it more slowly. This kind of discussion probes and stimulates
the child's reasoning because *he himself* constructs and formulates
the relationships. In this way he becomes aware of their generality,
i.e. as in the puppet study, he realises that reasons can be verified
by the person with whom he is talking. Thus he grasps an objective
view of the matter. This assists cognitive growth. This objective view
is concerned with the general principles, the meaning of what is being
said, and has little to do with the linguistic form of the utterances
in the conversation. The children selected for Studies 2–5 were
'intermediate' seriators and could describe the double relations of
individual items in a series provided they were prompted. They
therefore had at their command all the ingredients of action and
speech which should enable them to realise that they should make
double comparisons in the covered-set insertion tasks, but they did
not do so.

What was lacking? It appears to be the understanding of the *unit*
of opposing relations of each element in the series which comprises
the definitive feature of all asymmetrical series. The progress that
occurred after the intervention conditions (*b*), (*f*) and (*h*) (*Dialogue*,
Puppet and *Seriation Principle*) showed the children becoming
systematic in the double comparison use in the covered-set tasks i.e.
they checked the point at which to insert the extra item by comparing it with those on each side. Obviously at this point one of
these elements will be bigger than the extra item and the other will
be smaller. Following the other conditions (*Action, Didactic, Pairs,
Terminology* and *Controls*) children only made such double comparisons sporadically and this strategy was not sustained. Moreover the

analysis of the effective discussion in the puppet study suggests that the effort to grasp, not only the logical relations of the middle item to its neighbours, but also the objective verification and meaning of this unit of relations, was associated with advance in seriation. These observations should suggest some answer to what does occur between speech and cognition that bridges the gap between a loose agglomeration of skills and their effective synthesis into a logical unit of thought.

Changing theoretical context

Results of Study 1 onwards make it clear that 'language' is only usefully considered in relation to cognitive growth of young children in the form of speech in an action context. Children talk about what they are doing and it is in this setting that we should study the influence of speech upon learning. The original contention between Bruner (1964) and Piaget (1970) supported by Sinclair-de-Zwart (1967) overlooks two important combined features of the child's development, the communicative and referential *use* of speech. The child has the best opportunity of solving his present problems through conversation about them. Lasting and effective solutions arise as he discusses his ideas with others whose guidance helps him to select and unite definitive principles. He learns by means of this guiding discussion, how to formulate his thoughts, partly by realising the way that others view his expressed opinions and partly by appreciating those uniting principles which are effective and demonstrable.

Since Bruner's (1964) theories were expounded there has been a change of emphasis from considering the linguistic features of speech in cognitive development to appreciating its communicative and referential use. Bruner (1975a) speaks of 'the ontogenesis of speech acts'. Communication by interactive patterns of gesture are now thought to precede its spoken manifestation; (c.f. Ryan, 1974; Bruner and Sherwood, 1976; Trevarthen and Hubley, 1978). Once speech has been acquired its communicative importance is appreciated. For instance Bernstein (1973) admits his indebtedness to George Herbert Mead (1934). For Mead dialogue originates in gesture and culminates in words based in gesture which have come to have commonly agreed meanings. Indeed it is of great interest that Austin's (1962) philosophical analysis of speech led him to discard the notion that there could be 'statements' independent of a spoken context and which were either true or false. Instead, he suggested that any statement, whether spoken or written, whether public or personal, constrains the speaker or writer to be consistent with what he has suggested. In other words it is a personal commitment. Speech is thus a communicative activity and as such gives rise to negotiation, for the speaker must reflect on what he said in the light of other points of view. Seen in this way the speech of young children must be a growing point, especially when discussion occurs in a demanding situation where a more experienced person is guiding its progress. But there is more to it than this.

Learning through conversation: A synthesis of theories

Bruner (1975a, b) has emphasised the communicative attributes of speech outlined by Austin (1962). Many authors now stress the need to study speech functions and their influence upon cognitive development (e.g. Bernstein, 1973; Schlesinger, 1971; Bloom, 1970; Fillmore, 1968; Donaldson, 1977). Piaget's recent studies of 'cognisance' (1974a, b) – or 'the grasp of consciousness' are a detailed and subtle explanation of the child's learning. The child becomes aware of what he knows but does not yet understand. Awareness and clarification come about through *an interpretive process*. This process consists in reflection which is guided by extrinsic influences to which adjustments are made. Reflection is assisted by explication. However, if a child gains insight by explaining his problems this will occur most readily in conversation with others who draw his attention to features which need explanation. Piaget does not emphasise the rôle that conversation itself may play in the development of insight. Indeed the 'learning studies' of Inhelder *et al.* (1974) consisted in observations of the conversations of observers with children about problems the children were required to solve. The authors were interested in the children's pseudo-solutions as they tried to discover answers to the problems put before them. It was the children's reasoning as such which was the focus of the study. The nature of the conversation was not considered. This reasoning must take place in response to the investigator's questions which suggests that the dialogue itself offers an effective opportunity for the child to exercise his 'interpretive' powers. He is being drawn forward at the growing point of his understanding; being led from the known to the unknown. Piaget explains the process in terms of the child's cognitive activity. More than this is needed. For the child is responding to the demands of a communicative situation. By having to try to express his thought he begins to reflect upon what he has said and what it means to himself and to others. Polanyi (1962) in his study of "Personal Knowledge" outlines the transition from tacit understanding to knowledge which is explicit and disciplined. The process of explanation he sees as an heuristic which operates in the tension driven search leading from the known to the unknown. Polanyi elaborates the interaction of speech and cognition in this way:

> The domain of sophistication, – is formed by *not fully understood* symbolic operations which can be:
>   (*a*) a fumbling, to be *corrected* later by our tacit understanding.
>   (*b*) a pioneering, to be *followed up* later by our tacit understanding.
> More precisely speaking, we should say that we are referring in both these cases to a state of mental uneasiness due to the feeling that our tacit thoughts do not agree with our symbolic operations, so that we have to decide on which of the two to rely and which we should correct in the light of the other. (*ibid*. p. 93)

Although Polanyi is writing about adult problem solving and Piaget about the growth of knowledge in the child both appear to be describing a *purposeful interpretive activity*. However, neither of them is particularly interested in stressing the spoken negotiations which are patently essential to this interaction. But it does seem clear that speech in a guided discussion where the child is drawn to explain himself and thus reflect upon what he is saying is not just a 'catalyst' to his learning but is in itself a 'seed crystal'. Being part of the process of discovery it produces a new synthesis, or new level of understanding. This kind of conversation is likely to be one of the best opportunities for learning which may be provided by adults for their children in home and school. Unfortunately it may seem to be a relatively slow way of 'imparting knowledge'. If education is concerned to pack the child with facts teachers will see instruction as the quickest and most efficient strategy. However, if educators wish to stimulate the child's interpretive activity, by which he may then continue to resolve problems for himself, 'guided discussion' may well be the type of condition to which a child will respond best in his growing understanding and in the development of his reasoning powers.

Acknowledgements

The work of Study 1 was financed by a grant from the SSRC. Professor G. Trasler is to be thanked for his encouragement and for practical assistance in making provision for the whole project to be carried out with the material support of the Department of Psychology, University of Southampton. The author is most grateful for the benefit of advice and discussion with Professor W. P. Robinson, Dr E. J. Robinson, Dr W. M. Woodward, Dr P. H. Light and Dr D. Siddle. Permission to work in the schools was kindly granted by the Local Education Authority. Particular thanks are due to the teachers of the First Schools. They are: Miss E. F. Miller and staff at Mansell, Miss E. M. Neck, Mrs T. Woodward and staff at Highfield, Miss M. M. Jarvis and staff at Hollybrook and Mrs S. Stephens and staff at Hardmoor.

References

Austin, J. L. (1962). "How To Do Things With Words". Oxford University Press. Oxford

Bernstein, B. (1973). "Class, Codes and Control". Routledge, London

Bloom, L. (1970). "Language Development. Form and Function in Emerging Grammars". The M.I.T. Press, Cambridge, Massachusetts

Bruner, J. S. (1964). The course of cognitive development. *American Psychologist* 19, 1-15

Bruner, J. S. (1966). "Toward a Theory of Instruction". The Belknap Press of Harvard University Press, Cambridge, Massachusetts

Bruner, J. S. (1975a). The ontogenesis of speech acts. *Journal of Child Language* 2, 1-20

Bruner, J. S. (1975b). "The Social Context of Language". Paper presented at the BPS Scottish Branch, University of Stirling, January

Bruner, J. S. and Sherwood, V. (1976). Early rule structure: the case of peekaboo. *In* "Play. Its Role in Development and Evolution" (J. S. Bruner, A. Jolly and K. Sylva, Eds). Penguin Books, Harmondsworth

Bruner, J. S., Olver, R. R. and Greenfield, P. S. (1966). "Studies in Cognitive Growth". Wiley, New York

Donaldson, M. (1977). Development of conceptualisation. *In* "Development of Cognitive Processes" (V. Hamilton and M. D. Vernon, Eds). Academic Press, London

Fillmore, C. J. (1968). The case for case. *In* "Universals in Linguistic Theory" (E. Bach and R. T. Harms, Eds). Holt, Rinehart and Winston, New York

Heber, M. (1977). The influence of language training on seriation of 5-6-year-old children initially at different levels of descriptive competence. *British Journal of Psychology* 68, 85-95

Heber, M. (1978). "The Rôle of Language in Cognitive Development: Speech and Seriation in 5-6-year-old Children". Unpublished doctoral thesis. University of Southampton

Inhelder, B. and Piaget, J. (1964). "Early Growth of Logic in the Child". Routledge, London

Inhelder, B., Sinclair, H. and Bovet, M. (1974). "Learning and the Development of Cognition". Routledge and Kegan Paul, London

Mead, G. H. (1934). "Mind, Self and Society". The University of Chicago Press, Chicago

Piaget, J. (1962). "Play, Dreams and Imitation in Childhood". Routledge and Kegan Paul, London

Piaget, J. (1970). Piaget's theory. In "Carmichael's Manual of Child Psychology" (P. H. Mussen, Ed.) 2nd edn. John Wiley, New York

Piaget, J. (1974a). "La Prise de Conscience". Presses Universitaires de France, Paris

Piaget, J. (1974b). "Réussir et Comprendre". Presses Universitaires de France, Paris

Piaget, J. (1977). "The Grasp of Conciousness". Routledge, London

Piaget, J. (1978). "Success and Understanding". Routledge, London

Polanyi, M. (1962). "Personal Knowledge". Routledge, London

Ryan, J. (1974). In Early language development. "The Integration of a Child into a Social World" (M. P. M. Richards, Ed.). Cambridge University Press, Cambridge

Schlesinger, I. M. (1971). Production of utterances and language acquisition. In "The Ontogenesis of Grammar" (D. I. Slobin, Ed.). Academic Press, New York

Sinclair-de-Zwart, H. (1967). "Acquisition de Langage et Développement de la Pensée". Dunod, Paris

Sinclair-de-Zwart, H. (1969). In "Studies in Cognitive Development" (D. Elkind and J. Flavell, Eds). Oxford University Press, New York

Trevarthen, C. and Hubley, P. (1978). Secondary intersubjectivity. In "Action, Gesture and Symbol" (A. Lock, Ed.). Academic Press, London

Woodward, W. M. (1974). "Early Cognitive Development". Final Research Report. SSRC

9

Conflict and Cooperation as Opportunities for Learning

A-N. Perret-Clermont and M-L. Schubauer-Leoni

Is learning an individual process?

Is learning an individual process? When we visit schools at home or abroad whether they be 'traditional', 'informal', or 'child-centred' and in spite of the evident variety in the procedures used for teaching and learning, the learning process itself is almost universally viewed as a matter pertaining to the capacities and motivation of the individual child.

In some schools, teaching seems to be conceived as a matter of properly transmitting a certain body of knowledge, whose character is defined as relevant by the teacher, the school, other educational authorities or the 'culture' at large. This knowledge is directed at pupils by means of lectures or written texts, often to a whole class of children, sometimes to groups of children, and more rarely to individuals. Multiple copies of roneoed materials are likely to be identical for all pupils; textbooks themselves are prepared for thousands of children.

Although this information is transmitted to a group, paradoxically the individual pupils are not actually perceived by teachers as members of a group.

Many features of the environment can contribute to the isolation of the pupil during his learning. Even when desks and chairs are transformed from rows to groupings around tables, the pupil may be expected to be quiet as he works through a programme. The programme remains the same for all children; it is simply pursued individually. Essentially the pupil works by himself, and teachers assess his work on an individual basis also. The question is 'What can he manage on his own?'

But is it either necessary or desirable for effective learning that the child works essentially alone? While it may be true that there are occasions when a pupil needs to be alone to puzzle out something for himself or to concentrate undisturbed, we would like to question the common view that all learning is an activity requiring isolated concentration.

In this important respect many of the teaching methods sponsored by advocates of child-centred education are not importantly different from the methods of 'chalk and talk'. The child-centred conception and intention is to foster the learning processes *stemming from within the child*. He is again perceived as an individual with his own capacities, desires and questions, which are viewed as symptoms of his individual growth and activity. The school tries to provide for the development of these, often by devising *individualised* teaching treatments, which in turn contribute to a perception of the child as an individual, albeit a unique one.

Often the teachers, especially those who claim to practice child-centred education do indeed also work with small groups of children and place themselves at their disposal to help them to learn in a more personal manner. Notwithstanding this, the reasons teachers give to justify such attitudes are usually humanistic rather than pedagogic: 'Children need attention', 'It is good for them to learn to be sociable with friends' or 'It is more fun for them'. Only rarely are the reasons given linked to the cognitive processes involved in learning, e.g. 'A child must discuss his thoughts to fully understand them', 'He needs to try out his ideas on somebody else'.

Teachers are not the only people responsible for such a view of children and their learning. As Perret (1978a) argues, the theoretical models of intelligence that psychologists have constructed often contribute to a similar conception and serve to reinforce and justify such practices. The psychological assumptions of many assessment procedures make aptitudes and competencies properties or traits of the individual whose characteristics are then believed to determine whether or not he will be likely to benefit from a given educational treatment.

Developmental approaches in the field of the psychology of intelligence often call attention to the sequence of changes that occur in the characteristics of the child's cognitive capacities. Even if these may point successfully to the different educational needs of children at different development stages, they still consider the child as an isolated individual; and the stages themselves are seen as characteristics of individual growth.

Yet at the same time these approaches have maintained that the child grows up *within* an environment that can have differing impacts on the course his development will take; some environments are more likely than others to provide for the child's needs and thereby facilitate his growth and enable him to realise his proper potential. On this view of a child growing up 'isolated in his social environment' the educator's role is confined to protection and feeding of the intellect and emotions. He is like a gardener who supervises the needs of a plant for light, heat, water and fertiliser, but does not have an active role to play in the growing process of the plant, except through such interventions as pruning. But is this botanical analogy really useful for understanding the cognitive and social development of children? 'Pruning' can serve to remind us of educational treatments that interfere with the child's activity in order to shape into the expectations and plans of the adult. Metaphors of watering and feeding encourage an attitude of respect for the child's activity, but may lead us to neglect the extent to which the explicit or implicit *demands* of the environment play an active role in influencing the course of development. The developmental processes of human beings are likely to be more complex, subtle, and supple than those of plants. Too simplistic developmental analogies are misleading and fail to do justice to the wealth of sub-cultural and cross-cultural variation in children and adults. Cross-cultural studies point to variations from social group to social group both in the forms of stages of cognitive growth and the rates of progress through these. In so far as these differences are real and not simply artefacts of the research methodologies and conceptual frameworks used, the reasons for their existence will not be explained by referring to the traits of individual children.

Such explanations cannot provide the teacher or educational research worker with conceptual frameworks that enable them to understand how the educator's behaviour *does interact* with the pupil's learning. A more specific and deeper appreciation of the way these interchanges are relevant to learning and development could, we believe, help us to specify the social and cognitive characteristics of educational settings promotive both of the learning of specific skills and of the development of more general cognitive competencies. When psychological research can offer conceptual frameworks that accurately predict the interchanges between an individual and his social and cultural environment and their impact on cognitive growth, we believe it also offers the means to specify educative actions and assess the pupils' reactions to these.

Before we turn to examine this work, it is useful to consider briefly some of the consequences of sociological explanations of the differential achievement of children of different social groups in terms of the impact these have on educationalists' attitudes and practice. Although these approaches often make specific recommendations – or more often *post hoc* interpretations – about the environmental conditions judged to be appropriate for normal cognitive development of such children, they do not explain why and how the particular sociological character of such factors as housing conditions, parental occupations, declared child-rearing practices, social aspirations, access to cultural media and language standards, etc. interfere with or facilitate the child's learning. Are these mechanisms assumed to be obvious or trivial? We do not think they are either. Such psychological mechanisms as have been postulated have not been tested other than through simple correlational studies. Even in Bernstein's (1971, 1975) approach in which the functional role of language for the individual within a social setting and in a socio-cultural group is emphasised, the claims about differences in role relations and interpersonal relationships are not linked to psychologically based theories of learning.

It is only by going beyond this level of analysis that the social scientist can discover the psychological processes *mediating* any differential development of cognitive competencies. If the type of interpersonal relations which pupils have with adults does have an impact on the learning he achieves, it is important to identify which kinds of relationships are linked to which cognitive outcomes. We have examined these questions elsewhere (Schubauer-Leoni and Perret-Clermont, 1980) in terms of different cognitive outcomes. Here we focus upon varying the interpersonal relations to examine their impact on cognitive development.

The interchange between the child and the social setting: Communication, understanding and performance

In his current research Perret (1978a) demonstrates that the understanding which a young child has of a task will influence not only the level of performance he achieves, but also – and in the long term this may be more important – his communicative behaviour with his social environment. For example, it is only if the child already has some knowledge and ideas about the solution of a technical problem that he can or will ask questions of an adult or some other source of information for those matters that are arbitrary or conventional and not logical. Without a minimal level of understanding he will not be able to decide whether it is logical (and then he should find it out for himself) or arbitrary/conventional (in which case he must ask).

When at an earlier level of understanding the child is as yet incapable either of starting to solve the task or seeing that his suggested solution is wrong, he is also incapable of identifying the *kind* of help he needs – the type of relevant questions he could ask; hence he has great difficulty involving himself in an adequate interchange with his social environment about the task.

Observing older pupils of an Upper school involved in group work, Perret (1978b) has seen their cognitive activity deteriorating when they have failed to realise that they have not understood their teacher's instructions. Perhaps because they have not wished to constrain the approach of the students to the project proposed, the teachers have failed to be sufficiently explicit in their communication, and this defective communication has impeded the work of the adolescents concerned. These processes have two consequences when the pupil does not understand the nature of the task set, he is unlikely to be able to formulate constructive questions about his non-understanding. He does not know what to ask of the teacher. Under these circumstances he is unlikely to perform well.

The second consequence is made explicit in the work of Labov (1972) and Katz (1973) which reveals how the quality of the pupil's performance is sensitive to the social relationship obtaining on the occasion of its elicitation; the performance is richer when the pupil is at ease in his relations with the experimenter.

We suggest that ease of communication with the experimenter frees the subject to concentrate his efforts upon the task itself and saves him from the additional task of understanding and mastering the social relationship in which he is simultaneously involved. Given that adult and child are able to focus on the cognitive task set what is the possible relevance of the language used to the quality of the child's performance?

In an empirical study of relationships between children's mastery of Piagetian cognitive operations and their own semantic competence, Rommetweit (1976) offers striking examples of the importance of establishing common intersubjectivity between child and adult via linguistic prestructuring of the task. When presented with the drawings of circles shown in Fig. 1, some 7-year-old Norwegian children promptly pointed to the target object when it was called 'the second biggest snowball' but not when it was referred to as 'the second biggest white circle'.

Rommetweit shows how in tasks involving class inclusion, ordering and bi-variate classification children are sensitive to the interplay between what they see and what they hear. The operative capacities

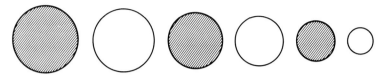

FIG. 1   Referential domain for choice of 'The one of the WHITE CIRCLES/ SNOWBALLS that is SECOND BIGGEST'

they reveal will depend on their semantic competence to understand what is made explicit in the instructions and their appreciation of what the adult has left implicit.

Rommetweit's concept of the 'architecture of intersubjectivity' is also useful as a framework for understanding the conditions that enable a teacher and a learner to achieve common intersubjectivity and hence to communicate effectively with each other. It is similar in thrust to Schaffer's (1979) observations of mother-infant interactions in the first months of life. He shows attention to important social prerequisites of cognitive development: the regularity of the rhythmic biological patterns in which the infant is involved (e.g. feeding) offers a basis for the mother to anticipate his behaviour and enter into a 'pseudo-dialogue'. This will gradually become more complex and flexible with greater intentional initiative being taken by the child. But it is clear that this important social and cognitive development is likely to come about *only if* the child's partners are willing and able to sustain his behaviour by responding *contingently* and appropriately in these exchanges. Contingency of the adult's responses linked to the direction of the baby's action is a necessary condition for achieving common inter-subjectivity between adult and child. It is within these pseudo-dialogues that the words and other features of behaviour to be learned are introduced and learned.

It appears that the types of inter-personal relationships that the child must establish influence both the level of his immediate task performance and the availability or not of opportunities for *learning*. Learning cannot occur independently of the social context which induces it; it cannot be reduced to matters of simple transmission of adequate information. Information transmitted will be more likely to be learned if the learner is a partner in an interactive communication process. Confining him to the role of a listener-receiver will be insufficient. It seems that information, perhaps even thinking itself, takes its relevance for the growing mind of the learner within his own contingent schemes of actions and his own cognitive grasping of tasks he faces.

It is also clear that any given task does not have the same social meaning for all children. Haroche and Pêcheux (1972) contrasted the problem-solving behaviour of factory workers and students. Reversals of differential superiority were shown to be related to the form in which the problems were set. Doise, Meyer and Perret-Clermont (1976) showed similar relationships between semantic content and cognitive performance in adolescents of different school streams.

It is also clear that any inter-personal relationship context does not have the same meaning for all children. The social distances between children and the experimenter (teacher) are not always the same. The adult is most often the person responsible for establishing and regulating the communication. Hence the children who lack the necessary information (often children of disadvantaged social groups) are also those who feel the greatest social distance with the adult (Perret, 1978a). It is not surprising then if they are also the children who least frequently pose questions. Differential levels of performance by children may reflect this differential distance between the child and the teacher. The experiment to be reported illustrates these problems.

Study 1:   Social context and performance: *the responses of 6-year-olds in Piaget's classic test of the conservation of liquids*

It is a general finding that performance on intelligence tests correlates with privilege of socio-cultural origin. Interpretations of these correlations vary, often assigning primary causation to one of three main sets of factors: social, psychological or biological. In view of the significance attached to performance on such tests as predictors of educational performance, it is important to elucidate the psycho-social processes that create these correlations.

Piaget claims that his theoretical framework is describing universal features of the development of intelligence. If this were so, the same cognitive performance should be manifested by a given child whenever and wherever it is studied – as typical of his stage of cognitive growth. Empirical studies refute this. The Piagetian school suggests that some environments are more likely to facilitate development than others, but does not say *how* or *why*. To assert that the sequence of emerging structures is universal, but that some social contexts reduce the rate of progress might be trivial if it were not for the possibly suspicious fact that the children who emerge as most advanced were very often (Dasen, 1977) precisely those from the same sub-culture as the authors of the reasearch; *viz.* Western middle-class. (Anyone who has tried to explain these results to students from Third World countries may have felt the risk of ethno-centrism that such an assertion carries.) It is possible that this kind of research is an example of social pre-constructs acting ethno-centrically as deform-ing prisms. Can such pre-constructs be dismantled at all by studying precisely how and why social factors affect cognitive development? We hope to illustrate how this might be achieved.

METHOD

The children investigated here were drawn from the First Grade classes of primary schools in seven villages near Locarno, Switzerland. We tested the thesis that children of different social backgrounds would be differentially sensitive to the characteristics of the social setting in which the cognitive level of their performance is assessed.

The hypothesis was tested in two ways. In the first the social conditions for presenting the traditional questions were varied. In the second the children were exposed to different kinds of social interaction previously found to be associated with progress in con-servation of liquids (Doise, Mugny and Perret-Clermont, 1975; Perret–Clermont, 1980; Mugny, Perret–Clermont and Doise (1981).

To achieve these aims the experiment was organised into three stages: a pre-test, exposure to different conditions of learning, and a post-test, essentially similar to the pre-test.

Subjects

It was not possible to draw a random or representative sample of children in the villages. In the state schools for which permission to conduct the investigation was granted, all first year children who were present were included in the sampling. The ages ranged from 5;9 to 6;9. School registers were used to extract declared parental occupa-tion, and although coarse, the information was sufficient to stratify the children into four groups in terms of the criteria presented in the Geneva Statistical Yearbook of Education:

Group 1: unskilled and semi-skilled workers

Group 2: qualified employees, small farmers, small shopkeepers, routine white collar workers

Group 3: schoolteachers, technicians, middle managers, etc.

Group 4: liberal professions, senior managers, directors, etc.

This categorisation had previously been shown to be associated with performance on Piaget and Szeminska's (1941) classic conservation of liquids task (Perret-Clermont, 1980).

Following this categorisation, children from Group 2 were omitted, Group 3 and 4 were combined as the 'privileged group' and Group 1 were labelled the 'underprivileged group'. The final sample comprised 82 boys and 77 girls: the privileged group consisting of 51 children (32 boys and 19 girls), the underprivileged group 108 children (45 boys and 63 girls). There were no known reasons for the apparent over-representation of boys in the privileged group.

Materials
The materials were those used in earlier experiments (Perret-Clermont, 1980): two identical 260 ml beakers A and A^1, a beaker C shorter and wider than A and A^1, an opaque bottle containing fruit juice, and drinking straws. For the second part of the pre-test a new set of beakers (E and E^1) was used, along with a beaker F of the same height, but wider. Two identical female dolls were used in one condition.

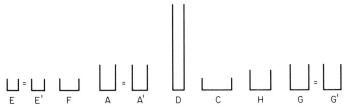

FIG. 2   Beakers used in experiments

Experimental conditions and procedure
Each child was tested individually in a separate room at the school by the experimenter (E) (female). Another adult (male) made notes about the conversation and significant events. After a relaxing conversation, the child (S) was shown the materials and invited to play 'a game with some juice' which he would be able to drink later if he so wished (see Perret-Clermont, 1980, pp. 44–45 for details). E asked each S a set sequence of identical questions about the relative quantities of fruit juice in A, A^1 and C (referred to as 'glasses' (bicchieri) in the instructions).

Pre-test: Phase 1 E asked S to pour equal quantities of juice into each of the two beakers, A and A^1. 'You must put juice in the 2 glasses so that they will both have just as much juice to drink. And now, have they both the same to drink or not?' When S was satisfied that the amounts were equal, E poured the liquid from beaker A into beaker C, and S was asked, 'Is there the same amount of juice in these two glasses or has one more or less or what do you think? S was then asked, 'Now I am going to pour (ancora una volta) the juice in glass C into this glass A. How far up this glass will the juice go?' S then poured the juice back into beaker A and was asked, 'And now is there the same amount of juice to drink in the two glasses or is there less in one or is there more in one or what do you think?' The third sub-phase repeated this procedure with A^1 instead of A, except that E made a counter-suggestion after the judgement following the first pouring. Conservers were told, 'Another child told me that there is more juice to drink in this glass (E points to A) because the juice goes higher up into it!' Whereas nonconservers were told, 'Another child told me that one glass is wider and the juice stays lower and one glass is thinner and the juice goes higher up into it but in both glasses there is just as much to drink. Is he right?' The rest of the sequence consisted of repeating the three sub-phases (but   omitting the counter suggestion).

Two conditions were used. In the first E and S had the beakers A and A^1. In the second the identical dolls each had a beaker A or A^1 and had to be given equal amounts of juice. This was for the three first sub-phases. Then the contexts were reversed. Those children who started sharing the juice between the experimenter and themselves continued by sharing it for the dolls – and vice versa. Just over half the children (51 underprivileged and 30 privileged) received the Experimenter-Child condition first; 57 under-privileged and 21 privileged children had the dolls first.

Subjects were also equally divided in the Experimenter-Child condition as to whether E or S had Beaker C: 41 Ss had beaker A while E poured from A^1 to C (AF condition). The other 40 poured from their own A^1 into C (CE condition).

For the sub-sample that started with dolls, the division into AF and CE applied to the first three questions after the counter-suggestion. Finally, 51 Ss from the underprivileged group kept their A, 57 used C; in the privileged group 27 kept A and 24 C.

Pre-test: Phase 2:   No dolls were used, and essentially the same procedure was followed except that beakers E, E^1 and F were substituted for A, A^1 and C. Subjects in AF in Phase 1 had a wider beaker F; those in CE had the thinner beaker E. No countersuggestions were made. Children were told that beaker E^1 was for them to use if they wanted to do so. At the end the child was asked from which beaker (E or F) he wanted to drink.

Hypotheses

1 *Privilege*   The privileged group should perform better on the conservation tasks overall, in line with previous findings (Coll-Salvador, Coll-Ventura and Miras-Mestros, 1974; Perret-Clermont, 1980).

2 *Social conditions of the task*   Children should perform better when directly involved in the task; the Experimenter-Child condition should give superior results to the Dolls condition (Doise *et al.*, 1976; Doise, Dionnet and Mugny, 1978; Lévy, 1980).

In addition when the fruit juice is shared between the experimenter and the child himself, and the child sees *E*'s juice transferred to a wider and shorter beaker C, his perception of the level reached may lead him to think his beaker has retained more; a conserving judgment requires him to 'rationalise' an apparently social inequality of distribution which is acting in his favour despite his inferior social status *vis-à-vis E*. Hence *S*s in the AF condition should be led to perform better to maintain a possible unusual privilege. This hypothesis was suggested by J. B. Rijsman on the basis of a pilot study which he conducted in Tilburg.

3 *Effect of social origin on the interpretation of the social conditions of the task*   While there is social distance between *S* and *E* for both privileged and underprivileged children, this is greater for the underprivileged. Hence differences due to both components of Hypothesis 2 should be greater for them.

Treatment for results

Criteria for conservation   *S*'s performance was evaluated on a 7-point scale ranging from no sign of conserving behaviour to full spontaneous mastery. This scale is finer than the one normally used; it takes account of discrepancies occurring on different judgements in the same test.

Non-conservers

NNC: Those *S*s who give no conserving judgments and cannot even predict what the level of juice in A^1 will be, when it is returned from C to itself.

NC: *S*s who predict constant equality of levels in A and A^1, but who judge amount has changed when the juice is poured into beakers of different dimensions. They pour equal *levels* of juice into E and F.

Intermediate

I_1: These *S*s behave like non-conservers in response to the first three questions but give a conserving judgment after the counter-suggestion. In the second part they pour unequal levels into E and F (visual compensation with no measurement).

I_2 : These Ss oscillate between conserving and non-conserving judgments throughout the test corresponding to none of the patterns described previously. They are not conservers.

Conservers

C_0 : While giving conserving judgments and supporting reasons during the first part of the pre-test, these Ss display non-conserving behaviour in the second part (i.e. they pour equal levels into E and F).

C_1 : These Ss give conserving judgments in the first part and make visual compensation when pouring into E and F.

C_2 : As C_1 but these Ss use beaker E^1 in the second part as a means of measuring the correct quantity for beaker F.

The Rank Sum Test with extensive ties was used to test trends where only two groups were contrasted; when three or more groups were used Jonckheere's general version of the test was used (Leach, 1979).

RESULTS

Hypothesis 1 The privileged children displayed a significantly higher level of mastery of conservation than the underprivileged children (The Rank Sum Test with extensive ties, $z = 3.97, p = 0.0001$).

TABLE 1
Cognitive level on conservation of liquid (pre-test) as a function of social origin

Social origin	Cognitive level							
	NNC	NC	I_1	I_2	C_0	C_1	C_2	N
Underprivileged	3	74	1	3	9	16	2	108
Privileged	1	16	3	1	13	14	3	51
N	4	90	4	4	22	30	5	159

Hypothesis 2 The Experimenter-Child condition gave higher performance than the dolls' condition ($z = 2.27, p = 0.01$) (see Table 2). These contextual differences yielded this difference, although they were effected only for the first part of the procedure.

Contrary to prediction, whether the child kept beaker A (AF) or changed it for the wider, shorter beaker C (CE) did not seem to make any difference ($z = 0.35, p = 0.36$) (see Table 3). This will be examined further later.

TABLE 2
Cognitive level on conservation of liquid (pre-test) as a function of
social conditions of task

Participants	Cognitive level							
	NNC	NC	I_1	I_2	C_0	C_1	C_2	N
Experimenter-Child	0	40	4	2	15	16	4	81
Dolls	4	50	0	2	7	14	1	78
N	4	90	4	4	22	30	5	159

TABLE 3
Cognitive level on conservation of liquid (pre-test) as a function of
Who has Which Beaker

Beaker possession	Cognitive level							
	NNC	NC	I_1	I_2	C_0	C_1	C_2	N
S has A and keeps it	2	43	1	3	10	17	2	78
S has A and changes it for C	2	47	3	1	12	13	3	81
N	4	90	4	4	22	30	5	159

TABLE 4
Cognitive level on conservation of liquid (pre-test) as a function of
social origin and social conditions of task

Social origin	Cognitive level							
	NNC	NC	I_1	I_2	C_0	C_1	C_2	N
Underprivileged								
Experimenter-Child	0	32	1	2	5	9	2	51
Dolls	3	42	0	1	4	7	0	57
N	3	74	1	3	9	16	2	108
Privileged								
Experimenter-Child	0	8	3	0	10	7	2	30
Dolls	1	8	0	1	3	7	1	21
N	1	16	3	1	13	14	3	51

Hypothesis 3 In Table 4 it appears that privileged children were unaffected by the manipulation of social context ($z = 0.37, p = 0.35$) and that the effect was due entirely to the behaviour of the underprivileged children ($z = 1.90, p = 0.028$). Keeping beaker A or exchanging it for beaker C again appeared to have no consequences for either privileged or underprivileged children (see Table 4).

EVALUATION OF RESULTS

When we derived Hypothesis 2 about the effects of social conditions upon performance, we reasoned in terms of the *whole* population of subjects; we were assuming general psychological principles. This is a traditional approach even when between-subjects variance is expected. In some respects the evidence appeared to support the validity of this assumption (Experiment-Child versus Dolls effect), but once this 'general' effect was analysed for sub-groups, its generality disappeared; it was seen to hold only for children in the underprivileged group. While this might be viewed as stemming from 'faulty' sampling and the application of statistical techniques to the whole sample before testing for differences within sub-groups, we may note that the empirical precedent from which the prediction was derived led us to expect a general rather than a specific to one group effect. [This is a frightening aspect of too much research in psychology and education. Theoretical models are erected which are literally global and universal. While these sometimes allow for there being *inter-individual* differences (often relegated to an 'error term' in the statistical analysis), these models seldom allow for *inter-group* differences. The subjects are usually chosen at random from the population regardless of their sociological characteristics.]

This is not simply an issue of the adequacy of the sampling. What should be the principles of sampling? What should be considered a proper population when planning research? Which wider social group memberships should be treated as possible relevant sources of variance? Whatever answers are given and whatever results are obtained, how can the interpretation be erected to the status of a 'general law', when it has been tested only on a specified population? And to understand that it is a specific population one should turn to sociology for help in defining the population and the proper criteria for sampling it.

And when typologies are drawn up, there remains the difficult task of interpreting the nature of the reality of the underlying categorisation erected: is it social or biological – or has it been induced by the methodology used? This last is as important a matter in psychology as in physics.

In respect of the particular study reported we have to disentangle the relevance of sex and social origin. Were the sex groups 'socially equivalent' or not?

Secondary analysis by sex, social origin and social conditions

These considerations led us to look back at the results and make a post hoc analysis. Was there another social categorisation, i.e. another sampling criterion, against which the subjects distributed non-randomly. For example, were there sex differences?

Taking the whole sample there was no statistical difference between the performances of the boys and girls, although there was a trend in favour of the latter ($z = 1.38, p = 0.08$) (see Table 5). This unexpected trend could have been due to there being proportionately more boys

TABLE 5

Cognitive level on conservation of liquid (pre-test) as a function of sex and social origin

Sex	Social origin	Cognitive level							
		NNC	NC	I_1	I_2	C_0	C_1	C_2	N
	Privileged	0	13	2	1	6	8	2	32
Boys	Underprivileged	2	27	0	1	2	11	2	45
	N	2	40	2	2	8	19	4	77
	Privileged	1	3	1	0	7	6	1	19
Girls	Underprivileged	1	47	1	2	7	5	0	63
	N	2	50	2	2	14	11	1	82
	N	4	90	4	4	22	30	5	159

than girls in the privileged group however. From an analysis controlling for social origins nothing emerged that helped to clarify the matter (priviledged group, $z = 0.88, p = 0.18$; underprivileged group, $z = 1.26, p = 0.10$ – in favour of boys). However within sex groups social origin discriminated between the girls ($z = 4.03, p = 0.00003$) much more strongly than it did between the boys ($z = 1.47, p = 0.07$). Should there have been a bias in the parental declaration of their occupations for the boys, that would have weakened any social origin effect in the results and that would also explain the over-representation of boys in our sample. If such was the case then it still remains plausible that boys tended to perform better than the girls overall.

Did social conditions operate equally for boys and girls? As Table 6 shows, they did not. There was no strong difference between

TABLE 6

Conservation as a function of experimental conditions, social conditions, sex and social origin

Sex	Social origin[a]	Condition	Conservation level							
			NNC	NC	I_1	I_2	C_0	C_1	C_2	N
Boys	P	Experimenter/Child	0	7	2	0	4	4	2	19
	U		0	11	0	0	0	4	2	17
	P	Dolls	0	6	0	1	2	4	0	13
	U		2	16	0	1	2	7	0	28
Girls	P	Experimenter/Child	0	1	1	0	6	3	0	11
	U		0	21	1	2	5	5	0	34
	P	Dolls	1	2	0	0	1	3	1	8
	U		1	26	0	0	2	0	0	29
Boys	P	Beaker A kept (AF)	0	8	0	1	5	5	0	19
	U		0	10	0	0	1	5	2	18
	P	Changes for C (CE)	0	5	2	0	1	3	2	13
	U		2	17	0	1	1	6	0	27
Girls	P	Beaker A kept (AF)	1	1	1	0	2	3	0	8
	U		1	24	0	2	2	4	0	33
	P	Changes for C (CE)	0	2	0	0	5	3	1	11
	U		0	23	1	0	5	1	0	30

[a]P, privileged; U, underprivileged

the experimenter-child and dolls conditions for boys ($z = 0.99$, $p = 0.16$), but the difference was highly significant for girls ($z = 2.56$, $p = 0.005$). Does this mean that the girls behaved like the underprivileged group did in the analysis testing the second hypothesis – in spite of or precisely because of the fact that dolls are usually more familiar to them than to boys?

Table 7 presents the results concerning the effect of the type of beaker received by the child. There were no differences for either boys ($z = 0.97$, $p = 0.16$) or girls ($z = 0.53$, $p = 0.29$).

From these results concerning the impact of the social context in this sample, sex was as much a relevant dimension of categorisation as social origin for performance. Just how these two are associated must await further exploration because of the sample's characteristics, but we can see the summary of the behaviour quite clearly in Table 8.

None of the four groups showed any effect on performance deriving from the type of beaker used. Boys showed no effect deriv-

TABLE 7
Conservation as a function of social origin and sex

Sex	Social origin[a]	Conservation level							
		NNC	NC	I_1	I_2	C_0	C_1	C_2	N
Boys	P	0	13	2	1	6	8	2	32
	U	2	27	0	1	2	11	2	45
	N	2	40	2	2	8	19	4	77
Girls	P	1	3	1	0	7	6	1	19
	U	1	47	1	2	7	5	0	63
	N	2	50	2	2	14	11	1	82

[a]P, privileged;   U, underprivileged

ing from the Experimenter-Child versus Dolls manipulation; neither did privileged girls. However the effect of the underprivileged girls was strong ($z = 2.74$, $p = 0.003$). The particular manipulation of social conditions of context was therefore very pertinent to estimates of the performance of this particular social group.

TABLE 8
Summary of the effects of variables on conservation

Subject variables	Experimental conditions			
	E/C *vs* Dolls		Beaker	Effect
	z	p	z	p
Boys, privileged	0.34	0.36	0.34	0.36
Girls, privileged	0.00	0.50	0.38	0.35
Boys, underprivileged	0.51	0.30	1.22	0.11
Girls, underprivileged	2.74	0.003	0.08	0.53

Study 2: Social context and learning

In Study 1 we have seen how children from different social categories reacted on the cognitive level to different social conditions of tasks performance. An apparently similar situation was not socially equivalent for all subjects. What applies to task performance may apply equally importantly to learning. Our thesis is that the same mechanisms are at work in both, and the second study observes the consequences for different social groups of providing different social conditions of learning.

There is still a lack of specific research methods and conceptual frameworks (Brun and Conne, 1979) for observing *directly* the dynamics of learning and the organisation of operatory structures. In Study 2 we limited ourselves to the construction of different situations likely to lead to different levels of learning, and we had to make inferences about the dynamics of the learning from the observable outcomes.

In a previous set of experiments reported elsewhere (Doise *et al.*, 1975: Perret-Clermont, 1980; Mugny *et al.*, 1981; Doise and Mugny, 1981), we have shown that when presented with certain kinds of interactions with partners about a cognitive problem, children who were non-conservers at pre-test were likely to display conserving behaviour on the post-test. Subjects were particularly likely to benefit when the interaction involves *socio-cognitive conflict* with one or more partners.

In the case of conservation a non-conserving child who has the necessary operatory prerequisites will be more likely to grasp and structure the idea of conservation, *viz.* learn it, when his partner is a conserver and is therefore proposing and defending a different answer than when his partner is a non-conserver making responses similar to those of the subject himself. In particular, non-conserving subjects interacting with conservers in a task requiring them to share some juice using beakers of unequal dimensions show more progress on post-test than those sharing with a non-conserving peer.

This hypothesis of the role of socio-cognitive conflict in development allows us to offer an alternative explanation for the demonstrated benefits of 'modelling' as a stimulus for conceptual growth (cf. Rosenthal and Zimmerman, 1978). We suggest that the presentation of a model may set into action a social conflict between the child's own initial perception of a problem and the one displayed by the person he is asked to observe. He is asked to overcome this conflict.

We would additionally suggest however that mere presentation of an alternative is less likely to induce socio-cognitive conflict than the direct confrontation of a true interchange with a partner; in such a dialogue the child will be more directly and contingently, involved in justifying (and if he fails, restructuring) his point of view. Confronted by a model alone the child has to abstract the meaning of the message that is there to be conveyed. He may also be puzzled as to why he is being presented with a model! The differences between modelling and direct interchange with a more advanced partner should be reflected both in the number of children likely to be affected by the experiences and by the extent of progress if they do change.

METHOD

Subjects

The sample of children was drawn from the population of Study 1. Children at the intermediate stage of conservation (I_1, I_2) readily learn to progress to the more advanced stage of conservation (Inhelder, Sinclair and Bovet, 1974), and hence only subjects who were non-conversers on the pre-test (NNC and NC) were retained in the sample for the second phase of the investigation. Other reasons such as absence, etc. reduced the sample to 69 subjects.

Among these only 11 were from the privileged social group; they were all assigned to Condition 2 (modelling) (see below). The other 58 from the underprivileged group were assigned as follows: Condition 1, 12 (3 boys, 9 girls); Condition 2, 19 (7 boys, 12 girls); Condition 3, 27 (12 boys, 15 girls).

Materials

Post-test materials were similar to pre-test beakers, but additional ones were included: D, which was taller and thinner than A and A^1; G and G^1 which were as tall as A and A^1 but wider; H which was shorter and wider than G and G^1 (see Fig. 2).

Experimental conditions and procedure

Children were seen twice after the pre-test. They experienced an 'experimental session' about two weeks after the pre-test and an individual post-test, essentially the same as the pre-test, approximately seven days after this.

Experimental session   The experimental session provided opportunities for learning in an interpersonal situation. Each *S* experienced interaction with a partner of one of three kinds: (*i*) Sharing juice with a peer who was a conserver on the pre-test; (*ii*) a situation in which conserving behaviour was modelled by a male adult; (*iii*) sharing juice with a peer who was a non-conserver on the pre-test.

Subjects in the peer interaction conditions (1 and 3) were asked to share between themselves some fruit juice presented in an opaque bottle, as described by Perret-Clermont (1980, p. 46); they were given beakers A and D and told they had to share the juice, and when agreement had been reached that they could drink the juice (if they wished to do so). Beaker A^1 was put at their disposal. In Condition 1 the non-conserving *S* was given the beaker A, while his conserving partner had the taller, thinner beaker D. The non-conserving *S* was given the opaque bottle and asked to start the sharing. In Condition

3, inevitably half the experimental Ss had A and half D, half of each beginning the sharing.

In Condition 2 the children individually observed the twin dolls. Initially S was asked to pour equal shares for the dolls; one having beaker A, the other having beaker D. Beaker A^1 was at his disposal. This procedure was then repeated and modelled by the co-experimenter who behaved as a conserver while S was invited to observe how he did it. (Because the child was a non-conserver matching liquids on levels, he was exposed to a result different from his own by the model.) Once the sharing had been completed by the adult, S was offered both beakers and invited to choose and drink from one of them. Throughout, the adult's behaviour was matched as closely as possible to the behaviour of the previous conserving child to control for the information made available to the child in both experimental groups.

Post-test   The first two parts of the post-test were like the pre-test, except that the countersuggestion was made after the fourth item. Children who had begun the pre-test in the Experimenter-Child condition began the post-test with the Dolls' conditions and vice versa. Similar controls were exercised for the distribution of beakers A and C, and E and F.

In a third part of the post-test S was required to pour equal quantities of juice for himself and E, one of whom had a beaker D and the other C (C was much shorter and wider than D). Beakers A and A^1 were at their disposal if they wished to use them. Half the children were given D, while the experimenter had C; for the other half this was reversed.

Finally E poured equal levels of fruit juice into the unequal beakers G and H (H was wider than G) and left G^1 empty. E then asked S what he thought about it. E additionally asked S to predict the level the juice would reach if poured from H to G. Those Ss who had had beaker D received H at this point and those who had had C received E.

The post-test ended with a task involving questions about the conservation of matter, using equal balls of plasticine, one of which was transformed by E into a pancake and back to a ball after judgements and predictions about quantity had been made. Two other transformations were also made: into a sausage and into 8–10 pieces.

Hypotheses

Hypothesis 1   Given the relatively strong learning effects anticipated, even in Condition 2 we expected similar post-test performances of Ss from the privileged and underprivileged social groups. Given adequate conditions (i.e. 1 and 2, but not 3) all children should learn. The effects under Condition 2 should be greatest for underprivileged girls, who have more to learn and whose final performance should reach the levels of the other groups.

Hypothesis 2   From previous research we would rank-order the three conditions in descending order of strength: 1, 2, 3. Condition 1 minimises social distance between interactants, personally involves S, and makes the cognitive conflict explicit; it should induce greater change than Condition 2 which leaves the basis of socio-cognitive conflict implicit and has high social distance. Condition 2 should be stronger than Condition 3 which has low social distance, but affords no socio-cognitive conflict. Underprivileged girls who have more to learn should be more sensitive to this.

Because subject numbers were likely to become small when testing Hypothesis 2, the tests made were confined to trend tests of the hierarchy 1, 2 and 3, and were not extended to comparisons between each and every other condition.

Hypothesis 3   We also expected that the 'experimental history' of S during the study would affect behaviour on the post-test. In particular those S who had shown sensitivity to the Experimenter-Child versus Dolls condition in the pre-test (*viz.* underprivileged girls) should react to this dimension on the post-test following experience of Condition 2, modelling – the child is external to the problem, as in the sharing of the juice between two dolls in the pre-test, and communication is less contingent.

However we would expect this differentiation to disappear when learning occurs after the directly involving interaction in Conditions 1 and 3.

We would also expect Conditions 1 and 3 to have differential effects on post-test behaviour. In Condition 1 Ss will have seen beaker D (thinner than A and 'perceptually' holding 'more' juice therefore) given to their conserving peer and will have heard him justify the fairness with conserving arguments about the apparent inequality of juice in spite of their equal social status. Subjects who then receive beaker A on the post-test and have to share with an adult who receives a C glass (wider and smaller) should consequently transfer more readily to the new situation in spite of the inequality of social status between adult and child and perform better than their peers who receive beaker C. However in Condition 3, Ss will not have heard such conserving arguments and might remember the experimental situation as an opportunity to share equally among peers.

Hence in the post-test the relative social status of adult and child should be important. They will feel that getting as much juice as the adult at the start is unfair and getting more (when the adult pours his own juice into C) even more awkward! It might even be suggested that those Ss who are given beaker A and had to transfer the juice into the wider beaker C may be afraid of losing the advantage they had been granted at the start and struggle (cognitively) to preserve it.

Treatment of results

The criteria used to assess performance for the first two sub-tests were the same as those used in the pre-test of Study 1 (Index 1). A second index (Index 2) took into account the whole post-test performance (including the third sub-test with beakers C and D): subjects were given one point for each correct answer.

RESULTS

Tables 9 and 10 set out the conservation performance on the post-test for all Ss. Table 11 summaries the differences found.

TABLE 9

Conservation levels of privileged boys and girls on post-test following modelling Condition 2

Sex	Conservation level							
	NNC	NC	I_1	I_2	C_0	C_1	C_2	N
Boys	0	4	0	0	2	1	0	7
Girls	0	3	0	0	0	1	0	4
N	0	7	0	0	2	2	0	11

Hypothesis 1   The summary of results in Table 11 shows no effects of either social origin or sex on the post-tests. This confirms the prediction that social origin would cease to be differentially associated with test performance and shows that the underprivileged girls 'recovered' from their earlier relatively poorer performance.

Hypothesis 2   Tables 12, 13 and 14 set out the results relevant to the hierarchy of effects between Conditions 1, 2 and 3 (interaction with C > modelling > interaction with NC) (Jonckheere test with ties). It was predicted that underprivileged girls would be most likely to exhibit this effect as they were the most likely to learn most being

TABLE 10

Post-test conservation levels as a function of experimental conditions and sex

	Conditions	Sex	Conservation level							
			NNC	NC	I_1	I_2	C_0	C_1	C_2	N
1	Interaction with	Boys	0	1	0	0	1	1	0	3
	conserver	Girls	0	3	0	0	4	2	0	9
		N	0	4	0	0	5	3	0	12
2	Interaction with	Boys	0	3	0	0	2	0	0	7
	modelling adult	Girls	0	6	0	0	5	0	1	12
		N	0	9	0	0	7	2	1	19
3	Interaction with	Boys	0	8	1	0	1	2	0	12
	non-conserver	Girls	0	9	0	2	4	0	0	15
		N	0	17	1	2	5	2	0	27

TABLE 11

Synopsis of post-test conservation level differences as a function of social origin, sex, and intervention conditions

Group		Difference	z	p
Condition 1	underprivileged	Sex	0.00	0.50
Condition 3	underprivileged	Sex	0.01	0.50
Condition 2	underprivileged	Sex	0.31	0.38
	Privileged	Sex	0.12	0.45
	All Ss	Sex	0.03	0.39
		Social origin	0.53	0.25
All Conditions	all Ss	Sex	0.06	0.47
		Social origin	0.33	0.37
	Boys	Social origin	0.01	0.49
	Girls	Social origin	0.38	0.35

the weaker on the pre-tests). The effect was predicted for the initial post-test, on the generalisation items of the post-test, and on the conservation of matter.

For the underprivileged girls the hierarchy was present both on initial post-test and on this score supplemented with the generalisation items; it was not present for the conservation of matter scores. For boys the effect did not achieve significance for Index 1; it did on Index 2 in which the generalisation items were included. (It should be noted that the test for conservation of matter used only a three point scale of achievement.)

TABLE 12
Conservation items passed on post-test as a function of experimental
conditions (underprivileged Ss)

Experimental conditions			Items passed[a]									
			0	1	1	3	4	5	6	7	8	N
1	Interaction with	Boys	0	0	1	0	0	0	1	0	1	3
	conserver	Girls	0	0	2	0	1	2	2	0	2	9
		N	0	0	3	0	1	2	3	0	3	12
2	Interaction with	Boys	0	0	2	1	0	1	1	0	2	7
	modelling adult	Girls	0	0	5	1	0	2	2	2	0	12
		N	0	0	7	2	0	3	?	2	2	19
3	Interaction with	Boys	0	0	8	0	0	2	0	0	2	12
	non-conserver	Girls	0	0	8	1	2	3	1	0	0	15
		N	0	0	16	1	2	5	1	0	2	27

[a]Post-test: 2nd index with generalisation items

TABLE 13
Conservation of matter as a function of experimental conditions
and sex (underprivileged Ss)

Experimental condition			Conservation of matter			
			NC	I	C	N
1	Interaction with	Boys	1	1	1	3
	conserver	Girls	4	1	4	9
		N	5	2	5	12
2	Interaction with	Boys	2	2	3	7
	modelling adult	Girls	4	2	6	12
		N	6	4	9	19
3	Interaction with	Boys	6	3	3	12
	non-conserver	Girls	7	6	2	15
		N	13	9	5	27

Hypothesis 3   The two relevant aspects of social history within the experimental session were the degree of personal involvement, as realised in the peer interactions (Conditions 1 and 3) versus the modelling condition, and the variations in beakers experienced. Data in Table 15, 16 and 17 show the results. As in the pre-test under-

privileged boys did not react to the differences in dolls *vs* experimenter presentation. Neither did the underprivileged girls remain sensitive to this dimension, if they have previously interacted with a peer within the experiment; in contrast observation of the model in condition 2 left them sensitive to the discrimination ($z = 1.90$, $p = 0.028$).

TABLE 14

Synopsis of the relative effects on conservation of the experimental conditions (underprivileged Ss)

Conservation tests		Test of order of Efficacy $1 > 2 > 3$		
		N	z	p
Conservation of liquids	Boys	22	1.30	0.09
(1st index identical to the pre-test index)	Girls	36	1.80	0.03
Conservation of liquids	Boys	22	1.57	0.05
(2nd index with generalisation items)	Girls	36	2.13	0.01
Conservation of matter	Boys	22	0.85	0.19
	Girls	36	1.11	0.13

TABLE 15

Post-test conservation performances as a function of experimental conditions, setting and sex

Experimental manipulation	Conditions of administration	Sex	Conservation level							
			NNC	NC	I_1	I_2	C_0	C_1	C_2	N
2 Modelling adult	Experimenter-Child	Boys	0	1	0	0	1	2	0	4
		Girls	0	1	0	0	4	0	1	6
	Dolls	Boys	0	2	0	0	1	0	0	3
		Girls	0	5	0	0	1	0	0	6
1 With conserver	Experimenter-Child	Boys	0	0	0	0	0	1	0	1
		Girls	0	1	0	0	0	2	0	3
	Dolls	Boys	0	1	0	0	1	0	0	2
		Girls	0	2	0	0	4	0	0	6
3 With non-conserver	Experimenter-Child	Boys	0	4	0	0	1	1	0	6
		Girls	0	4	0	1	2	0	0	7
	Dolls	Boys	0	4	1	0	0	1	0	6
		Girls	0	5	0	1	2	0	0	8

TABLE 16

Post-test conservation performances as a function of type of beaker and experimental conditions

Experimental condition	Beaker type	Sex	Conservation level							
			NNC	NC	I_1	I_2	C_0	C_1	C_2	N
2 Modelling	Beaker A kept (AF condition)	Boys	0	3	0	0	1	1	0	5
		Girls	0	1	0	0	2	0	1	4
	Beaker C kept (CE condition)	Boys	0	0	0	0	1	1	0	2
		Girls	0	5	0	0	3	0	0	8
1 Interaction with conserver	Beaker A kept (AF condition)	Boys	0	0	0	0	1	1	0	2
		Girls	0	0	0	0	1	2	0	3
	Beaker C kept (CE condition)	Boys	0	1	0	0	0	0	0	1
		Girls	0	3	0	0	3	0	0	6
3 Interaction with non-conserver	Beaker A kept (AF condition)	Boys	0	5	1	0	0	1	0	7
		Girls	0	7	0	1	0	0	0	8
	Beaker C kept (CE condition)	Boys	0	3	0	0	1	1	0	5
		Girls	0	2	0	1	4	0	0	7

Table 17 shows that boys were not responsive to the difference in beakers. The girls were differentially responsive if they had experienced conditions 1 or 3 but not if they had been exposed to modelling (Condition 2). After Condition 1, girls performed better if they kept beaker A (as the conserver did) and in Condition 3 after having beaker C (having a struggle not to be deprived?). These results are based on relatively low numbers of subjects and are not very strong; they are important, however, if corroborated in subsequent investigations. Indeed it seems that it is mostly those non-conserving subjects who had beaker A during the social interaction in Condition 3 who exhibited differential reactions to beaker arrangement in the post-test ($z = 2.15$, $p = 0.01$ for girls; $z = 1.42$, $p = 0.07$ for all subjects).

Certainly the results as a whole illustrate that the subjects's immediate social history in the experiment can account for at least part of his later capacity to offer responses in different social settings. We can further see from the 'type of beaker' effects for example that the 'social history' derives its meaning *only within a particular sequence* of events; as a function of prior experience it was either more *or* less facilitative to receive beaker C rather than A in the final post-test. In an important sense these are of course not 'type of beaker' effects, but interactions between the components of the

TABLE 17

Synopsis of post-test conservation effects as a function of all variables

Sex	Conditions of administration	Experimental conditions	N	Statistical effects	
				z	p
Boys	Experimenter-Child	2	7		not tested
	vs Dolls	1	3		not tested
		3	12	0.09	0.53
	Type of beaker	2	7		not tested
	AF *vs* CF	1	3		not tested
		3	12	0.28	0.39
	Distributing first	3	12	0.09	0.53
Girls	Experimenter-Child	2	12	1.90	0.03
	vs Dolls	1	9	0.74	0.22
		3	15	0.03	0.48
	Type of beaker	2	12	1.03	0.15
	AF *vs* CF	1	9	1.54	0.06 (AF > CE)
		3	15	2.14	0.02 (CE > AF)
	Distributing first	3	15	1.39	0.08

experimental history of the subjects and the socio-cognitive characteristics of the context in which the subject must perform. One of the
consequences of this observation is that at different moments in the
learning process the same social group of subjects is not equally
sensitive to the same dimensions, as for example in the case of the
underprivileged girls whose performance was not affected by type of
beaker on the pre-test, but was on the post-tests subsequent to
interchanges with peers.

EVALUATION OF RESULTS

In this experiment we provoked a cognitive structuring in children
in three phases (pre-test, learning session, and post-test) in order to
observe their cognitive evolution in reaction to their social environment. It is apparent that these reactions cannot be understood without taking into account the child's social position within the task
that he is asked to master and his anterior social position with respect
to related tasks. But we still need to refine our conceptual framework to explain how these positions relate to one another. We have
shown that the meaning of given social positions in an experimental

situation can be linked to previous social experience of this situation. But still it needs to be investigated how these social positions created within the experimental setting relate to the subject's positions within the wider social group: why are there no clear differences in our experiment between the boys and the girls of the privileged social group but marked differences in the underprivileged group? Why do boys of the two contrasted social groups differ from the girls? Why do girls in the underprivileged group seem to react like the 'most underprivileged'? If it is obvious that the social status of women and men in our society, of girls and boys within the families, is not equivalent in many situations, it still is not clear how these differences link with differences of the kind displayed in these results.

Learning: A process of performing and communicating within a social context

In earlier research (Perret-Clermont, 1980) evidence was produced that stresses the importance of social interaction and especially of cooperative activities among peers on the same task for the development of cognitive competencies in children. A series of experimental studies of different conditions of social interaction sustained the hypothesis that the socio-cognitive conflicts that these cooperative activities make possible are responsible for cognitive re-structurings that take place. The present experiment also suggests that the more the *object* of this conflict is clear for the child (for instance when he is directly involved, defending his share, etc.) the more it is likely to be fruitful for cognitive development.

But what makes this object clear? How does a child understand what the whole thing is about? How does he come to realise what is expected of him? How does he transfer his thinking from one social situation to another? Several authors have shown how the social components of a situation can affect the quality of a subject's performances. This we have also found in the performances exhibited in Study 1. But the second part of the present experiment tends to show that the same processes that are involved in the performing contexts are at work in the learning contexts. Performing and learning are related processes. When a child is asked to do something in a testing situation he must understand what is asked of him, and this he will do if the intersubjectivity he shares with the experimenter is sufficient and if he has practice in communicating his appraisal of the task in the form he is asked to produce. If not, he will need to learn to decode and interpret what is left implicit and what the expected answers are. A closer look at the effects of countersuggestions could be interesting in that respect since there is experimental evidence (Mugny, Doise and Perret-Clermont, 1976; Lévy, 1980) that these do have a cognitive effect on the subject. We would suggest that unless the subject already has full mastery and practice of the specific requirements involved, he will always be elaborating his response within the testing situation in which he has to produce it: 'learning' there, on the spot, to produce it. This elaboration will be for the subject more or less facilitated by the social context, its explicitness and its meaning within the social relation in which the child is involved.

At present, in the light of our current experimental data, it seems to us that the main difference found among the four social groups studied is that underprivileged subjects need more than their privileged peers and girls more than boys to be given *during the testing sessions* opportunities for cooperating - *and hence for engaging in socio-cognitive conflict*! - with the adult experimenter.

Given such opportunities either via direct adult-child interaction about a real activity that makes communication contingent or via the communication of what the expected behaviour is (modelling), or being introduced in a session in which socio-cognitive conflicts are facilitated by a peer presenting a different point of view – the differences in performances between the social groups can be considerably decreased.

Acknowledgements

We are pleased to acknowledge the financial support of the Fonds National de la Recherche Scientifique (W. Doise, G. Mugny, A-N Perret-Clermont, No. 1-706-078). We wish to thank W. Doise for the support he gave us in carrying out this study, M. Floriano for his help with data collecting, and L-O. Pochon for help in computer programming. We are very grateful to W. P. Robinson for his patient help with the translation of this contribution from French into English.

References

Bernstein, B. (1971). "Class, Codes and Control" Vol. 1. Routledge, London
Bernstein, B. (1975). "Class, Codes and Control" Vol. II. Routledge, London

Brun, J. and Conne, F. (1979). Approches en psychopédatogie des mathémati-ques. *Cahier No. 12 de la section des sciences de l'éducation.* Université de Genève, Genève

Coll-Salvador, C., Coll-Ventura, C. and Mira-Mestres, N. (1974). Genesis de la clasificacion y medios socio-economicos. Genesis de la seriacion y medios socio-economicos. *Annuaros de Psicologia* 10, 53–99

Dasen, P. R. (1977). Are cognitive process universal? A contribution to cross-cultural Piagetian psychology. *In* "Studies in Cross-cultural Psychology" Vol. 1. (M. Warren, Ed.). Academic Press, London

Doise, W., Dionnet, S. and Mugny, G. (1978). Conflict socio-cognitif, marquage social et développment cognitif. *Cahiers de psychologie* 21, 4

Doise, W., Meyer, G. and Perret-Clermont, A-N (1976). Représentations psycho-sociologiques d'élèves en fin de scolarité obligatoire *Cahier No. 2 de la section des sciences de l'education.* Université de Genève, Genève

Doise, W. and Mugny, G. (1981). "Le développement social de l'intelligence". Interéditions, Paris (in press)

Doise, W. and Mugny, G. and Perret-Clermont, A-N. (1975). Social interaction and the development of cogntiive operations. *European Journal of Social Psychology* 5, 367–383

Haroche, C. and Pêcheux, M. (1972). Facteurs socio-économiques et résolutions de problèmes. *Bulletin du CERP* 21, 101–117

Inhelder, B., Sinclair, H. and Bovet, M. (1974). "Apprentissages et Structures de la Connaissance". Presses Universitaires de France, Paris

Katz, I. (1973). Alternatives to a personality-deficit interpretation of Negro under-achievement. *In* "Psychology and Race" (P. Watson, Ed.). Penguin, Harmondsworth

Labov, W. (1972). The study of language in its social context. *In* "Language and Social Context" (P. Giglioli, Ed.). Penguin Education, Harmondsworth

Leach, G. (1979). "Introduction to Statistics: a non-parametrical approach for the Social Sciences". Wiley, New York

Lévy, M. (1980). Mémoire de thèse. Texte polycopié. Université de Genève, Genève

Mugny, G., Doise, W. and Perret-Clermont, A-N. (1976). Conflict de centrations et progrès cognitif. *Bulletin de Psychologie* 29, 199–204

Mugny, G., Perret-Clermont, A-N. and Doise, W. (1981). Interpersonal coordina-tions and sociological differences in intellectual growth. *In* "Progress in Applied Social Psychology" (G. M. Stephenson and J. H. Davis, Eds). Wiley, Chichester (in press)

Perret, J-F. (1978a). Contribution à une psychologie cognitive de l'enfant en situation pédagogique. *Communication au 'Congrès Développement de l'Enfant'.* CERCI, Lisbon

Perret, J-F. (1978b). A propos d'une expérience de 'travail indépendant': quel-ques réflexions psychopédagogiques. *Cahier No. 6 de la section des sciences de l'éducation* Université de Genève, Genève

Perret-Clermont, A-N. (1980). "Social Interaction and Cognitive Development in Children". Academic Press, London

Piaget, J. and Szeminska, A. (1941). "La Genèse du Nombre". Delachaux et Niestle, Neuchâtel and Paris. [English edition 1952, "The Child's Concep-tion of Number". Routledge, London]

Rommetweit. R. (1976). On Piagetian cognitive operations, semantic competence and message structure in adult-child communication. *In* "The Social Context of Language" (I. Markova, Ed.). Wiley, Chichester

Rosenthal, T. L. and Zimmerman, B. J. (1978). "Social Learning and Cognition". Academic Press, New York

Schaffer, H. R. (1979). Acquiring the concept of the dialogue. *In* "Psychological Development from Infancy" (M. H. Bornstein and W. Kessen, Eds). Erlbaum, New Jersey, 297–305

Schubauer-Leoni, M-L, Perret-Clermont, A-N (1980). Interactions sociales et représentations symboliques dan le cadre de problèmes additifs. *Revue Française de Didactique des Mathématiques* 1, 3, 297–300

10

Conversational Tactics and the Advancement of the Child's Understanding about Referential Communication

E. J. Robinson

Introduction

A number of authors have given advice about how adults should speak to children with the aim of improving their verbal communication skills. Certain strategies of language use are recommended, but the possibility that the child could benefit from talk *about* language use or *about* the process of communication seems not to have been considered. The assumption seems to be that the adult's own use of language when talking with the child somehow enables the child to extend his own language skills, and that this is all that is necessary for advancement of the child's skills. For example, C. and H. Rosen (1973) suggest that 'there are kinds of talk that are fanned into life and sustained by the teacher ... The teacher urges into articulation what is only half-formed and moves children towards new verbal ambitions' (p. 42). Similarly, Tough (1977) writes that *'Dialogue* is the means by which communication skills can most effectively promoted' (p. 21). She lists five strategies which the teacher may use in her attempts to 'foster' the child's use of language. In her discussion of these strategies there is no consideration of the possibility that the teacher might focus *directly* upon the quality of the child's utterance: 'While appraising what the child is doing with language, the teacher will look for opportunities in the course of the dialogue to help him think in ways that are new for him ... The teacher continues the dialogue, looking for a natural extension of the child's skill' (p. 24). Leach (1977) makes explicit that parents should not inform a child directly about the quality of his utterance: if the child says 'Why are bulls?', parents are advised 'Try not to say

"I don't know what you mean". Try instead to think what she is likely to mean' (p. 417).

Although supportive and extending conversation of the kind recommended by these authors may be important in the early stages of language acquisition, I shall argue that it is of little or no help in informing the child about certain aspects of the process of verbal referential communication. These authors ignore certain problems which the child appears to have, problems which could be lessened if he were given more accurate information about the quality of his messages. On the other hand saying to the child 'I don't know what you mean' and explaining why, may help him to learn about the requirements of effective communication.

I shall first present evidence to demonstrate deficiencies in the young child's understanding about verbal referential communication, and then show how his problems are maintained by the way adults commonly interact with young children.

Deficiencies in the young child's understanding about verbal referential communication

Evidence from a number of authors demonstrates that younger children are less likely than older ones (e.g. 5-year-olds as compared with 7-year-olds) to make comparisons between intended referent and other potential referents when they are formulating messages, interpreting them, or judging them. The evidence is consistent with the view that the young child does not know that a message should refer uniquely to whatever the speaker has in mind.

Typically in this work, a child speaker is asked to describe verbally one of a set of items for a real or imaginary listener. The speaker's task is to produce a message which identifies uniquely for his listener one of the items in the set.

Quality of messages

Whitehurst and his colleagues used a procedure in which the child was asked to identify for a listener one of a pair of triangles. Whitehurst and Sonnenschein (1978a) found that 5-year-olds gave informative messages when all that changed over trials was the value of the relevant dimension of the referent (which was marked for the child). For example, the referent might always be either the red triangle or the black triangle, while all the other differences remained constant over trials. When the relevant dimension varied over trials, however, (it might be colour, size or pattern), these children failed to give informative messages.

Judgments of message quality

Patterson and a number of colleagues (referred to by Patterson and Kister, 1978) gave kindergarten to Fourth grade children messages which referred to between one and eight potential referents. The youngest children judged all the messages to be adequate; the older ones were more likely to spot the inadequacy of the ambiguous messages.

Question-asking to reduce ambiguity

Several authors report that younger children are less likely than older ones to ask questions to clarify an ambiguous message (Alvy, 1968; Cosgrove and Patterson, 1977; Ironsmith and Whitehurst, 1978). Timidity appears not to be the problem for the younger children; they may simply not know that attempts to reduce ambiguity are appropriate.

Judgments of quality of questions

Bearison and Levey (1977) asked children from kindergarten to fourth grade to judge whether questions about sentences which had been read out were 'good' or 'bad'. The younger children were less skilful than the older ones at identifying the inadequate ones as 'bad'.

Judgments of quality of instructions

Markman (1977) gave 6-, 7- and 8-year-olds inadequate instructions as to how to perform a trick or play a game. She assessed whether the children had recognised the inadequacies by asking a sequence of questions which asked more and more explicitly whether anything had been omitted. The 6-year-olds tended to recognise inadequacies only when they attempted to carry out the instructions or saw them demonstrated.

Judgments of quality of instructions related to quality of recounting of those instructions

Robinson and Robinson presented children with pictorial instructions describing how to make two objects: a model hen and a papier mâché container. Some parts of the procedure were missing from the instructions. We made explicit that the instructions 'might not be good enough' and asked the children to comment on their quality. We answered any questions they raised about how to make the objects, then asked each child to tell children at another school how to make them (by speaking into a tape recorder), with the pictorial instructions still in front of them. We were interested in relationships between the child's comments on the instructions, that is the extent to which he noticed the omission in them, and the quality of his account of what the instructions were depicting.

We tested 45 children, of whom 25 were aged between 5-4 and 6-9, and 20 from 8;10 to 9;6.

RESULTS AND CONCLUSIONS

(*i*) There was no difference between the younger and the older children in the proportion who said they understood both sets of instructions (i.e. who said both sets were 'good enough' and that there was nothing else they would need to know if they were going to make the objects described): 7 of the 25 younger children answered in this way, as did 5 of the 20 older ones ($\chi^2 = 0.012, p = 0.9$).

(*ii*) Among those who said they did understand a particular set of instructions (either one set or both sets), the older children gave more complete accounts when recording for children at another school than did the younger ones. The children were prompted to give accounts as complete as they could by being asked questions when they said something ambiguous such as 'Then do that', so age differences in verbal fluency were probably not an important factor. The older children gave more information than the younger ones for both objects (*Fisher Exact Probability Tests*: Hen $p = 0.05$; Container $p < 0.01$).

(*iii*) Information given by the experimenter in answer to questions raised by the child was not scored when we evaluated the quality of the child's recording for other children. It was to be expected, therefore, that children who raised no questions (i.e. who judged the instructions to be adequate), would give better accounts than those who raised questions. This was true for the older children, but not for the younger ones: for the younger children, those who said they understood the instructions could give accounts just as poor as those who raised questions. (*Fisher Exact Probability Tests*, difference in quality of account between those who did and did not raise questions: older children, Hen $p = 0.05$; Container $p = 0.05$; younger children, Hen $p > 0.1$; Container $p > 0.1$).

(*iv*) There were differences between the age groups in the kind of question asked by those who did not understand a particular set of instructions (that is, 18 of the younger children and 15 of the older ones). Younger children were more likely than older ones to ask general questions such as 'What's that?' referring to a whole picture or sequence of pictures ($z = 3.8, p < 0.0001$), whereas older children were more likely than younger ones to ask specific questions referring to parts of a picture such as 'How do you get it so it isn't flat?' or 'What's this made of?' (S-test, $z = 2.1, p = 0.03$). It was also more common for older children to ask questions about features completely omitted from the instructions, such as 'I don't quite see how you make the head' when in fact there were no instructions as to how to make the head, although this difference between age groups did not reach statistical significance (S-test, $z = 1.8, p = 0.06$).

These results show that although the children of different ages were equally likely to judge the instructions to be inadequate, the older ones were better than the younger ones at assessing their own understanding. Whereas the older children who said they understood the instructions gave better accounts than did children who identified problems, this was not true of the younger children. Among those who said they did understand, older children gave better accounts than younger ones. Among those who identified problems, older children were better than younger ones at interpreting the pictures and noticing omissions and deficiences. The older children, it appears, were more likely than the younger ones to know whether or not they understood the instructions.

Judgments of message quality and the causes of communication failure

In a number of experiments, Robinson and Robinson have looked at the child's judgments about message adequacy and the causes of communicative success or failure, and have related these to aspects of his communicative performance. In the basic communication evaluation game, child and experimenter sit at opposite ends of a table with a screen across the middle. Both have identical sets of cards; commonly we have used line drawings of men, for example: a man with a red flower, a man with a blue flower, a man holding a red flag up high, a man holding a red flag down low, a man with a black pointed hat, a man with a black top hat. The drawings are chosen so that the child subjects will have a vocabulary adequate to describe the cards, but so that they frequently fail to give descriptions which identify a particular card uniquely. Child and experimenter take turns to be speaker. The speaker's task is to describe one of his drawings so that the other player, the listener, can pick up the same one on his side. The listener's rôle is passive in that he is not invited to ask questions in the face of an ambiguous message. On some of her turns as speaker, the experimenter deliberately gives an ambiguous message which refers to two of the cards, e.g. 'I've chosen one, it's a man with a flower' . . . Whichever one the child picks up, the experimenter shows that she was talking about the other. Communication failure has occurred because the speaker gave an ambiguous message. A similar situation occurs spontaneously on some trials when the child is speaker. Following the communication failure, the child is asked a standard sequence of questions, which we have called the 'Whose fault?' sequence of questions:

'We got different cards, we went wrong that time. Whose fault was that, mine, yours? Why? Did I/you tell you/me properly which one to pick?' If the child says 'No', he is asked 'What should I/you have said?' Finally, he is asked again 'Whose fault was it we went wrong? Why?'

That is, the child is asked to ascribe blame for communication failure, to give his reasons, and to judge whether or not the message was adequate. This questioning occurs when the child is in both the listener and the speaker rôle, and we have found empirically that he blames a particular role rather than an individual (himself or the experimenter).

Age-related differences in answers to the 'whose fault?' sequence of questions   There are strong age-related differences in children's answers to the 'whose fault?' sequence of questions. It is common among 5-year-olds for the listener alone to be blamed for the failure, on the grounds that he chose wrongly, and to judge the ambigous message to be adequate. By ages 7 or 8, it is becoming common for the child to blame the speaker for failure, on the grounds that his message was ambiguous, to judge the message to be inadequate and corrently identify at least one feature missing from the message (Robinson and Robinson, 1976a, b).

Variations of the procedure   Similar results are obtained if the child merely watches dolls sending messages to each other and makes judgments about their communication failures (Robinson and Robinson, 1977b), and if the child comments on more realistic communication failures depicted in drawings (Robinson and Robinson, 1977a). One set of drawings shows a boy, Steven, asking his mother for a drink. His mother gives him an orange drink but he really wanted a green drink. Whose fault was it that Steven did not get the drink he wanted? Younger children blame the mother, who gave the wrong drink, and judge Steven's message to be adequate, whereas older children blame Steven on the grounds that he gave insufficient information about what he wanted. Another modification which yields similar results is to ask the child following communication failure 'How would we make sure we got it right next time?' Children who answer the 'whose fault?' sequence of questions by blaming the speaker, indicate that the message must be improved next time, whereas children who blame only the listener in answer to the 'whose fault?' sequence, do not mention the message but instead suggest that they must 'try harder' or 'get it right' (Robinson and Robinson, 1978b).

Interpretation of results   We interpret these results in terms of the child's knowledge about ambiguous messages and their role in causing communication failure. Whereas children who blame the speaker and correctly identify the ambiguous messages clearly know that an ambiguous message may cause communication failure, those who blame the listener and judge ambiguous messages to be adequate do not reveal such knowledge. This interpretation is supported by data relating the child's judgments about communication failure to aspects of his communicative performance: in certain respects, listener blamers perform as if they were ignorant of the rôle of ambiguous messages in causing communication failure.

Relationships between judgments about ambiguous messages and communicative performance
   (*i*) When they are asked to make the listener's task difficult, speaker blamers but not listener blamers deliberately withhold information from their messages (Robinson and Robinson, 1978a).
   (*ii*) Speaker blamers are more likely than listener blamers to make comparisons between the cards in the set when producing their messages. We conclude this from the finding that speaker blamers improve the quality of their messages more than listener blamers when they can see the total set of cards from which the listener has to choose, as compared with seeing only the card they are to describe for the listener (Robinson and Robinson, 1978b).
   (*iii*) When they are instructing a listener how to build a Lego model which the listener cannot see, speaker blamers give better instructions than listener blamers in three respects: they give better descriptions of the individual pieces needed, give the information in a more appropriate sequence for building, and give more information about the positioning of the pieces.

Relationship between judgments about ambiguous messages and judgments about what was said   Further evidence consistent with the interpretation in terms of the young child's failure to recognise the importance of unique reference in a message comes from data relating judgments about ambiguous messages to judgments about what the speaker actually said.

Subjects   We tested 39 children aged between 5;2 and 6;10.

Procedure   Each child played two versions of the communication evaluation game. Following communication failures with one set of cards the child was asked to judge the adequacy of the message involved (it was in fact always ambiguous). The child was asked, 'Did I tell you enough about my card?' 'Could I have helped you any more?' If the child indicated that the experimenter had not said enough, he was asked 'What should I have said?' Similar questioning was used on up to two occasions when the child gave an ambiguous message and the experimenter chose wrongly. That is, we obtained judgments about the ambiguous messages both when the child was speaker and when he was listener.

Following communication failures with a second set of cards (which was presented first for half the children and second for the other half), the experimenter presented the child with either a disambiguated version of what had actually been said, with a correct reproduction, or with an altered version of the message. For example, if the message had in fact been 'I've got a man with a red flower' (the set of cards contained a big and a small red flower), when presenting the child with the disambiguated version the experimenter would say 'A man with a *big* red flower, is that what I/you said?' (if that was the card the speaker had chosen). If the child disagreed, he was asked 'What did I/you say?' The altered version of the message would be 'A man with a *blue* flower, is that what I/you said?' The three conditions (disambiguated versions, correct reproduction and altered version) were given both when the child was speaker and when he was listener.

RESULTS AND CONCLUSIONS

Each child was scored as successful in his message adequacy judgments if he said on every occasion that the speaker of an ambiguous message had not said enough (or could have helped more) *and* correctly specified what was missing from the message. Otherwise he was scored as unsuccessful. Each child was scored as successful in his judgments of what was said if on every occasion he rejected the disambiguated and altered versions of the ambiguous messages and correctly specified what had actually been said, and if he accepted the correct reproductions. Otherwise he was scored as unsuccessful. All the children correctly rejected the altered versions and accepted the correct reproductions, and there were no differences in either judgments of message adequacy or of what had been said according to whether the message was given by the child or by the experimenter.

However, children did differ in their judgments about the disambiguated versions of the messages, and these were related to their judgments about the ambiguous messages. Of those who successfully judged what was said, 21 were successful in their adequacy judgments and 1 was unsuccessful. Of those who were unsuccessful in judging what was said, 6 were successful in their adequacy judgments and 11 were unsuccessful ($\chi^2 = 13.6, p < 0.001$).

Children who judged ambiguous messages to be adequate also accepted the disambiguated version of the message as being what was actually said, whereas children who judged the ambiguous messages to be inadequate correctly judged that the disambiguated version was not actually produced. The former group of children appeared to be insensitive to the importance of the *extent* of reference of the message; messages which refer to the object the speaker had in mind are perhaps treated as equivalent whether or not they refer to other objects as well. Further evidence supporting this view is presented in Robinson and Robinson (1977b).

Relationship between judgments about ambiguous messages and reformulation of ambiguous messages in response to requests for help If the listener blamer does not understand that a message should identify the intended referent uniquely, then when he is asked to clarify an ambiguous message, he should be less likely than a speaker blamer to add information which reduces the number of choices available to the listener. In an experiment reported in more detail elsewhere (Robinson, 1978), child and experimenter played the communication game with a set of men drawings containing redundancy: all the men had blue flags; all the men with red flowers also wore boots, and all the men with blue flowers also wore shoes. We could code each item of information given by the child in terms of how much it reduced the number of cards to which the total message referred. We tested 58 children aged from 5;7 to 6;2. Following four communication failures the child was asked the 'whose fault?' sequence of questions, and on the basis of his awareness he was placed in one of four categories. Following two ambiguous messages given by the child, the experimenter said 'I don't know which one you mean. Can you help me?' The child's response was coded in terms of the extent to which it reduced the number of choices available to the listener. Although there was no difference between children in the four categories (associated with level of understanding about message inadequacy and the causes of communication failure) according to whether the child said something *new* in response to the request for help, there was a significant increase among children in the more advanced categories in the percentage of responses which reduced the number of choices available to the listener (S-test, p = 0.002). When the quality of message prior to the experimenter's request for help was controlled (in that we considered only messages which referred to two cards), the more advanced the child's answers to the 'whose fault?' sequence of questions, the more likely he was to give helpful information (p = 0.006).

Judgments about adequacy of instructions and behaviour when interpreting ambiguous instructions

The results of a pair of experiments by Flavell and his colleagues (Flavell, Spear, Green and August, 1979) support and extend the results presented above. Flavell and his colleagues asked kindergarten and Second grade children (mean ages 6;0 and 7;11 respectively) to listen to and attempt to carry out recorded instructions for making buildings. The instructions were presented as having been recorded by a girl, Kiersten, who had made the building corresponding to each set of instructions; the child subjects were to attempt to produce buildings exactly like Kiersten's. The children could replay the tape as often as they wished. When they had completed each building, they were asked two questions. Firstly, they were asked whether they thought their building was exactly like Kiersten's or whether it might be different. Secondly, they were asked whether Kiersten had done a good or a bad job of telling how to make the building. The children were videorecorded, and their reactions during building were analysed as well as their answers to the questions. There were 23 building tasks, for which 7 had clear and easy instructions and 16 had instructions which were inadequate in some respect – some had ambiguous references or contradictory directions.

In their answers to the first question (whether their building looked like Kiersten's), kindergarten children were more likely that Second graders to say their building was exactly like Kiersten's, whereas the older children were more likely not to know or to say theirs might be different. In answer to the second question, kindergarten children were more likely to judge that Kiersten had done a good job of telling, whereas Second graders were more likely to identify problems with the inadequate instructions. The analyses of the video-tapes showed that second graders were more likely to show signs of problem detection when they were attempting to carry out inadequate instructions. Some of the kindergarten children showed signs of puzzlement during building but in answer to the questions professed confidence both in their building and in the quality of the instructions. Flavell and his colleagues suggest that

The younger children do not realise the meaning, significance and implications of the transitory feelings of puzzlement, uncertainty, etc. that they may experience during the building period ... The children may be momentarily aware that they do not know which red block Kiersten wants them to use in Task 4 say, but may not interpret this awareness as indicating that a communication problem exists. (p. 43)

They also suggest that having made their interpretation of ambiguous instructions, the young children may forget that there had been a problem.

Consistent with the results of Robinson and Robinson was the finding that some kindergarten children but fewer Second graders said in answer to the first question that they had not carried out the instructions properly: this appears to be spontaneous listener blaming on the part of these children.

Flavell's analysis of the relationships between spontaneous non-verbal and verbal behaviour while attempting to interpret instructions on the one hand, and verbal judgments given after an interpretation has been made on the other, appears to be an important line of inquiry to follow up if we are to establish how the child comes to understand the role of ambiguous messages in causing communication failure.

Ways of improving the young child's performance and understanding about communication

As shown above, the findings of a number of research workers using different techniques are consistent in suggesting that the young child does not recognise the importance of unique reference in verbal communication. However, it appears that relatively simple interventions are effective in improving the young child's performance and/or understanding at least in the short term. The experiments to be described do not meet the criteria of good training experiments in that testing for generalisation and long term effects has been either absent or inadequate, but nevertheless results point to the importance of informing the child what the problem is when communication failure occurs, and telling him what is required of him.

Although it was shown above that young children tend not to make the necessary comparisons between intended referent and other potential referents, this is not necessarily because they cannot perform those comparisons. Robinson and Robinson (1978c) gave children two tasks requiring the same comparisons to be made. One was a description completion task in which the child completed a description of which of a pair of cards was/were turned down. The other task was a message evaluation task. While all children who successfully made the comparisons in the message evaluation task also made them in the description completion task, there were a number of children who were successful in the latter but not in the former: they could perform the comparisons but apparently did not recognise the relevance of doing so when judging the quality of messages.

Instructing the child to tell about differences

Whitehurst and Sonnenschein (1978b) used their procedure with pairs of triangles, one of which was designated for the child to describe for a listener. They asked 5-year-olds either to 'Tell me about the triangle with the star above it so that I know which triangle you are talking about' or to 'Tell me how the triangle with the star above it looks different from the other triangle'. The relevant dimension was varied over trials; it could be colour, size or pattern. The children who were asked to describe differences gave 73% informative messages, whereas those given the alternative instructions gave only 50%.

In a subsequent experiment, Whitehurst and Sonnenschein compared four methods of training children to give informative messages. The most effective method was to ask the child to tell so that the listener knew which one he was talking about, and then give him feedback about whether or not he had described differences: 'That's good, you told me how the triangle with the star above it was different from the other' or 'That's wrong, you did not tell me how the triangle with the star above it was different from the other'. This treatment produced 83% informative messages. Less successful treatments were (*i*) giving advice at the outset to describe differences with or without feedback about whether this had been done; (*ii*) asking the child to 'Tell which one' as in the most effective method but not giving informative feedback; and (*iii*) asking the child to 'Tell which one' and then give feedback about whether the message in fact told the listener which one had the star above it. Ignoring the details of these results, it is apparent that if the child is told to describe how the intended referent is different from a non-referent, he may be able to do so even though without these explicit instructions he does not.

Instructing the child about the extent of ambiguity in his message

(*i*) *Reformulation* In the experiment described earlier in which children who gave ambiguous messages were asked 'I don't know which one you mean. Can you help me?' we found that the more advanced the child's answers to the 'Whose fault?' sequence of questions (and therefore, we assume, the greater his understanding about ambiguous messages and their rôle in causing communication failure), the more likely his response was to give information which reduced the number of choices available to the listener. However, in a further experiment (Robinson, 1978) we gave the child more information about the listener's problem. The experimenter said 'I've got four/two (or however many cards the message referred to) like that, I'm not sure which one you mean. Can you help me?' Giving this additional information to the child brought the performance of the listener blamers up to that of the speaker blamers; there were no discernible differences between children in the different blame categories, even though there was still room for improvement among the children in each category. It appears that the listener blamers were capable of producing a message which referred uniquely to their chosen card, but that they needed to be prompted into doing so. Although the child may not be aware of the relationship betwen an ambiguous message and communication failure, if his listener points out in what way the message is ambiguous, the child knows what to do to help.

(*ii*) *Effects on performance and understanding* In another experiment (Robinson, 1978) we examined the effects on performance and understanding of giving the child explicit information about the inadequacies of his messages.

Subjects We tested 47 children aged from 5;2 to 6;5.

Procedure Each child played a game with the experimenter which involved dressing dolls. The players sat on either side of an opaque screen and had dolls with identical sets of clothes. One player selected a garment for her doll to wear and then described it for the other player so that he could choose the same garment. After each garment had been described, the players checked to see whether they had got the same one. The game was in three parts: at the beginning and the end, the game was played with a girl doll who had eight each of skirts, bouses and cardigans. At the beginning (the pre-test), only the child had turns as speaker, and at the end (the post-test), only the experimenter did so. In these pre- and post-tests, when an ambiguous message led to the listener's choosing wrongly, the child was asked the 'whose fault?' sequence of questions. In the middle part of the game, which involved boy dolls with eight each of six types of garment, the experimenter was listener throughout and responded in one of three ways to the child's ambiguous messages. For one third of the children she made a guess. For one third she said '*Which* one?' waited for the child's response and then chose as best she could. For the remaining children, the experimenter made explicit her problem with the child's message, e.g. 'Well there are four like that. I don't know whether it's got long or short sleeves and I don't know whether it's got stripes or checks (squares)'. Since most of the messages (258/282) did not uniquely identify the chosen referent, nearly all the children received six trials with one form of response to their ambiguous messages.

RESULTS AND CONCLUSIONS

The child's initial descriptions (i.e. before he had responded to the experimenter's comments on that particular trial) were given Ambiguity scores of 0, 1, 2 or 3 depending on whether they referred to 1, 2, 4 or 8 garments. The maximum Ambiguity score was 18; the children's scores obtained ranged from 4 to 16. On the basis of their answers to questioning in the pre- and post-tests, the children were placed twice into one of four categories: listener blamers, speaker blamers and two intermediate categories. The results can be summarised as follows:

(i) There was a significant relationship between category of blame on the pre-test and Ambiguity scores, with listener blamers tending to give poorer messages ($p = 0.01$).

(ii) Among those who were listener blamers on the pre-test (i.e. who displayed no understanding of ambiguous messages and their role in causing communication failure) those given explicit information about their ambiguous messages gave better messages (lower Ambiguity scores) than did those given the other two kinds of feedback ($p < 0.002$). There was no difference between the three feedback groups in the number of irrelevant attributes mentioned, so the children given explicit information were not merely learning to say more about their chosen garments.

(iii) Among those who were listener blamers at the outset, those given explicit information about the ambiguities of their messages performed significantly better in the post-test than those given either of the other two kinds of feedback ($p = 0.03$). That is, their understanding about ambiguous messages appeared to have improved.

The results of this experiment again suggest that merely making explicit to the child what the listener's problem is, enables him to improve the quality of his messages and also enables him to identify ambiguous messages.

Why does giving the child information improve his performance and understanding?

The results presented in the last section suggest that for children of the age tested in these experiments (about 5 years old), the problem is not a conceptual one but merely one of ignorance. Perhaps in their everyday lives these children are not given the information they need to develop their understanding about ambiguous messages and communication failure.

We analysed some data collected in Australia for other purposes, to begin to find out how adults deal with communication failure in their verbal interaction with children. Clough (1971) had recorded verbal exchanges in Melbourne pre-schools, involving teachers and children aged between 3;6 and 5;3. We inspected transcripts of 12 half-hour sessions. Cambourne (1971) had collected recordings of 28 Queensland children aged between 5 and 6;6, in verbal interaction with their teachers at school and their mothers at home.

The most common adult response to a child's inadequate message was for the listener to say 'What?', 'Pardon?' or use another conventional means for eliciting a repetition. A second common response was to solicit more information, by asking a question such as 'What sort of something?' 'Round the side where? You point to it'. Other ways were: to verbalise a guess, e.g. 'In a car?' 'The microphone?'; to verbalise alternatives meanings, e.g. 'Does she live in the country or the city?'; to repeat or expand the original message (an intiative of the speaker following an unsatisfactory response by the listener); to ignore the inadequate message. In none of the instances in the home did either person make explicit that a non-understanding or misunderstanding had occurred, and at school only five such examples were found, e.g. 'Oh I thought you meant that one', 'No, you misunderstood me'.

The particular speech samples analysed may not be generally representative of verbal exchanges between young children and adults, but the features identified raise the possibility that if young children were given more information about communication failures they might learn more quickly about the rôle of the message in successful and unsuccessful communication.

We carried out an experiment to see how children did in fact interpret the common adult ways of dealing with communication failure.
If a child says 'Have you seen my cardigan?' and the adult says
'Which one?' does the child realise that his request was ambiguous?
To find out, we constructed six snatches of dialogue between imaginary children and their mothers. In each case, the imaginary child had
lost an article of clothing (jumper, scarf, etc.) and asked his mother
for help. Each imaginary child was represented by a cardboard cut-
out doll, and the lost object was represented by a picture which was
attached in a 'thought bubble' near the doll's head as the dialogue
was presented. Each of the dolls said 'Mum, have you seen my
jumper/hat/trousers, etc. please?' and each of the mothers gave a
different reply. One of the mothers did know where the lost article
of clothing was, another one said she did not know, and the others
gave more or less explicit indicators of not understanding what was
wanted. The least explicit was 'Which gloves?' and the most explicit
was 'I don't know which cardigan you want. You've got two cardigans. You should tell me which one'. Following each snatch of dialogue we asked the child subject whether the imaginary mother had
understood *just* what was wanted, and whether the imaginary child
had said enough about what she wanted.

We found that our child subjects (aged between 5 and 6;6 years)
found it easier to identify the mother's nonunderstanding if she
made her problem explicit ('I don't know which cardigan you
want . . .') rather than just asking for the missing information ('Which
one?'). We suspected, therefore, that the common adult way of dealing with a child's inadequate messages, asking a question to extract
the missing information, was not the most effective way of informing
the child that his message was not understood. If communicative
failure occurs without the child realising it, how can he come to
understand its causes?

Relationship between mothers' ways of handling communication failure and children's understanding about communication

Is it the case that children who are given explicit information about
their ambiguous utterances acquire understanding about communication failure more readily than children who ambiguous messages are
dealt with in what appears to be the more common way? We have
been fortunate enough to have available in Bristol data which allowed
us to assess effects of mothers' ways of dealing with their children's
inadequate messages. Wells and his research team have collected a
large body of data consisting of mother-child vocal interaction.

Recordings were made at three monthly intervals in the child's home; the child wore a radio-microphone which transmitted to a receiver linked to a tape recorder. The tape recorder was pre-programmed to record 24 samples of 90 seconds each, at approximately 20 minute intervals throughout the day between 9 in the morning and 6 at night. No observer was present in the house while the recordings were being made, but in the evening the tape was played back to the mother who was asked to recall what had been happening during the day's speech samples. The tapes have been transcribed, and we have analysed some of these transcripts.

Procedure   We selected the transcripts of the 36 children in the Wells' sample whom we were able to find in time to test their understanding about communication close to their sixth birthday. We analysed transcripts of the recordings made at three monthly intervals between the ages of 2 years and 3;6, and for 32 of the children, a final recording made just before they started school at 5. Some of the transcripts were missing: for 31 of the children we had seven or eight transcripts available for the analysis; for 4 children we had six transcripts and for 1 child five transcripts.

From the transcripts we coded ways in which mothers dealt with communication failure when they were talking with their children. Usually when communication failure occurred the mother was coping with an ambiguous message given by the child, rather than dealing with the child's nonunderstanding of something she herself had said. We coded eleven different ways in which mothers dealt with communication failure. With most of these, the mother's nonunderstanding remained implicit; for example, the mothers made a conventional request for repetition such as 'Pardon?' or requested more information, or verbalised a guess about what the child meant, which might be either correct or incorrect. For example:

Request for more information:	*Child*: 'Does it go on that one?'
	Mother: 'Which one?'
	Child: 'This one'.
Guess – correct:	*Child*: 'This is going to come off'
	Mother: 'Your slipper is going to come off?'
	Child: 'Yes'
Guess – incorrect:	*Child*: 'That's a lucky colour, Ma, that's a lucky colour'
	Mother: 'What is? Orange?'
	Child: 'No, that colour is'
	Mother: 'Oh'

On some occasions some mothers made explicit to their children that they had not understood: they said, for example, 'I don't know what you mean', or 'I don't know what you're on about', or 'What do you mean?' For each of the 36 children we coded the number of occurrences of each of the eleven ways in which their mothers dealt with communication failure. Our expectation was that mothers who gave explicit information would have children more advanced in their understanding about communication failure than did mothers who used only the implicit ways.

As close as possible to his sixth birthday, we visited the child at school, and played three games with him. One was a communication evaluation game, in which we asked him the 'Whose fault?' sequence of questions following three communication failures. On the basis of his responses, we placed him in one of two categories: a more advanced one if on at least one occasion he blamed the speaker for failure and gave as a reason that the message had been inadequate. The child went into the less advanced category if he always blamed the listener for failure on the grounds that the listener had chosen wrongly. We did originally divide the children into a greater number of categories, but this proved not to be useful.

The second game we played with him at the age of 6 was to assess his skill at carrying out the comparisions necessary for judging the inadequacy of the messages in the communication game (Robinson and Robinson, 1978c). We wanted to be able to identify children who fell into the less advanced, listener-blaming category possibly only because they did not have the skill to make the comparisons necessary for speaker-blaming. If this was their problem we would not be surprised to find that they had failed to benefit from information about communication given by their mothers.

The third game was given for similar reasons: this was to assess children's skill at coping with distal, as opposed to proximal, causes. In previous work (Robinson and Robinson, 1978b) we have demonstrated that if he is to be a speaker blamer, the child must be able to handle distal causes: in our communication evaluation game, the speaker is a distal cause of communication failure, and the listener is a proximal cause. We wanted to be able to identify children who fell into the less advanced listener blaming category possibly only because they could not yet handle distal causes. We would not be surprised to find that these children failed to benefit from information about communication given by their mothers.

We had, then, two potential ways of coping with irregularities in our results: weakness at comparison skill and inability to handle distal causes. As it happened, we did not need to use either argument; there were no irregularities of these sorts.

RESULTS AND DISCUSSION

We compared mothers' ways of dealing with communication failures for the children in the less advanced, listener-blaming group, with those in the more advanced, speaker-blaming group.

(*i*) There was no difference between the two groups in the number of communication failures dealt with, nor in the number of different ways used by the mothers to handle communication failure.

(*ii*) There was no difference between the two groups in the frequency with which mothers used the various implicit ways of handling communication failure.

(*iii*) Explicit statements of nonunderstanding (such as 'I don't know what you mean') were given *only* by mothers whose children were in the speaker-blaming group. Sixteen of the mothers gave this kind of information to their children, and all those children were in the speaker-blaming group. None of the 10 children in the listener-blaming groups had mother who gave them this explicit information about nonunderstanding. This difference is significant at the 0.01 level.

Giving the child only implicit information that his listener has not understood may be effective in resolving the communication failure, but it is apparently less effective than explicit information when it comes to helping the child learn about ambiguous messages and their rôle in causing communication failure.

There were 10 children in the speaker-blaming group whose mothers did not, according to the transcripts, give them explicit information about nonunderstanding. This information occurred usually only once in the transcripts of the other 16 speaker-blamers, so it is quite likely that at least some of the 10 mothers did give this information but not when they were being recorded. Another possibility is that these children received this information from outside the home. A third possibility is that they attained their advanced state of understanding about communication without having received explicit information about their listener's nonunderstanding. However, we were unable to detect any other differences in the verbal behaviour of the mothers of listener-blamers and speaker-blamers.

We would certainly not argue that the giving of explicit information about ambiguity is sufficient for the development of understanding about the causes of communication failure; it may not even be necessary. It need not be given frequently. Indeed, it may be effective in promoting development only if it is given rarely. The children in our analysis of the Well's data who were told 'I don't understand' usually received this information only once in the $4\frac{1}{2}$ hours of recording. It could be that frequently given statements of the listener's nonunderstanding would be less beneficial or even harmful to the child's developing understanding about communication. The child's level of confidence that he can communicate effectively may need to be maintained, and telling him in detail about all the inadequacies of his attempts would possibly discourage him. It could also distract him from attending to the content area about which he is communicating; the young child is unlikely to be able to process information about the topic of communication and the process of communicating within the same short space of time.

Although we have no evidence that the children given explicit information were more advanced in their linguistic development than the others (there was no difference between the two groups on a 'combined language profile score' calculated at age $3\frac{1}{2}$ years by the Wells team, and no difference in scores on the English Picture Vocabulary Test at age 5 years, again given by the Wells team), I have argued elsewhere that it would be inappropriate to give the child explicit information about ambiguities in his messages whilst he is in the early stages of language acquisition (Robinson, 1978).

Despite these provisos, the evidence suggests that the way in which adults commonly handle communication failure in their verbal interaction with young children is not the best way for advancement of the child's understanding about communication.

Summary and conclusions

The evidence presented in the second section showed that both the young child's communicative performance and his verbal judgments about communication suggest that he does not know about ambiguous messages and their role in causing communication failure:

(a) In all but the simplest cases, younger children are less likely than older ones to give messages which identify the intended referent uniquely;

(b) They are less likely to ask questions to clarify ambiguous messages;

(c) They fail to recognise ambiguities and omissions when listening to or viewing instructions for performing a task;

(d) They judge both their own and others' ambiguous messages to be adequate, and fail to recognise the role of the speaker and his message in causing communication failure.

Associated with failure to identify ambiguous messages are:

(a) Failure to withhold information deliberately in order to make the listener's task difficult;

(b) Weakness at taking into account the total set of potential referents when producing a message;

(c) Weakness at giving instructions in an appropriate sequence and in supplying necessary information to a listener;

(d) Acceptance of a disambiguated version of the message as being what was actually said;

(e) Weakness at giving useful information when the listener to the child's ambiguous message asks for help.

In the third section it was shown that informing the young speaker about his listener's nonunderstanding and giving him the reasons for it, apparently enables him to improve both his performance and his verbal judgments of ambiguous messages:

(a) Asking the child to describe how the intended referent differs from other potential referents, rather than asking him to describe the intended referent for his listener, enables him to improve his performance;

(b) Telling the giver of an ambiguous message how many potential referents his message covers, enables him to give useful information when the listener asks for further help;

(c) Telling the child how many potential referents his ambiguous message covers and specifying the ambiguities, enables him to improve the quality of his subsequent messages and helps him to identify subsequently given ambiguous messages.

The reasons why improvement in the child's performance and understanding should be achieved in these ways were discussed in the fourth section, in which it was shown that in their verbal interaction with young children adults commonly handle communication failure using implicit rather than explicit means. Often they ask a question to elicit information missing from the child's utterance, without explicitly informing the child that they did not understand the original utterance. Experimental results suggest that the common adult ways of extracting from the child information missing from his message, may not be recognised by the child as indicators of nonunderstanding and message inadequacy. Communication failures occur without the child realising it. Mothers who do explicitly inform their pre-school children when they do not understand the child's utterance, have children who at the age of 6 are more advanced in their understanding about communication failure than do mothers who use only implicit means of handling communication failure.

It has been shown, then, that young children have difficulty in recognising the importance of certain requirements of effective verbal referential communication. Experimental results suggest that they can be helped simply by being informed what is needed. Commonly they are not given this information in their every day lives. As shown in the first section it is not only adults in their rôle of parents or teachers who omit to inform children effectively about ambiguities in messages; those who take on the rôle of experts in advancement of communication skills in children, make the same omission.

If we want our children to produce utterances which meet their listener's information requirements by avoiding ambiguity and unhelpful redundancy, rather than merely to speak fluently and confidently, and if we want them to behave appropriately as listeners by recognising their own nonunderstanding and asking questions when appropriate, why not inform them about the requirements of effective communication?

Acknowledgements

I am pleased to acknowledge the financial support of the Education Research and Development Committee of Australia for the earlier investigations and that of the Social Science Research Council of Great Britain for the later ones.

References

Alvy, K. T. (1968). Relation of age to children's egocentric and cooperative communication. *Journal of Genetic Psychology* 112, 275-286

Bearison, D. J. and Levey, L. M. (1977). Children's comprehension of referential communication: decoding ambiguous messages. *Child Development* 48, 716-720

Cambourne, B. L. (1971). "A Naturalistic Study of Language Performance in Grade I Rural and Urban School Children". Unpublished doctoral dissertation, James Cook University, Queensland

Clough, J. R. (1971). "An Experimental Investigation of the Effects of a Cognitive Training Programme on Educationally Disadvantaged Children of Pre-school Age". Unpublished doctoral dissertation, Monash University, Victoria

Cosgrove, J. M. and Patterson, S. J. (1977). Plans and the development of listener skills. *Developmental Psychology* 13, 557-564

Flavell, J. H., Speer, J. R., Green, F. L. and August, D. L. (1979). "The Development of Comprehension Monitoring and Knowledge about Communication". Unpublished manuscript, Stanford University

Ironsmith, M. and Whitehurst, G. J. (1978). The development of listener abilities in communication: how children deal with ambiguous information. *Child Development* 49, 348-352

Leach, P. (1977). "Baby and Child". Michael Joseph, London

Markman, E. M. (1977). Realizing that you don't understand: a preliminary investigation. *Child Development* 48, 986-992

Patterson, C. J. and Kister, M. C. (1978). "The Development of Listener Skills for Referential Communication". Paper presented at a conference on *Children's Oral Communication Skills*, University of Wisconsin

Robinson, E. J. (1978). "The Child's Understanding of Inadequate Messages and Communication Failure: A Problem of Ignorance or Egocentrism?" Paper given at a conference on *Children's Oral Communication Skills*, University of Wisconsin

Robinson, E. J. and Robinson, W. P. (1976a). Development changes in the child's explanation of communication failure. *Australian Journal of Psychology* 28, 155-165

Robinson, E. J. and Robinson, W. P. (1976b). The young child's understanding of communication. *Developmental Psychology* 12, 328-333

Robinson, E. J. and Robinson, W. P. (1977a). The child's understanding of life-like communication failures. *Australian Journal of Psychology* 29, 137-142

Robinson, E. J. and Robinson, W. P. (1977b). Development in the understanding of causes of success and failure in verbal communication. *Cognition* 5, 363-378

Robinson, E. J. and Robinson, W. P. (1978a). Explanations of communication failure and ability to give bad messages. *British Journal of Social and Clinical Psychology* 17, 219-225

Robinson, E. J. and Robinson, W. P. (1978b). Development of understanding about communication: message inadequacy and its role in causing communication failure. *Genetic Psychological Monographs* 98, 233-279

Robinson, E. J. and Robinson, W. P. (1978c). The roles of egocentrism and of weakness in comparing in children's explanations of communication failure. *Journal of Experimental Child Psychology* 26, 147-160

Rosen, C. and Rosen, H. (1973). "The Language of Primary School Children". Penguin, Harmondsworth

Tough, J. (1977). "Talking and Learning". Ward Lock, London

Whitehurst, G. J. and Sonnenschein, S. (1978a). The development of communication: attribute variation leads to contrast failure. *Journal of Experimental Child Psychology* 25, 454-490

Whitehurst, G. J. and Sonnenschein, S. (1978b). "The Development of Informative Messages in Referential Communication". Paper presented at a conference on *Children's Oral Communication Skills*, University of Wisconsin

11

Some Problems for Theory, Methodology, and Methods for the 1980s

W. P. Robinson

Introduction

Scientists are irritated by ambiguity. Lovers of literature relish it, on occasion. However, the ambiguity of the title of this book was not intended either to irritate scientists or to attract lovers; it simply reflects the realities of the contents. For some of the studies reported, aspects of communication function as independent variables relevant to children's learning and performance; a subsidiary distinction can also be made between those investigations in which variations in the communicative context of experimental situations serve to influence outcomes and those in which attempts are made to specify the kinds of other-child interaction most conducive to development. Other investigations include qualities of communicative performance (and understanding about communication) as dependent variables, trying to identify antecedents of variability observed. Several do both simultaneously, hence the titular ambiguity. Fortunately the contents of the chapters individually identify the rôles being played by the communication variables. As well as focusing on a particular set of empirical problems, each chapter also tries to specify the theoretical perspective that has underpinned the particular investigations chosen, thereby rendering it easier to assess the similarities and differences in terms of perspectives, methodology, and methods of enquiry.

While discussion of the contributions themselves would be a sufficient rationale for a final chapter, two other considerations make it desirable to set the work in a broader context, one romantic and one practical. Just as each New Year can be exploited to survey the states of our individual lives, so the beginnings of decades may cause us to pause and ask what the state of play is in the life of child development. Practically such an enquiry would seem to be particular apposite in relation to research into the development of communication, since this field seems destined to be a growth area, set to take off in terms of the number of research workers choosing to grapple with it. For those of us old enough to remember, it is tempting to note similarities with the state of studies of language development in 1960, even if we have no ideas comparable to those of Chomsky (1957) to serve as a point of departure. To have such an influence is not necessarily entirely beneficial, and perhaps we would be well-advised to ask ourselves about the limitations of any too uncritical enthusiasm for particular theoretical stances and modes of enquiry into the enthusiasm for work within a Piagetian perspective (subsequently referred to as ID, standing for intellectual development) that delayed the advancement of knowledge about language development (referred to as LD hereinafter). A parallel and partial enquiry into the enthusiam for work within a Piagetian perspective (subsequently referred to as ID standing for intellectual development) over roughly the same period can also be cautionary. Hence in this chapter I try to raise some alarm signals before the dangers arise, although such flashings mark no more than particular personal anxieties viewed from a developmental social psychological perspective; they do not pretend to originate from a systematic and comprehensive survey.

As developmental social psychologists in societies whose rhetoric at least propounds a doctrine of freedom of ideas, we are spared from direct control of our activities by official superordinate authorities, but we are not culture-free agents functioning outside time and space. Our thinking and actions are themselves influenced by norms similar in function to those whose character we study in our social groups. At given times in given places culturally-defined frames of reference limit the kinds of questions deemed proper to pose about topics, the kinds of statements that might be treated as acceptable answers. Methods of data collection and data processing are likewise subject to normative evaluation. These influences radiate from centres of power penetrating to colleagues at a distance. The American Psychological Association's Publication Manual sets limits to certain characteristics of the articles its journals are likely to publish. The prestigious journals through policy and selection help to define fashions of interest and propriety. Eminent experts set trends.

Strangely, we seldom pause to step back from the action to observe the *Zeitgeist* and *Zeitgeistlein* at work. It is perhaps surprising that more of our colleagues of bibliographic bent do not chart the temporal rise and fall of theories, topics, methods – and methodology. Such historical analyses might provoke more of us to ask whether or not our research is as sensible, constructive, and worthwhile as our actions presuppose. At the risk of being shown to be quite wrong by properly collated facts, I would hazard a number of guesses as to some of the dominant themes of the last two decades in the fields of LD and ID. We can note immediately that these two fields have commanded such attention and effort and are natural ancestors to studies of communication in development.

In terms of theoretical underpinnings the main thrusts in ID and LD derive from Piaget and Chomsky respectively, and we can ask about the strengths and weaknesses of these orientations for the study of communication in development.

In terms of general methodology the hegemony of a single paradigm in each field has meant that empirical studies have not focused on the relative merits of contesting hypotheses and explanations; rather they have been seen either as supporting the single theoretical position or as incompatible with it. Only a few researchers have proceeded to erect alternative stories. Much of the work in both fields has been descriptive rather than explanatory. Some of it has simply demonstrated co-variation of variables. In terms of methods and design, cross-sectional experiments eliciting relevant behaviour and short training experiments have been more common in ID, while LD has placed greater reliance on 'natural' longitudinal data, sometimes collected from very small numbers of children. In the former, tests of hypotheses have generally presupposed relations between variables to be monotonic, usually linear – in spite of the categorical qualities of Piagetian theory. In the latter, tests have not always been thought to be relevant. When tests have been used in either area, they have taken rejection of the null hypothesis as their anvil of decision-taking.

If these caricatures have a measure of validity, which approach should we adopt for studies of communication in development? Is either of these sets of ideas and methods appropriate and sufficient, and if so which? Are there important errors in either? Are important ideas and methods missing from both? If so, what are they, and are the portents favourable for their inclusion? Will it be difficult to persuade people to include them? Some habits should be easier to change than others. For example, there are no obvious reasons why tests for curvilinearity and other forms of relationship should not be used to replace, supplement, or complement tests of linear association. Where theoretical underpinnings can be shown to lead to expectations of non-linear relationships, appropriate testings are unlikely to be disputed by the gatekeepers to publication. On the other hand, it is more difficult, for example, to see a rapid advance towards the untilisation of the descendants of Bayesian statistical models, as a means to compare the efficacy of tightly predictive contrastive explanations across a range of studies; our explanatory stories simply do not yet approach the necessary quality of precision for such testing.

Such illustrations pale into insignificance beside some of our greater problems, one of which seems to evade discussion as much as cancer or death. My first professor advised me not to venture into studies of human motivation on the grounds that people perceive too great a discrepancy between what they are actually like and what they think they ought to be like for them to reveal the former. (A very unmaterialistic man himself, he counselled the buying of land as a more sensible career.) And what are our motives in conducting research? In terms of functions of language we would presumably agree that we should be trying to make important true statements within our universe of discourse; truth value should be pre-eminent over social functions of impressing, amusing, deceiving, or persuading either ourselves or others. But who can afford such luxuries? As social psychologists we know that the credibility of the source as well as the facts of matter influence others. The value (as opposed to the truth value) of our ideas is related to the value we individually command in the market place, both as cattle and as dealers in cattle. We each have to establish our reputations and maintain them if we are to have the opportunity to practise as developmental social psychologists, and these reputations are achieved mainly by personal contact and publication in high status journals. Not that either of these mechanisms is dispensable or undesirable *per se* – they function as the major means of filtering and disseminating knowledge, but both can exert pressures that are not entirely healthy. In a competitive marketplace an aspiring academic may decide it is more judicious to use analysis of variance to show that variable x is not randomly distributed by age or sex, where x is an up-and-coming variable. Rates of publication are easier to sustain with such short, safe descriptions than with larger projects which may advance original explanations. Alas descriptive facts only accrue significance in the context of explanation and may be more likely to enhance their authors' careers than our understanding of child development. Given those who take greater risks and whose ideas begin to influence others are also subject to the temptations of the market place and can begin to offer rhetoric rather than science. They are not always discouraged from doing so. Brecht's Mother Courage lamented the fate of countries

that needed heroes. Should we pity practitioners in academic disci-
plines that display a similar crutch?

Those of more puritannical bent have the problem of trying to
sort wheat from chaff, wisdom from word-spinning, good ideas from
bad ones – perhaps even asking unanswerable questions about the
motivation of the authors. Not very gentlemanly, but occasionally
necessary. Van den Berghe's (1970) satirical advice on how to be
a successful academic is too close to reality to be entirely amusing.
Perhaps we need to change the reinforcement schedules for research
and publication activity and observe an example of successful behaviour modification. Certainly we could begin to observe our corporate
activities mor critically, but this is a place for mentioning rather than
discussing these wider issues, and for the immediate purpose we need
to ask some questions about the recent history of research into intellectual development in general and language development in particular.

Theoretical perspectives

Strangely the two fields and their dominating theorists have had
different philosophical roots: Piaget is most easily linked to Kant,
Chomsky to Descartes. A third philosophical line running from neo-
behaviourism back to and beyond Hume has been heard only as a
weak counterpoint in either field. Neither Piaget nor Chomsky labels
himself as a psychologist. Piaget argues that Chomsky offers structure without genesis and that associative learning principles offer
genesis without structure. Both criticisms seem to be well-founded.
While transformational generative grammar helped to identify
sequences of likely syntactic mastery, no new mechanisms for learning them were suggested, and those extant were rejected. It was
inevitable that the Language Acquisition Device had to become very
rich in its innate programming. However, associative principles of
learning (Guthrie and Smith, 1921), especially if elaborated to incorporate rewards and punishments as selecting and stamping-in devices
(Ferster and Skinner, 1965), do provide conditions for changing at
least some kinds of behaviour, while essentially treating the child as
a reactive organism lacking in initial structures and cognitively-related
motivation. Although Piaget's theory offers both initial structure and
agentive properties to promote intellectual development, like
Chomsky's, it also has been criticised as essentially static rather than
dynamic, particularly by workers in Artificial Intelligence. Whether
these arguments are valid or not, I am not competent to assess; super-

ficially at least they look to be sensible and I can sympathasise with the spirit of the criticism; not only are the Piagetian stages couched in static terms, but the concepts of 'equilibration' and 'conflict resolution' (Piaget, 1971) lack specificity to a degree that programmers of computers cannot avoid.

But which are we to choose as our model of child development? Do we need to resurrect and integrate a Guthrie-Pavlov-Skinner model? Or are we to prefer an artificially intelligenced Piagetian child? Or Chomsky's? And do we need to integrate the hypotheses about 'modelling' which have enjoyed some support in language development studies and the development of moral behaviour?

'Modelling' or observational learning may be the easiest to assimilate to other theories of learning. That it occurs is well-established (Bandura and Walters, 1963), and some statements can be made about the condition under which it is more likely to occur. We can readily see that observational learning requires the child to make associations between actions, objects and events. Why are some learned and others not? Exactly the same difficulty arose with purely associative principles of learning themselves; they failed to be sufficiently selective. Certainly rewards and punishments conceived of in relational rather than categorical terms can be shown to affect the probabilities and rates of learning, as well as conditions of realisation in performance. So can manipulations establish sets in which the learner and arrangements of the environment that affect the salience and discriminability of stimuli.

While associative principles, whether 'pure' (Guthrie and Smith, 1921) or in the forms of classical (Pavlov, 1960) or operant conditioning (Ferster and Skinner, 1957), or even in the more intellectualised conceptions of Ausubel (1978), have to be accepted as potentially relevant to human development and learning, they appear inadequate to account for the active, agentive self-organising properties of children. If this is so, the solution is not to eliminate associative principles from accounts of human learning but to find their appropriate contexts of application, and they *seem* to be most in evidence when the child is a passive victim reacting to the environment rather than controlling it.

Increasingly psychologists are recognising the necessity to articulate some kind of updated cognitive developmental approach with associative principles of learning; neither is self-sufficient, both correspond to aspects of reality as currently evidenced. The problem is becoming one of deciding which influences are paramount in which domains of learning and performance and when. Piaget's system does not adequately describe or explain how the data get into the child in a form that the sensori-motor schemes or operational structures can get to work on. Not all learning involves the resolution of conflict between schemes or structures and reorganisation in terms of higher order principles, however. (Interestingly, in this volume Perret-Clermont illustrates how observational learning might be related to a cognitive conflict model of intellectual development; her contention is that its weakness in facilitating learning relative to focused and explicit confrontation and argument stems from the child's potential failure to appreciate the conflict which the behaviour of models can generate with his own thinking. Observational learning may also be associative without generating conflict, as suggested above.)

Whereas the cognitive development approach is weak in specifying determinants of data collection and assimilation, associative principles of learning lack a directive programming component, to select which associations may be learned or to analyse, coordinate or otherwise process the associations when they have been learned.

If these somewhat incoherent contentions are valid, then students of communication in development will have to see the child's learning as an articulated whole. He cannot be reduced to an Associative Child collecting data as it is given to him. He cannot be reduced to a Cognitive Developmental Child of deep intellectual processes. He is both: the deeper processes interpret and process the data; they also act to select them. But contiguity and potential rewards and punishments, and other aspects of environmental stimuli also affect the probability of data being collected. Such a perspective need not ignore Chomsky's contribution entirely. In so far as the acts of communication produced or received by a child are combinations of units constructed in accordance with rules, we have to describe and explain the decoding and encoding of these. The formulation of the psycho-communicative stages of generation is likely to be informed by the transformational generative approach, in respect of both longitudinal development and immediate performance. It is unlikely however that we shall pare communicative acts down to their syntax in the same manner that Chomsky stripped language, and we should of course arrive at a comparable impasse if we were to try to do so. While we may find it necessary to analyse acts of communication into semantic and pragmatic components, and we shall have to have superordinate semantic equivalents of lexico-grammar and phonology which include linguistic realisations, we shall have to see the four as articulated components of a single system. If we do this, we shall not omit such concepts of *tone unit* for example, from our analyses. What are the units of utterance? What is new in what is said and what is presumed to be shared? If Brazil (1978) is correct, much linguistic analysis, by omitting prosodic considerations, has missed (and still does miss) the very *raison d'etre* of utterances being made. While this does not imply that other components of the language system are developed solely in response to pragmatic needs at all points in development our acceptance of their salience at some points in development seems to be unavoidable (see Halliday, 1975) (cf. Bowerman, 1979, for examples of occasions where pragmatic considerations may not provide a motivating principle). While then, the study of communicative acts will require a four level analysis for adult behaviour (but may not need as many for babies), we will also need to be careful not to omit crucial components of the systems of communication, and just as we need to see the child-learner as a whole we shall need to re-integrate the components of communication into a coherent whole.

If we incorporate the pragmatic component properly we shall be in no danger of forgetting that communication is between people as well as between a person and his environment; hopefully we shall also remember that communication between people can be about the environment both physical and social. Chomsky was simply not concerned with those kinds of problem in language development. Piaget originally was, in at least two respects. His contribution to the development of moral judgement (Piaget, 1932) is still an essential introduction to the subject, but a Piagetian perspective has yet to be systematically utilised to study children's perception and thinking about the child's own self, other people, social processes, and social structure. Investigations directed to those topics would seem to be an essential part of the enterprise, if we are to describe and explain developing variations in communicative acts in relation to Hymes' (1967) SPEAKING (Setting, Participants, Ends, Art Characteristics, Key, Instrumentalities, Norms and Genre). But these do not function solely as determinants of subsequent variations.

As an example we may select participants as one of the more important of Hymes' list of factors. Strangely perhaps, Piaget's (1926) original suggestions about the environmental contingencies relevant to development of speech have been generally neglected; he cited arguing with peers as a spur to the abandonment of egocentrism in speech. Peers rather than parents were emphasised only because his contention was that parent's would be skilled in guessing what children meant even if their verbal forms of expression were inadequate, an observation generally consistent with the observations of the behaviour of both parents and teachers reported by E. J. Robinson in this volume. The efficacy of dialectical confrontations with peers for promoting understanding of conservation is strongly evidenced in the chapter by Perret-Clermont and Schubauer-Leoni (see also Doise, Mugny and Perret-Clermont, 1975). That it is the kind of communication rather than than the character of the antagonist is illustrated by Perret-Clermont and Schubauer-Leoni for conservation of amount in liquids, by Heber for seriation, and by E. J. Robinson for one of understanding about effective referential communication. Each of these learnings involves the child in a re-structuring of his thinking, and other people are both the most sources of challenge to his initial solution and the most likely to offer him (or render available to him) alternative more satisfactory solutions in a form to which he can accommodate. But as well as these re-programmings, children are also accumulating ways of finding out things from others and propositional knowledge to relay to others, and the chapters by McGlaughlin *et al.*, Hartmann and Haavind, and W. P. Robinson illustrate variations in communicative behaviour of mothers associated with variation in their children. These chapters are asocial in so far as their analyses of children's speech concentrate on the representational function of language (there are no data about children's speech in the service of regulating the states and behaviour of others or themselves, their marking of rôle relations, their identity and states etc.), but within their domains of focus they yield results consistent with the joint constructionist, associative model of the child posited in this chapter. They stress the efficaciousness of conversation in which mothers' behaviour is consistent with constructionist-associative theories of child development (the extent to which mothers explicitly believe in such a theory has yet to be determined) and of conversations in which mothers' success in establishing and maintaining communication with the child. The characteristics of such facilitatory activity are discussed in greater detail elsewhere (Wells and Robinson, 1981).

This emphasis upon the quantity and qualities of other-child interaction and conversation has its parallels in work on very young children. Halliday (1975) has illustrated the social and pragmatic character of the earliest functions of child speech and more generally a shift in perspective occurred in the mid-1970s that began to take due note of the readily observable fact that new-born babies interact with people as well as things. What is more it was recognised that their interaction with things can be importantly mediated by the actions of other people. Trevarthen (Trevarthen and Hubley, 1978) has proposed concepts of primary and secondary inter-subjectivity to refer to the triangular relations in the system. Bruner (1975) has stressed the role of 'joint action' in early development. To re-introduce joint action with caretakers into the picture has the additional advantage that it may remind us that there are effective and emotional components that will enter into the learning process. Piaget's focus of interest excluded these. Conceptions of reward and punishments in associative learning theories tended to focus upon needs to avoid pain, to eat and to drink to the exclusion of the states of well being derived from contact comfort (Harlow, 1953) or phatic communion (Malinowski, 1935). Bruner and Trevarthen are much more strongly social, and in emphasising the biological adaptive-ness of desing characteristics that programme the infant to interact with its primary caretaker(s) in certain ways yield a portrait of a baby of spirit and flesh as well as intellect. Their babies can smile and cry, cuddle and commune in the ways that babies do. Piaget's baby is too much of an observer of social living and too little of a participant; too much of an embryonic physicist, and not enough of a social psychologist.

The future is promising in several respects. If we can incorporate associative principles of learning into a neo-Piagetian framework (see Boden, 1979) and integrate these with a view of the child that recog-nises him as a social being *ab initio*, we shall be thinking of the development of the child as a whole. This should reduce the chances of our descriptions and explanations exaggerating certain aspects to the exclusion of others as we have tended to in the past. Too many psychological theories (and philosophical views of man) have adopted explanatory framewords which appear to be valid for the initial puzzles that they are used to solve but lose plausibility as they are stretched to become all-embracing. Although it is quite proper to explore a theory to its limits, and these can only be discovered by proceeding beyond, their proponents and adherents seem to be reluctant to say, 'This far and no further'. From the times when Greek philosophers first spawned a wide diversity of -isms, we seem to have had difficulty in defining the boundaries of these views of man and integrating them into a balanced and realistic system. Although they have been brilliantly formally operational in their constructions of possible worlds, they have forgotten the empirical constraint that in one sense there is only one real world, and that the job of scientists is to describe and explain this one as it is. We are concerned with the world as it might become, but only within the constraints of empiri-cal and not logical possibility.

The portrait of the child that is now emerging is perhaps beginning to take on a more obvious realistic quality and we can perhaps be optimistic as we move into the 1980s, that we are omitting fewer necessary perspectives than heretofore.

Methodology

EXPLANATION AND DESCRIPTION

At a high level of abstraction the ends of the enterprise are not contentious: they are to describe and explain the development of human beings through childhood at psychological levels of analysis from appropriate psychological perspectives. Other things being equal, explanations which have predictive power are preferable to those which do not. Explanations that are associated with demonstrable and detailed control of relevant behaviour are better than those not so associated. At least in our rhetoric we emphasis explanation as well as description; in our behaviour however description seems to have been pre-eminent, if we accept that the two terms may be used contrastively and that explanations are more concerned with answers to questions of 'How?' and 'Why?', whereas descriptions derive from 'What?', 'Who?', 'When?', 'Where?' and 'Which?', we do not need to proceed to assert their independence from each other; it would be misguided to do so. Explanations are inevitably and indissolubly linked to descriptions, and descriptions set limits to explanations by structuring the categories and relations to be explained. Ideally both are developed together in any field of interest, each influencing the other. Sadly descriptions and extensions and refinements of descriptions seem to have been of greater concern than the construction and testing of alternative explanations for what has been described.

For example, in respect of psychological explanations of ID of children, such items as age, ethnicity, gender, or socio-economic status have no explanatory power in and of themselves. And yet how often are questions in respect of a phenomenon posed in those terms? Are there gender differences? Are there sub-cultural differences? If there are, these only become interesting to psychologists if we can begin to specify pscyhological reasons for these differences occurring. Variations across such categories or along such dimensions may be empirically associated with psychological variations in the incidence or character of the phenomena in focus, but demonstrations of such covariation serve only to *locate* what has yet to be explained. Such mapping may be useful initial steps from which putative explanations can be constructed, but this will happen only if we can identify and suggest other psychological variables that distribute non-randomly against the biological, sociological, or cultural variables we have used, and which can be shown to mediate the behaviour in question.

Even when we have moved from more distal levels of analysis into the realms of psychology we still have to be careful in our discrimination of sub-levels of explanation within the discipline. Differential attitudes of parents cannot be used to explain empirically correlated differences in the behaviour of children without further specification of the processes by which attitudes are mediated to the children. Explanations of children's behaviour that appeal to parental attitudes only are one of many examples that implicitly seem to rely on extra-sensory perception by the child. How does he know what his father's attitudes are? And why should his behaviour be influenced by them? We have to link attitudes or other hypothetical constructs of this kind to the behaviour of the parents – being careful to specify the characteristics of the context in which the behaviour is manifested. And having done this we have still only reached a point at which we can describe the data made available to the child (see Messer, this volume). To know how he will react and what initiatives he might display we need to know about the child's own psychology: adequate theories of motivation, attention, perception, learning, remembering, thinking and action are essential prerequisities of our being able to link the child's immediate and imminent behaviour to his past experience. This assertion should not be taken to imply that the explanations of behaviour lie wholly within the child himself as an individual; but only that some of the essential determinants of his behaviour have to be sought within him. The specification of child-other-environment interaction processes will also be an integral part of such explanations. Just as drawing where rivers run and towns stand locates but does not explain how or why they came to be where they are at the point in time of the map-making, so demographic (as its etymology asserts) data locate variations awaiting explanation or re-description prior to explanation.

None of the chapters in this collection confines itself to a demographic description of covariation; each tries to offer explanations either for individual differences or for developmental changes in children's intellectual development. At first sight the data of Messer and Sylvester-Bradley might appear to be mainly descriptive, but both authors offer a theoretical rationale for their studies. Messer's interest in the synchrony of wordings and actions presupposes the importance of contiguity as a factor relevant to learning. His demonstrations of differential emphasis presuppose the advantages of rendering what is supposed to be in focus clearly discriminable from what is in the background; both are integrated within recent approaches to word-meaning mastery. Sylvester-Bradley offers a new perspective on the functional significance of negativity that includes ideas of stimulus satiation and needs for achieving and maintaining optimal levels of arousal. All the adult-child studies reported examine interaction *per se*. Those which include socio-economic status or sex as discriminating variables (McGlaughlin *et al.*, Perret-Clermont and Schubauer-Leoni, and W. P. Robinson) attempt to explain why these variables discriminate at a psychological level. Emiliani *et al.* move away from the child to offer explanations of adult interaction with nursery school children in terms of the ideology and beliefs the adults have about such children. Hartmann and Haavind try to make explicit why differential treatment by mothers should affect development in their children, as do both Robinsons. Heber and Perret-Clermont and Schubauer-Leoni look directly at types of interaction which might promote learning, dependent upon the theory of learning being probed – and emerge with similar preferences. Freeman *et al.* attempt to explain the reasons for variations in children's apparent understanding of preposition-based instructions to locate objects.

Although none of the explanations offered for the data presented could be claimed to be comprehensive systematic accounts in tight and unique correspondence with data they do endeavour to come close to the child's thinking and/or learning processes and to the determinants of his performance. The ends are clearly to explain as well as describe. To that extent each can refute any charge of being blindly empirical, presenting facts and leaving them for other colleagues to explain.

TYPES OF EXPLANATION

Ignorance of itself would be a sufficient reason for glossing over the detailed philosophical and substantive issues surrounding the difficulties of justifying any preferences for one mode of explanation rather than another, but in so far as each of us is looking for explanations we each have to have some appreciation of the kinds we might find acceptable. Once we cease to defend extreme positions of either inherited or environmental determinism, we are also less likely to think in terms of linear cause-effect relations of an all-or-none variety; we are less prone to see behaviour as made up of effects having single traceable causes. Our frames of reference become probabilistic when thinking about particular occasions for learning and/or performance. Our representations of developmental achievements made may remain strong in their implicational relations however; we may still seek to identify necessary and/or sufficient conditions. This can be so whether we are working within a neo-Piagetian framework of an accumulation of potentially incompatible schemes to be rendered more coherent by reorganisation or whether we are treating complex behaviour as shaped coordinations of simpler combinations and units. Complementary to ideas of necessary and sufficient conditions are those of facilitating and inhibiting conditions. Most of the chapters are couched within this kind of probabilistic framework. Only E. J. Robinson makes a claim about the occurrence of mothers' explicit statements of non-understanding being a sufficient condition of the early appearance of the child's understanding that inadequate messages can cause communication failure; and that is of course limited to the range of variation within the particular population studied. Presumably for a mother to have made the relevant kind of remark once to a year-old baby would not have resulted in the development of understanding occurring earlier. The other chapters looking at development are explicitly or implicitly couched in terms of facilitating and/or inhibiting conditions. If mothers talk in certain ways in certain contexts this increases the probability that the child will learn X rather than Y. The individual differences studies of Hartmann and Haavind, McGlaughlin *et al.*, and W. P. Robinson exemplify this kind of expectation. We may also note that at least three chapters recognise that not only is the development of some capacities and skills seen as probabilistic, there may also be *more than one* route or course for developments to follow. While Heber, Perret-Clermont and Schubauer-Leoni, and E. J. Robinson severally found one mode of treatment more efficacious for learning than the others utilised, none claimed that there was only one kind of environmental manipulation or occurrence that would facilitate learning. Such disjunctive possibilities have been neglected too often in the past. We have, for reasons which are obscure, preferred conjunctive hypotheses, perhaps because our previous training encourages us to approach problems with such limiting assumptions (see Bruner, Goodnow and Austin, 1956).

Methods of study

TYPES OF OBSERVATION

No arguments have so far been addressed to the controversies about the advantages of case studies versus systematic sampling, experiments versus observations, cross-sectional versus longitudinal studies, behaviour itself versus respondent's accounts of their behaviour. Each author has assumed that the particular method adopted was appropriate to the question under scrutiny. While Sylvester-Bradley illustrated arguments with photographs drawn from relatively intensive observations of a small number of mother-child pairs, McGlaughlin *et al.* have recourse to statistical procedures requiring larger sample sizes. Since none of the studies was concerned to estimate the incidence of occurrence of certain features in definable populations, sample surveys were not necessary. Whether the sampling of the behaviour was sufficient either in numbers of subjects or in the amount of data obtained from each subject to merit the conclusions drawn would have to be argued separately for each study.

Every chapter has been concerned with language and its use either as independent or dependent variable or both, and during the 1970s strong positions were adopted on the issue of whether speech should be sampled only in its everyday occurrence. None of the work reported in this volume resulted from unobtrusive observation, although most of it has striven to elicit behaviour in semi-natural situations or checked relations between experimental and observational results. For the purists this would not be sufficient and it may be helpful to set out arguments to anticipate adverse criticisms of those who reject results and interpretations derived from contrived situations.

Are we to observe natural or artificial (unnatural?) behaviour? The point of making this distinction can be misunderstood as well as abused. In so far as the distinction is of use then in the short run preferences for one or the other presumably ought to be made in the light of the objectives of the particular piece of research. In the longer term descriptions and explanations of phenomena have to apply to behaviour *wherever* it occurs, regardless of the conditions of observation.

What is meant when we claim tnat a piece of behaviour is 'natural'? What we can observe is limited by time and place. It is limited by the cultural and biological characteristics of both the observed and the observer. Certain aspects of what is true here and now may not have been true in the past and many not be so in the future. Somewhere other than here they may not be true now. Hence to observe samples of everyday life is to take a sample of the possible, and we ought not to endow these extracts with unwarranted status. This point is not always acknowledged by advocates of unobtrusive observation. As scientists we are interested in what can and cannot be empircally true, as well as in which of the possibilities are realised in particular periods in the history of particular cultures.

We must also beware of an essentialist fallacy in another direction as well. Human beings are part of nature, and our factories and armaments are as much a part of the natural order as termite nests and snake bites. Within our field of developmental social psychology it is occasionally said that writing and reading, for example, are harder for children than listening and speaking because they are less natural. The argument can be developed several steps, but in the end cannot be sustained; at the end of the chain either all four are natural or all four are artificial. (Quick appeals to essence or what is natural were not included among the strong modes of answering in chapter 6, it may be recalled.)

There is a third sense in which the distinction can be misleading. It is empirically and logically impossible to create behaviour in an artificial setting that could not occur outside that setting. Science cannot transcend itself! If a relationship can be demonstrated in a laboratory, it must be possible for it to exist outside, in natural circumstances. We can misinterpret behaviour observed in a laboratory and we can make false inferences from laboratory observations, but we cannot produce the impossible. In part, any preference for the laboratory rather than the field or vice versa ought to depend upon whether we are trying to describe and explain things as they are in everyday life (at given times in given places or as they might be, given different environmental conditions). If we want to know how as a matter of fact children come to express conserving judgements we should, at some stage, have to observe them longitudinally in their everyday environments. If we are interested in how they *could* learn to make such judgements, laboratory studies may suffice. If we are interested in both, we have to study both. E. J. Robinson's chapter exemplifies the double approach. She recognises there may be more than one way for children to learn that messages can be too general and hence ambiguous and that if we ask which of the routes are followed outside the laboratory we should need to conduct sample surveys with extended observations. She does not add that the publication of the results of the work on television or in a 'Woman's Weekly' might change what happens to be the case in the everyday world very rapidly – a principle that can be extended to any behaviour that is amendable to control.

In recent years, particularly in respect of LD, arguments about natural versus artificial settings for data collection have been juxtaposed with questions about the role and relevance of the observer. Does the observer interfere with the behaviour of the observed, and if so does it matter? Two ways of minimising interference have been suggested, one straightforward, the other superficially strange. If the observed is unaware of the fact that he is being observed, there would seem to be no immediate scientific difficulty. In studies of child development the measurement procedures do not extract energy from what is being observed. It is a false analogy to allege comparability with those problems in physics where the amount and kind of energy required for measurement can be a significant fraction of that in the system under examination. To maintain repeated and/or intensive unobtrusive observation may not be possible, and while there are no scientific difficulties of principle some investigators also judge such observation to be morally wrong. The weakness of the approach lies both in the difficulty of achieving or maintaining it sufficiently to collect the requisite data and in the work loaded upon the observers. If the relevant event are rare they may miss them. By denying themselves the possibility of deliberately eliciting relevant behaviour or of talking about the problems with the observed they forego potentially valuable sets of data. The strengths of the method are not to be denied.

The alternative form of unobtrusive observation is to become a participant in the everyday life of those being observed. While this immediately precludes the possibility of non-interference, it can enable long-term and direct observation relevant to the problems in hand.

Although it may be rash to try to make generalisations about the proper occasions for unobtrusive or participant observation, there are at least two phases of research in which it benefits are likely to be considerable. The first is during the exploratory phase of research, the period during which the investigator is very ignorant and is still trying to define the research problem in ways which can be systematically investigated. The second is when any laboratory studies being pursued or explanations being offered are in danger of losing touch with the substantive problems they are intended to illuminate. Keeping an intermittent eye on everyday life can be a useful and occasionally a salutary corrective to the way theory is developing. It is extraordinary and frightening how many researchers in child development do not seem to interact with children outside the laboratory. In respect of my own work with low SES mothers and their children I have been told that I as a middle-class male of some maturity could not hope to communicate successfully with

such people. While I would not pretend to claims that I can invariably communicate successfully with all people on a large range of
matters and may well be in error in the inferences I draw in chapter
6, I am disagreeably surprised when such criticism emanates from
people who will readily admit that they have not themselves talked
either with low SES children or with their mothers. My reply to
such criticism has to be that the critic go and check for himself
whether or not he can find the specify the communication barriers
that exist; there comes a point where disagreement, potential or
actual of this kind requires that the disputants both have first-hand
experience of the contentious issue. First-hand experience as an
interacting observer would seem to be necessary for any pretending
researcher in child development.

If the decision taken leads to the adoption of a method that
involves extraction of data from persons in deliberately contrived
situations, at least two possible dangers exist. The first is that the
situation so modifies the behaviour of the observed that it ceases to
be a sample of everyday behaviour collected under controlled conditions when the intention was to obtain such a sample. The second
is that false inferences may be drawn because the experimenter is
deluded about the extent and quality of his control over the situation. Particularly with subjects who are importantly different from
oneself – and children are archetypically problematic – there is a
danger of attributing one's own interpretation of what is required
for the performance to the subject – and being wrong. Are the principles regulating the behaviour of the subject what you think they
are? Ignoring the solipsist fallacy, this remains a great challenge to
the ingenuity and imagination of the observer, perhaps particularly
when working with young children, who may not know 'the rules
of the game'. In this connection both Freeman et al., and Perret-
Clermont and Schubauer-Leoni worry this point with tenacity.
Freeman et al. could not ask their children what they thought the
experimenter was trying to find out. They had to contrive alterations
to the procedure that would tease out what kinds of meaning (semantic) their children applied to the prepositions being studied and how
their experimental behaviour was influenced by these manipulations.
To consider a seemingly slight point first – and one whose relevance
is also demonstrated by the Swiss team. What has been the immediately experimental history of the child? The prior experience with
the waste-paper baskets set some of the children to respond in
particular ways. Perret-Clermont and Schubauer-Leoni could expose
similar influences at work. In neither case were these effects treated

as error-variance; they were viewed as crucial influences upon the children's behaviour. Experimental psychologists have long concerned themselves with 'set'. Animal psychologists retain detailed biographies of previous experiments in which their animals have taken part and often take the precaution of using experimentally naïve animals. While young children may be experimentally naïve, they are never lacking in a biography and one that may be situationally relevant. For many experiments the observer expects the child not only to cooperate fully but understand what is expected of him and to do his best – but in what respects? Hartley (1980) has recently demonstrated how easy it can be to change scores of young children of low socio-economic status on the Matching Familiar Figures Test. With several kinds of instructions and experience he was able to produce dramatic increases in the 'reflectiveness' of low SES children. What is to count as a good performance on that test? Is it speed of completion or absence of error or a combination of the two? These data were consistent with an interpretation that claimed that the low SES children he tested accorded priority to speed. By simple instructions he could shift this priority. (It might also be mentioned that one reason Hartley pursued this line of enquiry was that he observed that MFF-diagnosed 'impulsive' children could spend a quarter of an hour choosing sweets in the corner shop, seemingly reflecting upon the choices.) While it may be psychologically interesting that children of different social groups interpret task demands differently, it is important not to account for such differential performance with a wrong interpretation. We have of course to be wary of the opposite disposition. 'How do we know the children interpreted the situation sufficiently similarly to make an adequate test of the hypothesis?' could become a catch-all dismissive question. Certainly experimenters will have to (and should) pay more attention to this problem in the future than some of us did in the past, but it is only a helpful question if we can advance constructive hypotheses that could be relevant to any differential performance observed. Perhaps one implication of the work of Freeman et al., and Perret-Clermont and Schubauer-Leoni is that we should increasingly use a variety of instructions and procedures across a batch of experiments before we make claims to explanations that exclude differential interpretation of the situation by the children participating. Certainly one implication of their work and of that of many others is that we should endeavour to make our instructions as comprehensible and explicit as possible to the children concerned. As Markman (1977) and we (E. J. Robinson, 1978) have argued and found, children have to learn what it is not to understand. They will willingly admit that they 'understand' what to do because they do not know what it is to not understand. Consistent with these suggestions, Patterson and her colleagues (Patterson and Kister, 1978) have shown that younger children may not ask questions in the face of inadequate instructions even when explicitly told they are free to do so.

Before we leave matters of method three other points may be made briefly. It might be said that too seldom in the past have we combined four components in our studies: what people do, what they report as the reasons for their behaviour, and when and why these are not always congruent. Many large surveys have relied entirely on mothers' verbal reports about what they do, and have not proceeded to follow up these answers in either of two directions; they have not checked whether what the mothers report corresponds to their behaviour and neither have they enquired into the reasons why mothers adopt the strategies or tactics reported. Three chapters include studies which have or are checking out correspondences or reasons. McGlaughlin et al. have data not reported here that will have a bearing on the matter. Emiliani et al. are finding out why the adults in their nursery talk as they do. W. P. Robinson endeavoured to check the accuracy of maternal reports indirectly both by making predictions about the children's behaviour and by observing mother-child interaction in a subsequent investigation. (It would have been better to have checked a sub-sample of the mothers in the original investigation.) It would also have been informative to have discussed with the mothers why they answered as they did. For example, if in these interviews low SES mothers had frequently mentioned they would have liked to say more in answer to their children's questions, but did not know what to say, this would have corroborated the interpretation finally offered and greatly strengthened its plausibility. The 1970s witnessed a revival of the maxim 'If you want to know, why not ask them?'. Somewhere along the line social psychologists became too suspicious of the accuracy of peoples' accounts of the reasons for their behaviour. Freud encouraged us to be wary, especially of accounts relating to aspects of the dark self. The Introspectionists tried to observe their imageless thoughts. Edwards (1957) warned us of the tendency of people to give socially desirable answers. The strict behaviourists managed to classify any speech as subjective and unreliable. However none of these touch on the question of what people can and are willing to give valid accounts about. We have been reminded of what we have known all along as ordinary human beings that people can give perfectly adequate accounts of some of their behaviour, in appropriate circumstances. All we have to ensure is that topics are those for which the accounts are likely to be valid and that we establish appropriate circumstances for the recording of them. The arguments apply *mutatis mutandis* to children.

The implications of the various points addressed to the question of choice of methods to studies of communication in development are perhaps even more eclectic than those following upon the discussion of choice of theoretical perspectives. Each method mentioned has its strength and weaknesses. The appropriateness of each is limited by the specific questions which are to be answered. While particular choices can only be made in the light of the contemporary state of the art and the resources available, in the long run *all* available methods need to be used and shown to yield mutually consistent results if we are to check and double-check the quality of our descriptions and explanations.

DESIGN AND STATISTICS

Design and statistics make good servants, but bad masters. Discussion about empirical work within the Piagetian framework may even be said to have suffered in the past from a difficulty of the slightly higher order but that has implications for design and statistics. It is a difficulty I am tempted to attribute to language-concept differences between French and English. French has no synonym for 'experiment'; English has no equivalent lexical item for the French 'experience'. English speakers have striven for objectivity, reducing the experimenter to an impersonal unbiased recorder, and the connotation of 'experiment' perhaps encourages them to believe that this goal can be achieved. The French 'experience' recognises the interpretive component integral to acts of perception. English-speakers are seduced towards a delusion of objectivity. Hence perhaps our proneness to forget that any psychology experiment is a social situation and can never be otherwise (see Freeman *et al.*, and Perret-Clermont and Schubauer-Leoni for examples of the dangers). It is not just that the 'subjects' may not interpret the demands of the task in the way the experimenter intended because the instructions are insufficiently explicit or not believed, but that the perceived social relationship between the respondent and the victim may also be problematic and influenced the outcomes in ways not known to the experimenter. One response to worries about differential interpretation by respondents has been to standardise procedures, but paradoxically total uniformity of stimulus presentation leads to a lack of psychological equivalence if there is systematic variation in the meanings of included words or actions linked to individually or socially-based differences between children. While we may try to standardise our procedures as much as possible within an experiment, we must also find it necessary to vary them systematically across a matrix of experiments with similar objectives, simply to show that any one particular set of instructions, procedures or materials is not responsible for generating results that mislead us.

With that proviso, the English-speaker notions of the objective quality of experiments still leads them to hope that training in detachment and scepticism will enable them to elimininate their personal prejudices when recording and processing data, and that by externalising these activities for others to insepct, they may be able to achieve objectivity.

The French-speaking psychologist should be less likely to suffer from such a delusion. His temptations may lie in another direction. He may be prone to see empirical investigations more as guides to his own interpretations than as reports for subsequent public scrutiny. He may interrogate and expose children to a variety of experiences intended to probe the plausibility of his ideas. If these are confirmed the eventual report may derive its authority more from the credibility of the interpretation than from the qualities of the data displayed. These may be proffered mainly as illustrations to demonstrate the sense of the interpretations. Some of those studying language development in the Chomsky tradition also behaved a little like this, for reasons perhaps more plausibly attributed to differences in the methods emphasised in linguistics as contrasted with those of child psychology rather than as a consequence of thinking in French, however.

The point of the opposition is not to make claims about the behaviour of Gallic and Anglo-Saxon experimenters. It is simply to set up an opposition for consideration, and to argue that a synthesis of the two approaches is both feasible and desirable. Our specifications of procedures should be rendered as reproducible at a distance as possible. Abbreviation of these, and the difficulties of conveying the ambience of the experimental situation through wordings may in part be responsible for variability and apparent anomalies of results. Video-recordings of experimental situations can reveal ambience in a way that adverbal and adjectival qualification cannot. Once we concede that social factors are significant determinants of children's behaviour in experimental situations, we are under the onerous obligation of describing the social context of these situations. Who sits where and on what? Is the experimenter soft-spoken and successfully amiable? Is the procedure followed in a light business-like manner or is it allowed to be playful? The work reported by E. J. Robinson has been imagined by some people to present children with traumatic decisions. To ask young children 'Whose fault? can be imagined to trigger feelings of guilt or shame, and no doubt the question could be posed in a manner that might have such consequences. It has been suggested that young children would be reluctant to blame an adult experimenter. That the results show children willing to answer the question and to blame the experimenter if that is the outcome of their analysis does not remove the suspicions of a reader in the same way as a film might. Such worries have been frequently voiced about work on LD, where portraits are drawn of big alien interviewers intimidating children into silence and grunts. This kind of worry has already been voiced about communication and its development (see the chapter by W. P. Robinson). No obvious solution commends itself.

For problems of design as such we can restrict comment to the issue of preferences for cross-sectional and longitudinal data. We have to recognise that the analysis of relatively infrequent sampling of natural speech on small numbers of children proved to be an ardous time-consuming task (see Brown, 1973). Even that analysis paid relatively little attention to prosodic, lexical, semantic and pragmatic components of the children's speech. Mothers' speech was used only for limited tests of certain hypotheses. Conversational structure and process was not included. Neither was context of situation. Naturalistic studies of communication in development would require these components to be included as well. The task looks daunting. One day some brave and persistent people may decide to embark upon longitudinal studies that extend over several years. There is of course no need to construe 'longitudinal' to mean more than a few months, and it must be hoped that the proportions of longitudinal to cross-sectional studies may be better balanced and better coordinated than they have been in either LD or ID.

We might also hope for some changes in the analytic statistics employed. The type of statistical test used should be consistent with both the distributional character of the data and with the psychological theory which justifies the study. The most common but by no means universal error in both ID and LD has been to use statistical tests that have presupposed quantitative variations on variables when the underlying theoretical model has been expressed in categorical form, often a sequential form. For example, if the psychological

model claims that the appearance of facility B always and only follows the appearance of A, then data are only consistent with it if no
cases of B without A occur in the data, and the statistical test selected
ought to be appropriate for the theory. While we may concede some
degree of unreliability to measurements made, arguments could be
advanced for subsequent more intensive exploration of deviant cases.
If these cannot be explained and their occurrence can be reliably
demonstrated then the problem is to construct a better explanation
rather than to consign such children to error variance.

Traditionally in science deviant cases have been seen as the challenge to theory, but in child psychology we have tended to neglect
their significance, partly because both our theories and measurements
have lacked precision. Should our explanations of some aspects of
the development in communicative capacities and skills take the
form of sequences, it may be hoped that we shall adopt appropriate statistics and be tough-minded in an examination of relations
between data and theory.

The studies reported in this volume in no case pretent to a foundation in such tight theories, but it may be noted that non-parametric
rather than parametric tests are used in each of the investigations for
which the psychological theorising is couched in terms of categorical
or rank order scaling.

Concluding remarks

In some respects this chapter has been pretentious, offering advice
and suggestions on a variety of issues in a relatively haphazard fashion.
Although fools may rush in where angels fear to tread, we cannot all
be angels, and there is perhaps some merit in trying to see what the
errors of the past have been in the hope that we can learn from these.
In the section on theoretical perspectives it was argued that the errors
in the fields of ID and LD have derived mainly from imagining that
one perspective was able to cope with more than it could. Similarly
in the discussion on methods, it was suggested that protagonists have
erred by stressing the strengths of their own preferences and the
weakness of others, meanwhile forgetting the reciprocal possibilities
of their antagonists. If the validity of the several arguments is
accepted the resolution of the apparent dilemmas is to offset the
different kinds of weakness by employing all the methods available
and obtaining consistent results. Experts on design and statistics
would be able to expand greatly on the few comments offered about

that topic, as could methologists. While the general tenor of the commentary has been optimistic it is perhaps in respect of theory that it is easiest to be less so. Life for us, as developmental psychologists interested in communication, would be easier if we had several strong theoretical positions from which we could generate mutually inconsistent empirical predictions. Given those conditions, researchers would be less tempted to pursue the kinds of descriptive studies whose prevalence is regretted in the methodology section.

However such theories are unlikely to emerge *sui generis*, and it should become easier to construct such grander theories in the future if we ensure that at least the individual efforts of the kinds reported in this volume each tries to offer explanations as well as descriptions of the limited questions they address. Micro-theories in contest will require macro-theories to replace them.

References

Ausubel, D. P. (1978). "Theory and Problems of Child Development" (2nd edn). Grune and Stratton, New York

Bandura, A. and Walters, R. H. (1963). "Social Learning and Personality Development". Holt, New York

Bowerman, M. (1979). The rôle of meaning in language acquisition. Paper presented at *Annual Child Language Seminar*, Manchester, England

Boden, M. A. (1979). "Piaget". Fontana, Glasgow

Brazil, D. (1978). "Discourse Analysis". Final Reports, Social Science Research Council, London

Brown, R. (1973). "A First Language". Penguin, Harmondsworth

Bruner, J. S. (1975). The ontogenesis of speech acts. *Journal of Child Language* 2, 1–19

Burner, J. S., Goodnow, J. J. and Austin, (1956). "A Study of Thinking". Wiley, New York

Chomsky, N. (1957). "Syntactic Structures". Mouton, The Hague

Doise, W., Mugny, G. and Perret-Clermont, A-N (1975). Social interaction and the development of cognitive operations. *European Journal of Social Psychology* 5, 365–383

Edwards, A. L. (1957). "The Social Desirability Variable in Personality Assessment and Research". Holt, New York

Ferster, C. B. and Skinner, B. F. (1957). "Schedules of Reinforcment". Appleton-Century-Crofts, New York

Guthrie, E. R. and Smith, S. (1921). "General Psychology in Terms of Behavior". Appleton–Century–Crofts, New York

Halliday, M. A. K. (1975). "Learning How to Mean". Arnold, London

Harlow, H. F. (1953). Motivation as a factor in the acquisition of new responses. *In* "Current Theory and Research in Motivation". University of Nebraska Press, Lincoln, Nebraska

Hartley, R. L. (1980). Impulsitivity and reflectivity in working class children. Unpublished Doctoral Dissertation, London

Hymes, D. (1967). Models of the interaction of language and social setting. *Journal of Social Issues* 23, 8–28

Malinowski, B. (1935). "Coral Gardens and their Magic". American Book Company, New York

Markman, E. M. (1977). Realizing that you don't understand: a preliminary investigation. *Child Development* 48, 986–992

Patterson, C. J. and Kister, M. C. (1978). "The Development of Listener Skills for Referential Communication". Paper presented at a *Conference on Children's Oral Communication Skills*, University of Wisconsin

Pavlov, I. P. (1960). "Conditioned Reflexes". Dover, New York

Piaget, J. (1926). "The Language and Thought of the Child". Routledge, London

Piaget, J. (1932). "The Moral Judgment of the Child". Routledge, London

Piaget, J. (1971). Piaget's theory. *In* "Carmichael's Manual of Child Psychology" (P. H. Mussen, Ed.). Wiley, New York

Robinson, E. J. (1978). "The Child's Understanding of Inadequate Messages and Communication Failure: A Problem of Ignorance or Egocentrism?" Paper presented at a *Conference on Children's Oral Communication Skills*, University of Wisconsin

Trevarthen, C. and Hubley, P. (1978). Secondary intersubjectivity. *In* "Action, Gesture and Symbol: The Emergence of Language" (A. Locke, Ed.). Academic Press, London

Van den Berghe, P. (1970). "Academic Gamesmanship". Abelard, New York

Wells, C. G. and Robinson, W. P. (1981). The Role of adult speech in language development. *In*. "Progress in Social Psychology" (C. Fraser and K. Scherer, Eds). Cambridge University Press, Cambridge

Author Index

Subject Index

European Monographs in Social Psychology

Series Editor: **HENRI TAJFEL**

H. GILES (*ed*)
Language, Ethnicity and Intergroup Relations, 1977

H. TAJFEL (*ed*)
Differentation between Social Groups: Studies in the Social Psychology of
Intergroup Relations, 1979

M. BILLIG
Fascists: A Social Psychological View of the National Front, 1979

C.P. WILSON
Jokes, Form, Content, Use and Function, 1979

J.P. FORGAS
Social Episodes: The Study of Interaction Routines, 1979

R.A. HINDE
Towards Understanding Relationships, 1979

A-N. PERRET-CLERMONT
Social Interaction and Cognitive Development in Children, 1980

B.A. GEBER and S.P. NEWMAN
Soweto's Children: The Development of Attitudes, 1980

S.H. NG
The Social Psychology of Power, 1980

P. SCHÖNBACH, P. GOLLWITZER, G. STIEPEL and U. WAGNER
Education and Intergroup Attitudes, 1981

C. ANTAKI (*ed*)
The Psychology of Ordinary Explanations of Social Behaviour, 1981

In Preparation

H. BRANDSTÄTTER, J. H. DAVIS and G. STOCKER-KREICHGAUER (*eds*)
Group Decision Making

J.P. FORGAS (*ed*)
Social Cognition: Perspectives in Everyday Understanding

H.T. HIMMELWEIT, P. HUMPHREYS, M. JAEGER and M. KATZ
How Voters Decide: A Longitudinal Study of Political Attitudes
extending over Fifteen Years

P. STRINGER (*ed.*)
Confronting Social Issues: Applications of Social Psychology, Vol. 1